ELVIS
A MUSICAL INVENTORY
1939-55

ELVIS
A MUSICAL INVENTORY
1939-55

Richard Boussiron

MUSIC MENTOR BOOKS
York, England

British Library Cataloguing-in-Publication Data
A catalogue record for this book is available from the British Library.

ISBN 0 9519888 7 5

Published worldwide by Music Mentor Books *(Proprietor: G.R. Groom-White)*
69 Station Road, Upper Poppleton, York YO26 6PZ, North Yorkshire, England.
Telephone/Fax: +44 (0)1904 330308   *email:* music.mentor@ntlworld.com

Front cover photo by William S. Randolph.

Cover by It's Great To Be Rich, York.

Printed and bound in Great Britain by Antony Rowe Ltd, Eastbourne, East Sussex.

In memory of

Elvis Aaron Presley
(1935-77)

Samuel Barnes
(1946-90)

Graham Metson
(1934-85)

PUBLISHER'S NOTE

Richard Boussiron died suddenly on 3 May 2004,
shortly before this book went to press.
We feel it is fitting that he is also remembered here.

Richard Boussiron
(1964-2004)

Acknowledgments

This book is based on the research of two independent American record collectors/researchers, Samuel Barnes and Graham Metson. The bulk of their investigations took place in the seven years from 1968 to 1975, although their work also continued beyond that point.

Focusing solely on Elvis, Sam carried out extensive research in Mississippi and around the Memphis area between 1968 and 1975. In 1970, he negotiated an exclusive agreement with Marion Keisker to publish the definitive record of the legendary Sun sessions based on her comprehensive personal notes. (In her role as Sun's administrator, Marion meticulously chronicled all of Elvis' sessions in a series of notebooks, then transferred basic information from these onto the company's official files. She took the notebooks with her when she left Sun in 1957.) For obvious reasons a closely-guarded secret, Marion's records were considerably more detailed than the company's own files and contained a great deal of hitherto unknown information about lost takes, unissued titles and — in some instances — entire deleted sessions. Understandably, she was not prepared to let them out of her sight and Sam was therefore obliged to manually transcribe all the data. I would have liked to include some reproductions of Marion's notes in this book; unfortunately, it is not known what became of them after her death.

Graham meanwhile researched Elvis' jam sessions and pieced together details of his live appearances from public performance copyright records and radio and TV station archives. He also collected similar information on Eddie Cochran, Gene Vincent and other Fifties' rock'n'roll artists.

Progress on this mammoth undertaking was slow, and Sam and Graham worked in constant fear of Presley's manager, Parker, who was extremely litigious at the time and had already blocked the appearance of several other unofficial Elvis books. In fact, it wasn't until after Elvis' death in 1977 that they were finally able to work without inhibition.

I began assisting with research for the project in 1983, but sadly both Graham and Marion passed away soon after. Following Sam's death in 1990, I undertook to complete the book in their memory and devoted myself to researching the origins of all the songs, which Sam and Graham had not been able to supply due to lack of time.

I am immensely grateful to Bill Beard (editor of *Eddie Cochran Connection*), Alasdair Blaazer, Trevor Cajiao (editor of *Now Dig This*), Dave Clarke, Stuart Colman, Bill Daniels, Phil Davies, Colin Escott, Henk Gorter, Daniel Gugolz, Martin Hawkins, Shane Hughes, Dik de Heer, Tom Kelly, Adam Komorowski, Victor Pearlin, Dave Penny, Jean Marc Pezet, Bill Pearson, Fred Rothwell, Robert Stallworth, Gerry Stonestreet, Chris Strachwitz, Tapio Vaisanen, David Vanacloig, Billy Vera, Tony Watson, Graham Weaver and Tony Wilkinson for their invaluable assistance in this respect, and also to Alan Balfour, Steve Cairns, John Garst, Wanda Feathers, Peter Guralnick, Ernst Jorgensen and George R. White for the additional information they provided.

Last but not least, I would like to thank — and dedicate the book to — Carvel Lee Ausborn (Mississippi Slim), Bill Black, Reverend W. Herbert Brewster, Pastor Heywood C. Brown, Irwin Chandler, Sherwin Evans, D.J. Fontana, Oleta Grimes, Marion Keisker, Scotty Moore, Sam Phillips, Vernon and Gladys Presley, Lisa Marie

Presley, Reverend Frank W. Smith, James Tipler, Marcus Van Story and all the bluesmen, gospel masters, hillbilly stars, and rockabilly cats and chicks who ever crossed Elvis' path for just being there.

Richard Boussiron
Boulogne, February 2004

Contents

Introduction

Elvis Presley's unique fusion of white and black American music styles and culture gave birth to rockabilly and helped to create a new art form that changed Western popular culture forever: rock'n'roll.

This 'musical inventory' is an attempt to catalogue the many songs that Elvis knew, liked and sang during his childhood and early career — arguably his most interesting and creative period — to build up a picture of his musical development throughout that time. Also included is a Sun sessionography compiled directly from Marion Keisker's personal notes. Although not 100% complete, they nevertheless contained a wealth of new information about Elvis' historic recording sessions.

By its very nature, a work such as this will always remain incomplete, and it would be pretentious and misleading to describe it as 'definitive' or the last word on the subject. As everyone knows, Elvis was a music lover who sang in all manner of places throughout his life, so it is both natural and inevitable that certain titles will be missing: it is impossible to catalogue absolutely everything he sang between 1939 and 1955.

I wanted this book to be uncomplicated and easy for everyone to use — amateurs and specialists alike — so I have simply presented the 'hard facts' without photographs, very much in the spirit of the *Blues Records* books of Mike Leadbitter, Neil Slaven, Les Fancourt and Paul Pelletier.

However, I must emphasise that this is an *inventory*, not a discography. It was Samuel Barnes' and Graham Metson's intention to compile a detailed catalogue of songs known to Elvis over a specific period, rather than a traditional discography, and I have tried to respect their wishes. So, while some information about Elvis' record releases has been included to help orientate the reader, this book does *not* contain exhaustive details of all releases. Numerous works of this nature already exist all over the world.

For the benefit of researchers, I have also included details of the earliest known recording of each song, as well as Elvis' probable sources — records he would have heard on the radio, on jukeboxes, at Charlie Hazelgrove's record store in Memphis, and elsewhere. His primary source of religious songs would, of course, have been church services and gospel singings; however, popular gospel records — particularly those he heard on the radio — would have been an important secondary source and have therefore also been listed.

It is my sincere hope that this book will contribute to our knowledge and understanding of Elvis Presley's early life and career, and in doing so will become a lasting testament to the work of my two good friends, Sam and Graham.

Now, let us step back in time and walk in Elvis' footsteps...

Technical Notes

The information in this book is presented in seven Sections, each focusing on a different aspect of Elvis' early life/career. Within each Section, every session or personal appearance has been allocated a two-part number. For example, the sixth session or appearance listed under Section 1 is shown like this:

These numbers, rather than page numbers, are used for all cross-references and index entries.

Basic information on non-religious titles is presented as follows:

Title of show [where applicable]
Location
Date / Time
Personnel   Instruments

TITLE [ALTERNATIVE TITLES] *(composer)*
Historical information.

✱ Original by [name, label, catalogue number, year of release]
◆ *Elvis' sources:* [name, label, catalogue number, year of release]
◯ Details of subsequent recordings by Elvis.

For ease of reference, only the lead/main artist's name is listed under 'Original by' and '*Elvis' sources*' (eg 'Mildred Bailey' not 'Mildred Bailey with Benny Goodman & His Orchestra'). This also avoids potential conflicts where the names of acts were occasionally styled differently (eg Roy Acuff & *The* Smokey Mountain Boys, Roy Acuff & *His* Smokey Mountain Boys).

There are a few exceptions. For example, Billy Ward & His Dominoes are listed in full to distiguish them from the post-Ward Dominoes. Where pertinent, prominent band vocalists are listed after the name of the ensemble thus: 'Tommy Dorsey – Voc. Frank Sinatra'.

For similar reasons, catalogue numbers of singles have in most cases been listed without prefixes and suffixes.

Records listed under 'Original by' are the earliest known recorded examples of the song in question. There is no suggestion that Elvis ever heard them, although he might have done so in some instances.

Records listed under '*Elvis' sources*' are those he is likely to have heard during his formative years — predominantly hits of the day. It is clear from his early repertoire that Elvis soaked up a wide variety of pop, country and R&B influences. While this involves some conjecture, it is hoped that this section will give the reader a useful insight into the sounds that inspired the future King.

This basic information is supplemented in many instances with additional data. For example, Section 4 (*The Sun Sessions*) contains details of playing times, RCA master numbers, the release history of individual takes, etc.

Due to a lack of information and many contradictions between the few sources that do exist, it has proved impossible to pinpoint the majority of release dates with any degree of certainty. For this reason, only the year of release is shown.

Religious titles are presented in a similar format, but usually with additional details about their origins, since most pre-date the sound recording era. Since Elvis' primary source for all of these is most likely to have been church gatherings, contemporary religious recordings he may have heard/been influenced by are listed as '*Elvis' radio sources*'. There were, of course, many other more obscure recordings of the same titles.

A word of explanation is also necessary regarding Negro spirituals. Although the majority of these originated among black slaves in the South, they were widely embraced by whites during the Nineteenth Century and were constantly reworked and reborn as lyrics and melodies were adapted by successive performers. As a result, many spirituals have several variants and/or alternative titles.

It may also appear strange to read that certain spirituals were first heard in white, rather than black churches. There is, however, a very simple explanation for this: although the first independent black church in the East opened in Silver Bluff, South Carolina in 1774 and Absalom Jones founded the first black church in Philadelphia in 1794, there were actually very few black churches in existence until the late 1800s. It goes without saying that African Americans sang spirituals in less formal surroundings (in the fields, at camp meetings, etc) significantly earlier than this.

◆ SECTION 1 ◆

Tupelo 1939-48

This section focuses on Elvis Presley's earliest years and the many musical influences he absorbed as a child from church, school, radio and the streets of East Tupelo and Tupelo town, Mississippi (East Tupelo merged with Tupelo proper in 1946). Thanks to Samuel Barnes' timely and exhaustive investigations, we at last have details of some of the songs Elvis knew and sang as a young boy.

The First Assembly of God Church
206 Adams Street, East Tupelo, Mississippi
Between 1939 and 1948 (exact dates unknown)
As with most families in the South, religion played a major role in the life of the Presleys. The First Assembly of God Church, which was just around the corner from their home, was built in 1937. Its architect and first preacher was Gains Mansell, uncle of Elvis' mother, Gladys. He was replaced during 1944 by Pastor Frank Smith from Meridian, Mississippi. Occasionally, other ministers like Pastor Heywood C. Brown and Rev. Parks would subsitute.

There is a wonderful story told by Gladys Presley about her three-year old son slipping off her knee during a service, climbing up onto the platform and joining in with the choir. Another story tells how he used to rush home from school to catch the daily half-hour black gospel show on local radio station WELO. Of course, the attraction of the music remained with him for the rest of his life.

The following list of hymns and spirituals was compiled from the joint recollections of half a dozen members of the First Assembly of God Church, Tupelo during four extensive expeditions in 1968, 1971, 1974 and 1975 around Tupelo and southern Mississippi. Many of these were of black origin, just as many hymns of white origin were sung in black churches.

In the South during the 1930s and 1940s, the same hymns and spirituals varied in rhythm, phrasing and tempo depending on the musical sensibilities of individual ministers, and also which particular church they were sung in. Thus, ministers gave each hymn or spiritual their own touch. There were no established rules and each minister had the freedom to create their own personal version for their congregation. For example, the classic **I SHALL NOT BE MOVED** *might have been sung slowly, or in a more rhythmic uptempo fashion, depending on how the minister chose to interpret it. So, any two churches in Mississippi might have sung the same hymn differently, depending upon the ministers officiating there.*

In Tupelo, Elvis was influenced first and foremost by the guitar arangements of Pastors Brown, Smith and others — not by any white or black gospel performers he may have heard on the radio during the 1940s. For instance, his version of **WORKING ON THE BUILDING** *(recorded in October 1960 for the LP 'His Hand In Mine') was inspired by the arrangement he heard in Tupelo during the 1940s played by Pastors Brown and Smith which, according to the* *former, employed the same guitar intro. It is the most 'rootsy' cut on the LP — the handclapping being a throwback to his time as a young child in the church at Tupelo.*

Similarly, Elvis' renditions of **DOWN BY THE RIVERSIDE, FARTHER ALONG, I SHALL NOT BE MOVED** *and* **JESUS WALKED THAT LONESOME VALLEY** *at the 'Million Dollar Quartet' session of 4 December 1956 used exactly the same rhythm and phrasing as Pastors Smith and Brown all those years earlier.*

AMEN *and* **AMAZING GRACE** *differ inasmuch as, when Elvis sang those in the 1970s, he did so with a wealth of musical experience behind him, and arranged them in his own vision — as he did with many other gospel songs and spirituals during his career. It goes without saying that he sang them very differently than he would have done in Tupelo in 1947. By 1972, Elvis had one gospel EP and three gospel LPs to his credit and possessed total mastery of the idiom.*

BEFORE THIS TIME ANOTHER YEAR *(Traditional)*
Negro spiritual. Heard in black churches in the South from circa 1870; in white churches from circa 1875.

✱ Original by Odette & Ethel (Columbia 14169) 1926.
◆ *Elvis' radio source:* Jubalaires (Decca 48085) 1944.
                     Harmoneers (King 4233) 1946.
                     Dixieaires (Coleman 5977) 1948.

COME DOWN MY LORD *(Traditional)*
Negro spiritual. Heard in black churches in the South from circa 1895; in white churches from circa 1897.

✱ Original by ?

EVERYTIME I FEEL THE SPIRIT *(Traditional)*
Negro spiritual. Heard in black churches in the South from circa 1868; in white churches from circa 1871.

✱ Original by the Morehouse College Quartet (OKeh 40268) 1924.
◆ *Elvis' radio sources:* Harmonizing Four (Decca 48018) 1943.
                     EVERYTIME THAT I FEEL THE SPIRIT
                            Golden Gate Jubilee Quartet (Bluebird 8328) 1939.

FARTHER ALONG *(Stevens)*
Hymn composed in 1937 by Rev. W.B. Stevens in 1937. Heard in white churches in the South from 1937; in black churches from 1938. (Based on **FARTHER ALONE**, *a hymn composed in 1880 by an unknown Missourian preacher. Heard in white churches in the South from circa 1880; in black churches from circa 1883.)*

✱ Original by Deacon Guy Cherry
                      (Library Of Congress field recording, Tupelo, Mississippi May 1939).
   Original commercial release by ?
◆ *Elvis' radio sources:* Roy Acuff (Conqueror 9433) 1940.
                   Roy Acuff (Conqueror 9667) 1941.
                   Roy Acuff (Columbia 20480) 1948.
                   Stamps Quartet (Columbia 20337) 1948.
◉ Elvis later recorded this title at RCA Studio B, Nashville on 27 May 1966 (released in 1967 on LP *How Great Thou Art*, RCA-Victor LPM/LSP-3758). Also recorded at the *Million Dollar Quartet* session at Sun Studio, Memphis on 4 December 1956 (released in 1990 on 2-LP/CD *The Million Dollar Quartet*, BMG/RCA 2023-1-R / 2023-2-R).

I KNOW DE LORD HAS LAID HIS HANDS ON ME *(Traditional)*
Negro spiritual. Heard in black churches in the South from circa 1882; in white churches from circa 1884. Many variations.

✱ Original **I KNOW THE LORD LAID HIS HANDS ON ME**
                               Fisk University Jubilee Quartet (Victor 16895) 1911.
◆ *Elvis' radio source:* Cleveland Colored Quartet (Gold Tone 116) 1947.

I'M GOING THROUGH *(Traditional)*
Negro spiritual. Heard in black churches in the South from circa 1899; in white churches from circa 1901.

✱ Original by the Norfolk Jazz & Jubilee Quartet (Paramount 12749) 1927.

JESUS IS RISEN FROM THE DEAD *(Traditional)*
Negro spiritual. Heard in black churches.in the South from circa 1865; in white churches from circa 1867.

✱ Original by ?

JESUS WALKED THAT LONESOME VALLEY *(Traditional)*
Negro spiritual. Heard in black churches in the South from circa 1880; in white churches from circa 1882.

✱ Original **JESUS WALKED THIS LONESOME VALLEY** by Mrs. Shaw
                          (University Of Texas field recording, San Antonio, Texas, May 1941).
   Original commercial release by ?

(WE'LL UNDERSTAND IT BETTER) BY AND BY *(Tindley)*
Hymn composed in 1905 by Rev. Charles Albert Tindley. Heard in black churches in the South from circa 1906; in white churches also from circa 1906. (Not to be confused with **BYE AND BYE***, as first recorded by the Nazarene Congregational Church Choir (Gennett 6004) 1926.)*

✱ Original by unidentified black female quartet
                          (direct-to-disc 78 rpm field recording near Drew, Mississippi, January 1906).
   Original commercial release by ?
◐ Elvis later recorded **BY AND BY (WHEN THE MORNING COMES)**, a variant of this title, at RCA Studio B, Nashville on 27 May 1966 (released in 1967 on LP *How Great Thou Art*, RCA-Victor LPM/LSP-3758).

WORKING ON THE BUILDING *(Hoyle/Bowes)*
Gospel song composed in 1934 by W.O. Hoyle and Lillian Bowles. Heard in white churches in the South from 1934; in black churches from ?

✱ Original by the Blackwood Brothers (no details, reportedly released on own label) 1934.
◆ *Elvis' radio sources:* **WORKING ON A BUILDING** by the Carter Family (Bluebird 5716) 1934.
                          J.E. Mainer's Mountaineers (King 543) 1946.
                          Five Blind Boys Of Mississippi (Coleman 5968) 1948.
                          Soul Comforters (DeLuxe 1157) 1948.
                          Soul Stirrers (Aladdin 2020) 1948.
                          Swan's Silvertone Singers (King 4248) 1948.
◐ Elvis later recorded this title at RCA Studio B, Nashville on 31 October 1960 (released in 1960 on LP *His Hand In Mine*, RCA-Victor LPM/LSP-2328). *[Also see introductory note to this section.]*

YOU HEAR THE LAMBS A-CRYIN' [HEAR DE LAM'S A-CRYIN'] *(Traditional)*
Negro spiritual. Heard in black churches in the South from circa 1865; in white churches from circa 1870.

★ Original by the Fisk University Jubilee Quartet (Columbia 3596) 1921.

The First Assembly of God Church
206 Adams Street, East Tupelo, Mississippi
April 1942 and January 1944 (exact dates unknown)

*In 1968, Samuel Barnes tracked down Pastor Heywood C. Brown (then 72 years old) in Hurley, Mississippi. Pastor Brown substituted at the First Assembly of God Church in April 1942 and January 1944, and had retained his music files over the years. He remembered Elvis singing the following hymns and spirituals in the choir and/or with his parents in early 1944. [See also comments to **1.1**.]*

AMAZING GRACE *(Newton/Carrell/Clayton)*
English hymn composed in 1779 by reformed slave trader Rev. John Newton; music by James P. Carrell and David S. Clayton added in 1831. Popularised in the USA by the Baptist song leader, Singin' Billy Walker (1809-75). Initially heard in white churches in the East from 1780 onwards. By 1835, it had spread to all churches in the South.

★ Original by the Wisdom Sisters (Columbia 15093) 1926.
◆ *Elvis' radio sources:* Dixie Hummingbirds (Apollo 108) 1946.
                       Fairfield Four (Bullet 292) 1948.
                       Mahalia Jackson (Apollo 194) 1948.
O Elvis later recorded this title at RCA Studio B, Nashville on 15 March 1971 (released in 1972 on LP *He Touched Me*, RCA-Victor LSP-4690).

AMEN *(Traditional)*
*Negro spiritual. Heard in black churches in the East from circa 1796. Heard in white churches in the South from circa 1800; in black churches from circa 1865. (NB. There are two spirituals titled **AMEN**. This is the one which begins 'Amen, oh lawdy! Amen, have mercy!' — not to be confused with the other **AMEN**, which Elvis sang as a medley with **I GOT A WOMAN** in his 1970s concerts, which begins with the word 'Amen' repeated five times.)*

★ Original by ?
◆ *Elvis' radio sources:* Luvenia Nash Singers (Excelsior 148) 1946.
                       Wings Over Jordan Choir (RCA-Victor 3242) 1948.

FATHER ABRAHAM *(Traditional)*
Negro spiritual. Heard in black churches in the South from circa 1867; in white churches from circa 1869.

★ Original by unidentified group of older men and women
       (Library of Congress field recording, St. Austin's Church, Cockrum, Mississippi, May 1939).
    Original commercial release by ?

GLORY, GLORY, HALLELUJAH *(Traditional)*
Negro spiritual. Heard in black churches in the South from circa 1867; in white churches from circa 1869. Not to be confused with **GLORY! GLORY! HALLELUJAH (BATTLE HYMN OF THE REPUBLIC)** *or the spiritual called* **HALLELUJAH,** *first recorded by the Cotton Belt Quartet (Paramount 12530) 1927.*

✱ Original **SINCE I LAID MY BURDEN DOWN** by Elders McIntorsh & Edwards
(OKeh 8698) 1929.
Original **WHEN I LAY MY BURDENS DOWN** by Blind Roosevelt Graves & Uaroy Graves
(Paramount 12974) 1929.
Original **GLORY, GLORY, HALLELUJAH** by Mother McCollum (Vocalion 1591) 1930.
◆ *Elvis' radio sources:* Golden Gate Quartet & Mother McCollum (Thesaurus 1151) 1941.
Sunlight Jubilee Singers (Down Town 2008) 1946.
Five Blind Boys Of Mississippi (Coleman 6000) 1948.
Soul Stirrers (Aladdin 2027) 1948.

GOD CALLED ADAM *(Traditional)*
Negro spiritual. First heard in the USA's first black church — St. Thomas' in Philadelphia, founded in 1794 by Absalom Jones. Heard in white churches in the South from circa 1798. Was reborn with new lyrics in 1865 following the Civil War and heard in white and black churches throughout the South thereafter.

✱ Original by ?

GO TELL IT ON THE MOUNTAIN *(Traditional)*
Negro spiritual. Heard in black churches in the South from circa 1865; in white churches from circa 1867.

✱ Original by ?
◆ *Elvis' radio source:* Famous Jubilee Singers (Bullet 294) 1948.

I SHALL NOT BE MOVED *(Traditional)*
Negro spiritual. Heard in white churches in the South from circa 1930; in black churches from ?

✱ Original by the Taskiana Four (Victor 20183) 1926.
◉ Elvis later recorded this title at the *Million Dollar Quartet* session at Sun Studio, Memphis on 4 December 1956 (released in 1990 on 2-LP/CD *The Million Dollar Quartet*, BMG/RCA 2023-1-R / 2023-2-R).

IT'S MY TIME, PRAISE THE LORD *(Traditional)*
Hymn by unknown composer. Heard in white churches in the South from circa 1810; in black churches from ?

✱ Original by ?

THE OLD RUGGED CROSS *(Bennard)*
Hymn composed in 1913 by Rev. George Bennard. Heard in white churches in the South from circa 1930; in black churches from ? A hit in 1921 for Homer Rodeheaver & Virginia Asher (Victor 18706).

✱ Original by Homer Rodeheaver & Virginia Asher (Victor 18706) 1921.
◆ *Elvis' radio sources:* Silvertone Jubilee Quartette (Vocalion 04799) 1938.
Pilgrim Travelers (Specialty 357) 1948.

19

O, SINNER MAN *(Traditional)*
Negro spiritual. Heard in black churches in the South from circa 1865; in white churches from circa 1868.

✱ Original by ?

Elvis Presley's home between 1944 and 1947 (exact dates unknown)
The Presleys lived at several different addresses in East Tupelo between 1944 and 1947: Kelly Street until 8 August 1945; Berry Street until 18 July 1946; Commerce Street until unknown date; 510½ Maple Street until unknown date. They then moved to Mulberry Alley near the fairgrounds in Tupelo town centre until September 1947; and finally to 1010 North Green Street, Shakerag, where they remained until they moved to Memphis on 6 November 1948.

Mrs. Oleta Grimes was Elvis' teacher in 1944-45 at East Tupelo Consolidated School (Lawhon Elementary), as well as a neighbour and frequent visitor to the Presley household. Below is a list of songs that Mrs. Grimes recalled teaching to Elvis or heard him sing at home around that time.

A LEAF ON A TREE *(Traditional)*
Elvis sang this traditional song to his class on his last day at Milam Junior High School in Tupelo (5 November 1948). On 6 November, he moved with his parents to Memphis.

✱ Original by ?
◆ *Elvis' source:* Elvis was taught this song in school by Mrs. Grimes around 1944.

DIXIE HIGHWAY *(Kahn/Donaldson)*
A hit in 1922 for Aileen Stanley (Victor 18935).

✱ Original by Aileen Stanley (Victor 18935) 1922.
◆ *Elvis' sources:*   Marion Harris (Brunswick 2318) 1922.
                              Aileen Stanley (Victor 18935) 1922.

DOWN BY THE RIVERSIDE [STUDY WAR NO MORE] *(Traditional)*
Negro spiritual. Heard in white and black churches in the South from circa 1865. Pop hit in 1953 for the Four Lads (Columbia 40005) and in 1954 for Gary Crosby (Decca 28955).

✱ Original by Evangelist Homer Rodeheaver (Rainbow 1044) 1923.
◆ *Elvis' radio sources:* **STUDY WAR NO MO'** by the Golden Echo Quartet (DeLuxe 1005) 1945.
                                       Dixieaires (Continental 6072) 1947.
◉ Elvis later recorded this title at the *Million Dollar Quartet* session at Sun Studio, Memphis on 4 December 1956 (released in 1990 on 2-LP/CD *The Million Dollar Quartet*, BMG/RCA 2023-1-R / 2023-2-R). Also as a medley with **WHEN THE SAINTS GO MARCHING IN** at Radio Recorders, Hollywood on 12-13 May 1965 (released in 1966 on LP *Frankie And Johnny*, RCA-Victor LPM/LSP-3553).

GOD BLESS AMERICA *(Berlin)*
Song written in 1918 by Irving Berlin for the revue, 'Yip, Yip, Yaphank', but rejected by the composer as being too solemn. As war again threatened Europe in 1938, Berlin reworked the song, which was premiered on national radio on an Armistice Day (11 November) broadcast by the popular soprano, Kate Smith. It was an immediate sensation, providing Smith with hits in 1939, 1940 and 1942 and Bing Crosby with a hit in 1939. It has since become the unofficial national anthem of the USA.

✱ Original by Kate Smith (Victor 26198) 1939.
◆ *Elvis' sources:*   Kate Smith (Victor 26198) 1939.
                    Bing Crosby (Decca 2400) 1939.

HELLO SUNSHINE HELLO *(Tobias)*

✱ Original by Eddie Cantor (Victor 21982) 1929.
◆ *Elvis' source:* Elvis was taught this song in school by Mrs. Grimes.

THE LONESOME ROAD *(Austin/Shilkret)*
Song from the Broadway musical, 'Show Boat'. A hit in 1928 for Gene Austin (Victor 20198), in 1929 for Nat Shilkret (Victor 21996), in 1930 for Ted Lewis (Columbia 2181) and in 1939 for Bing Crosby (Decca 2257).

✱ Original by the Blue Ridge Duo *[Gene Austin and George Reneau]* (Edison 51515) 1924.
◆ *Elvis' sources:*   Sister Rosetta Tharpe (Decca 2243) 1938.
                    Bing Crosby (Decca 2257) 1939.
                    Maxwell Davis (4 Star 1027) 1945.

MY BLUE HEAVEN *(Whiting/Donaldson)*
Million-seller in 1927 for Gene Austin (Victor 20964). Also a hit in 1927 for Paul Whiteman (Victor 20828), and in 1928 for Seger Ellis (OKeh 40928), Sammy Kaye (Vocalion 04199), Nick Lucas (Brunswick 3684) and Don Vorhees (Columbia 1129).

✱ Original by Paul Whiteman – Voc. Bing Crosby, Jack Fulton, Charles Gaylord,
                                Al Rinker and Austin Young (Victor 20828) 1927.
◆ *Elvis' sources:*   Gene Austin (Victor 20964) 1927.
                    Jimmie Lunceford (Decca 712) 1936.
                    Sammy Kaye (Vocalion 04199) 1939.
                    Jesse Cryor (G&G 1032) 1946.

THE OLD RUGGED CROSS *(Bennard)*
Hymn composed in 1913 by Rev. George Bennard. Heard in white churches in the South from circa 1930; in black churches from ? A hit in 1921 for Homer Rodeheaver & Virginia Asher (Victor 18706).

✱ Original by Homer Rodeheaver & Virginia Asher (Victor 18706) 1921.
◆ *Elvis' radio sources:*   Silvertone Jubilee Quartette (Vocalion 04799) 1938.
                          Pilgrim Travelers (Specialty 357) 1948.

OL' MAN RIVER *(Hammerstein/Kern)*

Song from the Broadway musical, 'Show Boat'. A hit in 1928 for Al Jolson (Brunswick 3867), Paul Robeson (Victor 35912), Paul Whiteman (Victor 21218) and the Revelers (Victor 21241), and in 1934 for Luis Russell (Perfect 15995). R&B hit in 1948 for the Ravens.

✱ Original by Paul Whiteman – Voc. Bing Crosby (Victor 21218) 1928.
◆ *Elvis' sources:* Al Jolson (Brunswick 3867) 1928.
       Revelers (Victor 21241) 1928.
       Paul Robeson (Victor 35912) 1928.
       Paul Whiteman – Voc. Bing Crosby (Victor 21218) 1928.
       Luis Russell – Voc. Sonny Woods (Perfect 15995) 1934.
       Paul Robeson in the 1936 film, *Show Boat.*
       Golden Gate Jubilee Quartet (Bluebird 8190) 1939.
       Ravens (National 9035) 1947.

ON THE MISSISSIPPI *(MacDonald/Carol/Sloane)*

Song from the Broadway musical 'Hanky Panky'. A hit in 1913 for the American Quartet (Victor 17237), Billy Murray (Edison Amberol 1637) and Sousa's Band (Victor 17249).

✱ Original by Gene Greene (Pathe 544) 1913.
◆ *Elvis' source:* Elvis was taught this song in school by Mrs. Grimes.

OVER THE RAINBOW *(Arlen/Harburg)*

Song from the 1939 film, 'The Wizard Of Oz'. A hit in 1939 for Larry Clinton (Victor 26174), Bob Crosby (Decca 2657), Judy Garland (Decca 2672) and Glenn Miller (Bluebird 10366).

✱ Original by Judy Garland (Decca 2672) 1939.
◆ *Elvis' sources:* Larry Clinton – Voc. Bea Wain (Victor 26174) 1939.
       Bob Crosby (Decca 2657) 1939.
       Judy Garland (Decca 2672) 1939.
       Glenn Miller (Bluebird 10366) 1939.
⦿ Elvis sang the opening line between recording other songs at RCA Studio A, Hollywood on 31 March 1972. This was filmed by MGM for *Elvis On Tour*, but wasn't included in the final edit. Released in 1989 on bootleg CD *The Complete On Tour Sessions (Volume 1)* (Vicky 0211).

Elvis Presley's home, Berry Street, East Tupelo, Mississippi
1945 (exact date unknown)

In 1971, Samuel Barnes tracked down Sherwin Evans (then 60 years old) in Preston, Mississippi. Mr. Evans was a carpenter who had worked with Elvis' father, Vernon in Como, Mississippi in 1942. He visited the Presley home once in 1945 and recalled Elvis singing the following song:

HUCKLEBERRY FINN *(Hess/Lewis/Young)*

A hit in 1917 for comedy-musical duo Van & Schenck (Victor 18318).

✱ Original by Sam Ash (Columbia 2245) 1917.
◆ *Elvis' source:* Elvis was taught this song in school by Mrs. Grimes.

1.5

Elvis Presley's home, 1010 North Green Street, Tupelo, Mississippi
1947 (exact dates unknown)

In 1971, Samuel Barnes tracked down Irwin Chandler (then 54 years old) in Clara, Mississippi. Mr. Chandler was a carpenter who had worked with Elvis' father, Vernon in Como, Mississippi in 1942. He visited the Presley home twice in 1947 and recalled Elvis singing the following songs:

BLUEBIRDS IN THE MOONLIGHT *(Robin/Rainger)*
Song from the 1939 animated film, 'Gulliver's Travels'. A hit in 1939 for Glenn Miller (Bluebird 10465) and in 1940 for Benny Goodman (Columbia 35289) and Dick Jurgens (Vocalion 05081).

✱ Original by Mildred Bailey (Columbia 35289) 1939.
◆ *Elvis' source:* Gladys Presley sang and taught this song to her son.

THE LAST LONG TRAIL *(Traditional)*
Traditional cowboy song.

✱ Original by ?
◆ *Elvis' source:* Gladys Presley sang and taught this song to her son.

1.6

Shakerag, Tupelo, Mississippi
1947 and 1948 (exact dates unknown)

Eulysses Mayhorn was a black man who ran a grocery store at 580 North Spring Street in the predeominantly black Shakerag district of Tupelo. Elvis saw the following bluesmen perform outside his store: Arthur 'Big Boy' Crudup, David 'Honeyboy' Edwards, Tommy McClennan, Johnny Shines, Bukka White and Sonny Boy Williamson [Rice Miller]. Elvis lived at 1010 North Green Street, Shakerag between September 1947 and November 1948, and often heard neighbours playing blues on guitar and harmonica, or on their phonogram. This is where he learned about the blues.

ABERDEEN, MISSISSIPPI BLUES *(White)*

✱ Original by Bukka White (OKeh 05743) 1940.
◆ *Elvis' source:* Bukka White (OKeh 05743) 1940.

BABY PLEASE DON'T GO *(Williams)*

✱ Original by Big Joe Williams (Bluebird 6200) 1935.
◆ *Elvis' source:* Big Joe Williams (Bluebird 8969) 1942.

BAD LUCK BLUES *(Austin)*

✱ Original by Ma Rainey (Paramount 12081) 1924.
◆ *Elvis' source:* Ma Rainey (Paramount 12081) 1924.

BLUES BEFORE SUNRISE *(Carr/Blackwell)*

★ Original by Leroy Carr (Vocalion 02657) 1934.
◆ *Elvis' source:* Leroy Carr (Vocalion 02657) 1934.

CARELESS LOVE (BLUES) *(Handy/Williams/Koenig)*
Composition by W.C. Handy, Spencer Williams and Martha Koenig based on a traditional Irish ballad. A hit in 1925 for Bessie Smith (Columbia 14083).

★ Original by Bessie Smith (Columbia 14083) 1925.
◆ *Elvis' sources:*   Bessie Smith (Columbia 14083) 1925.
                  Lonnie Johnson (OKeh 8635) 1928.
                  Riley Puckett (Columbia 15747) 1932.
                  Riley Puckett (Bluebird 5532) 1934.
                  Delmore Brothers (Bluebird 7436) 1938.
○ Elvis made a private recording of this title at Memphis Recording Service (Sun Studio) on 5 June 1954 [see **4.4** for details].

COTTONFIELDS *(Traditional)*
Folk-song of black origin dating from the 1850s popularised by Leadbelly during the 1940s. A 16-inch acetate recorded by him for WNYC (New York) in November or December 1941 is currently in the Smithsonian-Folkways Archive.

★ Original by ?
○ Jam during rehearsals at MGM Soundstage, Hollywood on 15 July 1970. Released in 1998 on bootleg CD *Get Down And Get With It* (Fort Baxter 2204). Officially released in 2000 on CD box set *Elvis – That's The Way It Is: Special Edition* (BMG/RCA 07863 67938-2).

DROP DOWN MAMA *(Estes)*

★ Original by Sleepy John Estes (Champion 50048) 1935.
◆ *Elvis' source:* Sleepy John Estes (Champion 50048) 1935.

HIGHWAY 51 *(Jones)*

★ Original by Curtis Jones (Vocalion 03990) 1938.
◆ *Elvis' source:* Curtis Jones (Vocalion 03990) 1938.

I'M SO GLAD *(James)*
Not to be confused with Ida Cox's **I'M SO GLAD** *(Paramount 12965) 1929.*

★ Original by Skip James (Paramount 13098) 1931.
◆ *Elvis' source:* Skip James (Paramount 13098) 1931.

KOKOMO BLUES

★ Original by Scrapper Blackwell (Vocalion 1192) 1928.
◆ *Elvis' sources:*   Scrapper Blackwell (Vocalion 1192) 1928.
                  OLD ORIGINAL KOKOMO BLUES by Kokomo Arnold (Decca 7026) 1934.

LEND ME YOUR LOVE

★ Original by Peter Chatman *[Memphis Slim]* (Bluebird 9028) 1942.
◆ *Elvis' source:* Peter Chatman (Bluebird 9028) 1942.

MIDNIGHT SPECIAL
Prisoner song thought to have originated at the Texas State Prison Farm at Sugar Land. Popularised by Leadbelly, who recorded his first version of it for the folklorist Alan Lomax at the Louisiana State Penitentiary, Angola, in July 1934. R&B instrumental hit in 1948 for Tiny Grimes (Atlantic 865).

★ Original by Sodarisa Miller (Paramount 12306) 1925.
◆ *Elvis' sources:* Delmore Brothers (King 514) 1946.
　　　　　　　　　　 Leadbelly (Disc 6043) 1946.

MY GAL IS GONE *(Whittaker)*

★ Original by Tampa Red (Bluebird 7010) 1937.
◆ *Elvis' source:* Tampa Red (Bluebird 7010) 1937.

RAINY DAY BLUES *(Lofton)*

★ Original by Poor Boy Lofton (Decca 7049) 1935.
◆ *Elvis' source:* Poor Boy Lofton (Decca 7049) 1935.

STAGGER LEE [STAGOLEE, STACK O'LEE (BLUES)] *(Traditional)*
Folk-song of black origin first published in 1910. Instrumental hit in 1924 for Fred Waring's Pennsylvanians (Victor 19189).

★ Original **STACK O'LEE BLUES** by Fred Waring's Pennsylvanians (Victor 19189) 1923.
◆ *Elvis' sources:* **STACK O'LEE BLUES** by Ma Rainey (Paramount 12357) 1926.
　　　　　　　　　　 BILLY LYONS AND STACK O'LEE by Furry Lewis (Vocalion 1132) 1927.
　　　　　　　　　　 STACK O'LEE BLUES by Mississippi John Hurt (OKeh 8654) 1929.
○ Jam recorded during rehearsals at MGM Soundstage, Hollywood on 15 July 1970. Released on bootleg CDs *A Dinner Date With Elvis* (Presto CD-1021) and *Get Down And Get With It* (Fort Baxter 2204).

TROUBLE IN MIND *(Jones)*

★ Original by Thelma La Vizzo (Paramount 12206) 1924.
◆ *Elvis' sources:* Richard Jones (Bluebird 6563) 1936.
　　　　　　　　　　 Georgia White (Decca 7192) 1936.
　　　　　　　　　　 Lucky Millinder – Voc. Rosetta Thorpe (Decca 4041) 1942.
　　　　　　　　　　 Bertha 'Chippie' Hill (Circle 1003) 1946.
　　　　　　　　　　 Bob Wills (Columbia 37306) 1947.
　　　　　　　　　　 Duke Henderson (Modern 20-632) 1948.

◆ SECTION 2 ◆

WELO Appearances 1944-48

It has been known for some time that Elvis appeared on WELO on several occasions — most famously in July 1944, when he sang **OLD SHEP**. Samuel Barnes' investigations at the radio station uncovered details of this plus more than a dozen other appearances. All songs played on air — whether on record or performed live — were declared by WELO for copyright purposes. However, the station's files were incomplete, so it is possible that Elvis also made other appearances for which records no longer exist. Indeed, a recently discovered letter from Gladys Presley to a friend implies that Elvis frequently performed on the show.

Radio station WELO was founded in May 1941 by Charles Boren and was based at 212 South Spring Street, Tupelo, Mississippi. A pilot for an amateur talent show, the *Black & White Saturday Jamboree*, was broadcast in March 1943. Named after its sponsor, the Black & White hardware store (above which WELO's offices were located), it became a regular Saturday feature for many years. The programme was broadcast live from the Lee County Courthouse at 200 East Jefferson Street in Tupelo and was hosted by local hillbilly star, Mississippi Slim (Carvel Lee Ausborn). Slim was the older brother of one of Elvis' school friends, James Ausborn, and was some eleven years older than Elvis.

Between 1944 and 1948, the *Black & White Saturday Jamboree* went out immediately after Slim's own show, *Singin' And Pickin' Hillbilly*, first broadcast as a pilot on Saturday, 15 April 1944. It aired daily from 12.15 to 12.30 pm and typically consisted of five or six songs interspersed with commercials, announcements and jokes. In August 1944, *Singin' And Pickin' Hillbilly* moved to a 12.30 to 12.45 pm slot. In 1945, it was extended to thirty minutes (12.30 to 1.00 pm). In 1948, Slim moved to WSIX in Nashville, and the *Black & White Saturday Jamboree* continued without him on WELO.

Elvis' appearances on the *Black & White Jamboree* were sporadic. It is not known whether he ever accompanied himself on guitar — his mother bought him one in 1946 — but there were certainly some occasions when he either sang unaccompanied or with Mississippi Slim backing him on guitar. Bill Mitchell, who played fiddle in Slim's band, also remembers them backing the lad on at least one occasion. (Interestingly, future Sun artist Billy Lee Riley also appeared on the show in 1946 at the age of thirteen.)

2.1

Black & White Saturday Jamboree (WELO)
Lee County Courthouse, Tupelo, Mississippi
Saturday, 15(?) July 1944
Elvis Presley   Vocal
Mississippi Slim   Acoustic guitar
Lew Reibert   Announcer

This was Elvis' first-ever radio appearance. Radio engineer Archie Mackey recalled that Elvis sang two songs accompanied by Mississippi Slim on guitar. In 'The Real Elvis: Good Old Boy', Vince Staten claims that Elvis made his radio debut on the 'Black & White Jamboree' on 15 May 1944. This is impossible, as 15 May 1944 was a Monday. Similarly, in 'Elvis: A Radio History From 1945 To 1955' Aaron Webster erroneously cites both 15 May 1944 (page 8) and 15 April 1944 (page 237).

OLD SHEP *(Foley/Arthur)*

✱ Original by Red Foley (Decca 5944) 1941.
◆ *Elvis' source:* Red Foley (Decca 5944) 1941.
O Elvis later recorded this title at Radio Recorders, Hollywood on 2 September 1956 (released in 1956 on LP *Elvis*, RCA-Victor LPM-1382).

UNKNOWN TITLE

2.2

Black & White Saturday Jamboree (WELO)
Lee County Courthouse, Tupelo, Mississippi
Saturday, ? February 1945 (exact date unknown)
Elvis Presley   Vocal
Lew Reibert   Announcer

WON'T YOU RIDE IN MY LITTLE RED WAGON *(Griffin)*

✱ Original by Hank Penny (Vocalion 05438) 1939.
◆ *Elvis' source:* Hank Penny (Vocalion 05438) 1939.

Black & White Saturday Jamboree **(WELO)**
Lee County Courthouse, Tupelo, Mississippi
Saturday, ? May 1945 (exact date unknown)
Elvis Presley   Vocal
Charles Boren   Announcer

MY DIXIE DARLING *(Carter)*

✱ Original by the Carter Family (Decca 5240) 1936.
◆ *Elvis' source:* Carter Family (Decca 5240) 1936.

Black & White Saturday Jamboree **(WELO)**
Lee County Courthouse, Tupelo, Mississippi
Saturday, 7 July 1945
Elvis Presley   Vocal
Mississippi Slim   Acoustic guitar
Bill Mitchell?   Fiddle?
Others?
Lew Reibert   Announcer

LITTLE WOODPECKER SONG *(Ausborn)*
This song was composed by Mississippi Slim and was originally conceived as a lullaby. He later recorded a demo of it for Sun circa 1955/56, possibly with altered lyrics.

◆ *Elvis' source:* Mississippi Slim taught this song to Elvis.

2.5

Children's Day Talent Contest **(WELO)**
Mississippi–Alabama Fair & Dairy Show, **Fairground, Tupelo, Mississippi**
Wednesday, 3 October 1945
Elvis Presley   Vocal

Elvis was entered for this talent show by his school principal, Mr. J. D. Cole, on the recommendation of his teacher, Mrs. Oleta Grimes. He actually came 5th, not 2nd as has previously been claimed by various writers.

OLD SHEP *(Foley/Arthur)*

✱ Original by Red Foley (Decca 5944) 1941.
◆ *Elvis' source:* Red Foley (Decca 5944) 1941.
⚬ Elvis later recorded this title at Radio Recorders, Hollywood on 2 September 1956 (released in 1956 on LP *Elvis*, RCA-Victor LPM-1382).

2.6

Black & White Saturday Jamboree (WELO)
Lee County Courthouse, Tupelo, Mississippi
Saturday, ? November 1945 (exact date unknown)

Elvis Presley	Vocal
Mississippi Slim	Acoustic guitar
Bill Mitchell?	Fiddle?
Others?	
Lew Reibert	Announcer

THE LONESOME ROAD *(Austin/Shilkret)*
Song from the Broadway musical, 'Show Boat'. A hit in 1928 for Gene Austin (Victor 20198), in 1929 for Nat Shilkret (Victor 21996), in 1930 for Ted Lewis (Columbia 2181) and in 1939 for Bing Crosby (Decca 2257).

★ Original by the Blue Ridge Duo *[Gene Austin and George Reneau]* (Edison 51515) 1924.
◆ *Elvis' sources:* Sister Rosetta Tharpe (Decca 2243) 1938.
　　　　　　　　　 Bing Crosby (Decca 2257) 1939.
　　　　　　　　　 Maxwell Davis (4 Star 1027) 1945.

2.7

Black & White Saturday Jamboree (WELO)
Lee County Courthouse, Tupelo, Mississippi
Saturday, ? March 1946 (exact date unknown)

Elvis Presley	Vocal
Charles Boren	Announcer

I NEED THE PRAYERS OF THOSE I LOVE *(Vaughan)*
Hymn composed by James D. Vaughan, 'the father of Southern gospel'.

★ Original by the Delmore Brothers (Bluebird 7672) 1937.
◆ *Elvis' source:* Delmore Brothers (Bluebird 7672) 1937.

2.8

Black & White Saturday Jamboree (WELO)
Lee County Courthouse, Tupelo, Mississippi
Saturday, ? June 1946 (exact date unknown)

Elvis Presley	Vocal
Lew Reibert	Announcer

MOTHER, QUEEN OF MY HEART *(Rodgers)*

★ Original by Jimmie Rodgers (Victor 23721) 1932.
◆ *Elvis' source:* Jimmie Rodgers (Victor 23721) 1932.

2.9

Black & White Saturday Jamboree (WELO)
Lee County Courthouse, Tupelo, Mississippi
Saturday, 14 September 1946

Elvis Presley	Vocal
Mississippi Slim	Acoustic guitar
Bill Mitchell?	Fiddle?
Others?	
Lew Reibert	Announcer

WE THREE (MY ECHO, MY SHADOW AND ME) *(Robertson/Cogane/Mysels)*
A hit in 1940 for Tommy Dorsey (Victor 26747) and in 1941 for the Ink Spots (Decca 3379).

✱ Original by the Ink Spots (Decca 3379) 1940.
◆ *Elvis' sources:* Tommy Dorsey – Voc. Frank Sinatra (Victor 26747) 1940.
　　　　　　　　　　 Ink Spots (Decca 3379) 1940.

2.10

Black & White Saturday Jamboree (WELO)
Lee County Courthouse, Tupelo, Mississippi
Saturday, ? January 1947 (exact date unknown)

Elvis Presley	Vocal
Lew Reibert	Announcer

MY ROSE OF ALABAMA *(Steele)*
Patriotic song composed in 1846 by S.S. Steele.

✱ Original by ?
◆ *Elvis' source:* Elvis learned this song at East Tupelo Consolidated School (Lawhon Elementary)
　　　　　　　　　 in 1944.

2.11

Black & White Saturday Jamboree (WELO)
Lee County Courthouse, Tupelo, Mississippi
Saturday, ? April 1947 (exact date unknown)

Elvis Presley	Vocal
Mississippi Slim	Acoustic guitar
Bill Mitchell?	Fiddle?
Others?	
Lew Reibert	Announcer

BLIND CHILD *(Delmore)*

✱ Original by the Delmore Brothers (Bluebird 6915) 1937.
◆ *Elvis' source:* Delmore Brothers (Bluebird 6915) 1937.

2.12

***Black & White Saturday Jamboree* (WELO)**
Lee County Courthouse, Tupelo, Mississippi
Saturday, ? April 1947 (exact date unknown)
Elvis Presley   Vocal
Lew Reibert   Announcer

DADDY AND HOME *(Rodgers/Williamson/McWilliams)*

✱ Original by Jimmie Rodgers (Victor 21757) 1928.
◆ *Elvis' source:* Jimmie Rodgers (Victor 21757) 1928.

2.13

***Black & White Saturday Jamboree* (WELO)**
Lee County Courthouse, Tupelo, Mississippi
Saturday, ? December 1947 (exact date unknown)
Elvis Presley   Vocal
Lew Reibert   Announcer

BLUE MELODY *(Dumont)*

✱ Original by Hank Penny (Vocalion 04826) 1939.
◆ *Elvis' source:* Hank Penny (Vocalion 04826) 1939.

2.14

***Black & White Saturday Jamboree* (WELO)**
Lee County Courthouse, Tupelo, Mississippi
Saturday, 21 February 1948
Elvis Presley   Vocal
Lew Reibert   Announcer

YOU ARE MY FLOWER *(Carter)*

✱ Original by the Carter Family (Decca 5692) 1939.
◆ *Elvis' source:* Carter Family (Decca 5692) 1939.

2.15

Black & White Saturday Jamboree (WELO)
Lee County Courthouse, Tupelo, Mississippi
Saturday, ? May 1948 (exact date unknown)
Elvis Presley   Vocal
Lew Reibert   Announcer

SOUTHERN MOON *(Delmore)*

✱ Original by the Delmore Brothers (Bluebird 6841) 1937.
◆ *Elvis' source:* Delmore Brothers (Bluebird 6841) 1937.

◆ SECTION 3 ◆

Memphis 1948-54

The experience of moving from a small country town to the big city at the age of thirteen had a profound effect on Elvis, and it reportedly took him quite some time to adjust to his new surroundings. More positively, however, it also exposed him to the sights and sounds of America's urban black culture that were to have such a tremendous influence on both his appearance and his music. It also presented him with the opportunity to listen to and meet many other musicians, and ultimately become a performer and recording artist himself. As the list below demonstrates, the teenage Elvis was already a big fan of the styles that formed the cornerstones of his career: gospel, pop ballads, hillbilly, blues and R&B.

The First Assembly of God Church
1084 East McLemore Avenue, Memphis, Tennessee
Between 1950 and 1952 (exact dates unknown)

Rev. James E. Hamill, pastor of the First Assembly of God Church, recalled Elvis singing the following hymns and spirituals in the choir and/or with his parents.

I'LL FLY AWAY *(Brumley)*
Hymn composed in 1931 by Rev. Albert E. Brumley. Heard in black churches in the South from the 1930s; in white churches from around the same date.

✱ Original by Rev. J.M. Gates (Bluebird 8504) 1940.
◆ *Elvis' radio sources:* Rev. J.M. Gates (Bluebird 8504) 1940.
Selah Jubilee Singers (Decca 7831) 1941.
Chuck Wagon Gang (Columbia 20599) 1949.
Sensational Nightingales (Coleman 6028) 1949.
Sister Marie Knight (Decca 48253) 1951.
Southern Sons Quartette (Trumpet 164) 1951.
Trumpeteers (OKeh 6890) 1952.

MOSES SMOTE THE WATER(S) *(Traditional)*
Negro spiritual. Heard in black churches in the South from circa 1880; in white churches from ?

✱ Original by the Golden Gate Quartet. Recorded in September 1941 on a 16-inch transcription disc (Thesaurus 977). A second recording made in December 1941 was commercially released in 1946 (Columbia 36937).
First commercial release: Kings Of Harmony Jubilee Quartette (King Solomon 1007) 1944.
◆ *Elvis' radio source:* Golden Gate Quartet (Columbia 36937) 1946.

SWING LOW, SWEET CHARIOT [SWING DOWN, SWEET CHARIOT] *(Traditional)*
Negro spiritual. Heard in black churches in the South from circa 1872; in white churches from circa 1874. Many variants, most notably **SWING DOWN CHARIOT (LET ME RIDE)**. *A hit in 1910 for the Fisk University Jubilee Quartet (Victor 16453).*

✱ Original recording on cylinder by the Standard Quartette (Columbia, no number) 1894.
Original recording on 78 rpm by the Fisk University Jubilee Quartet (Victor 16453) 1910.
◆ *Elvis' radio sources:*   Charioteers (Brunswick 8468) 1939.
        Charioteers (Columbia 35693) 1940.
        Deep River Boys (Pilot 5149) 1946.
        Wings Over Jordan Choir (Queen 4154) 1946.
        Harmonaires (Varsity 5008) 1947.
        SWING DOWN, CHARIOT by the Golden Gate Quartet
         (Columbia 37834) 1948.
        Luvenia Nash Singers (Excelsior 155) 1949.
        SWING DOWN CHARIOT by the Dixieaires (Sunrise 2117) 1950.
        Sister Rosetta Tharpe (Decca 48160) 1950.
        Bill Monroe (Decca 46325) 1951.
        Ames Brothers (Coral 60634) 1952.
○ Elvis later recorded this title at RCA Studio B, Nashville on 31 October 1960 (released in 1960 on LP *His Hand In Mine*, RCA-Victor LPM/LSP-2328). He re-recorded it at United Artists Recorders, Hollywood on 23 October 1968 for the film *The Trouble With Girls* (released 1969). This version appeared in 1983 on LP *Elvis: A Legendary Performer (Volume 4)* (RCA-Victor CPL1-4848). He also recorded a live version at the Bloch Arena, Pearl Harbor in 1961.

East Trigg Baptist Church
1189 East Trigg Avenue, Memphis, Tennessee
Between 1950 and 1952 (exact dates unknown)

East Trigg was a black church run by the charismatic Rev. W. Herbert Brewster, whose Sunday evening sermons were broadcast over WDIA in Memphis. Elvis and his friends often attended the exciting services there. In July 1970, Samuel Barnes interviewed Rev. Brewster, who recalled Elvis singing the following songs, and also that he sometimes stayed behind after services to play piano.

AIN'T THAT GOOD NEWS *(Traditional)*
Negro spiritual. Heard in black churches in the South from circa 1890; in white churches from ?

✱ Original by the Birmingham Jubilee Singers (Columbia 14408) 1929.
◆ *Elvis' radio source:* Heavenly Gospel Singers (Bluebird 8047) 1939.

DEEP RIVER *(Traditional)*
Negro spiritual. Heard in black and white churches in the South from circa 1870. A hit in 1927 for Paul Robeson (Victor 20793).

✱ Original by Clark Carroll (Columbia 128D) 1923.
◆ *Elvis' radio sources:* Deep River Boys (Associated 60.917) 1946.
                          Wings Over Jordan Choir (Queen 4140) 1946.
                          Harmonaires (Varsity 5007) 1947.
                          Ames Brothers (Coral 60633) 1952.

DIDN'T IT RAIN *(Traditional)*
Negro spiritual. Heard in black churches in the South from circa 1920; in white churches from circa ?

✱ Original by Deacon Leon Davis (OKeh 8426) 1926.
◆ *Elvis' radio sources:* Golden Gate Quartet (OKeh 6529) 1941.
                          Golden Gate Quartet (Columbia 37475) 1947.
                          Harmonaires (Varsity 5007) 1947.
                          Sister Rosetta Tharpe (Decca 48054) 1947.
                          Golden Gate Quartet (Columbia 30042) 1948.
                          Trumpeteers (Score 5003) 1948.
                          Elder Charles Beck (Apex 606) 1949.
                          Sallie Martin Singers (Specialty 391) 1950.

THE LORD'S PRAYER *(Traditional)*
Traditional hymn. Heard in white churches in the South from circa 1820; in black churches from circa 1865. Pop in 1949 for Perry Como (RCA-Victor 0436). R&B hit in 1950 for the Original Five Blind Boys (Peacock 1550).

✱ Original **THE LORD'S PRAYER & 23RD PSALM** by Len Spencer (Columbia A-1035) 1911.
◆ *Elvis' radio sources:* Heavenly Gospel Singers (Bluebird 7133) 1937.
                          Sarah Vaughan (Musicraft 525) 1947.
                          Perry Como (RCA-Victor 0436) 1949.
                          OUR FATHER by the Original Five Blind Boys *[Of Mississippi]*
                                      (Peacock 1550) 1950.
                          Myrtle Jackson (Coral 65047) 1950.
                          Orioles (Jubilee 5045) 1950.
                          OUR FATHER by Brother Joe May (Specialty 388) 1950.
                          Mahalia Jackson (Apollo 245) 1951.
                          OUR FATHER by the Sensational Nightingales (Decca 48205) 1951.
                          Sons Of The Pioneers (RCA-Victor 4347) 1951.
                          Harmonizing Four (Gotham 775) 1952.
                          Dinah Washington (Mercury 70263) 1953.
◉ Elvis later made a private recording of this title at Monovale Drive, Hollywood in the autumn of 1960. He subsequently recorded it at RCA Studio B, Nashville on 16 May 1971 (released in 1996 on CD *A Hundred Years From Now (Essential Elvis Volume 4)*, BMG/RCA 66866-2).

3.3

Brief list of songs Elvis is known to have sung at Lauderdale Courts, at school (during recess) and elsewhere between 1949 and 1953 (exact dates unknown)

COOL WATER *(Nolan)*
Pop hit in 1941 for the Sons Of The Pioneers (Decca 5939), and in 1949 for Vaughn Monroe with the Sons Of The Pioneers (RCA-Victor 2923). C&W hit in 1947 and 1948 for the Sons Of The Pioneers (Decca 46027). R&B hit in 1948 for Nellie Lutcher (Capitol 15148).

✱ Original by the Sons Of The Pioneers (Decca 5939) 1941.
◆ *Elvis' sources:*   Sons Of The Pioneers (Decca 46027) 1947.
            Jimmy Wakely (Sterling 213) 1947.
            Nellie Lutcher (Capitol 15148) 1948.
            Vaughn Monroe with the Sons Of The Pioneers (RCA-Victor 2923) 1948.
            Four Tunes (RCA-Victor 3967) 1950.
            Bing Crosby + Andrews Sisters (Decca 28419) 1952.
○ Elvis later made a private recording of this title at his army house at 14 Goethestrasse, Bad Nauheim, West Germany circa April 1959 (lost).

GOIN' HOME *(Domino/Young)*
Crossover (pop and R&B) hit in 1952 for Fats Domino.

✱ Original by Fats Domino (Imperial 5180) 1952.
◆ *Elvis' source:* Fats Domino (Imperial 5180) 1952.

I'M MOVIN' ON *(Snow)*
Crossover (pop and C&W) hit in 1950 for Hank Snow (RCA-Victor 0328).

✱ Original by Hank Snow (RCA-Victor 0328) 1950.
◆ *Elvis' source:* Hank Snow (RCA-Victor 0328) 1950.
○ Elvis later recorded this title at American Sound Studio, Memphis on 15 January 1969 (released in 1969 on LP *From Elvis In Memphis*, RCA-Victor LSP-4155).

IT'S TOO SOON TO KNOW *(Chessler)*
Crossover (pop and R&B) hit in 1948 for the Orioles (It's A Natural 5000). R&B hit in 1948 for Ella Fitzgerald (Decca 24497), the Ravens (National 9056) and Dinah Washington (Mercury 8107).

✱ Original by the Orioles (It's A Natural 5000) 1948.
◆ *Elvis' sources:*   Deep River Boys (RCA-Victor 3203) 1948.
            Ella Fitzgerald (Decca 24497) 1948.
            Ravens (National 9056) 1948.
            Dinah Washington (Mercury 8107) 1948.

LAWDY MISS CLAWDY *(Price)*
R&B hit in 1952 for Lloyd Price (Specialty 428).

✱ Original by Lloyd Price (Specialty 428) 1952.
◆ *Elvis' source:* Lloyd Price (Specialty 428) 1952.
○ Elvis later recorded this title at RCA, New York on 3 February 1956 (released in 1956 on EP *Elvis Presley*, RCA-Victor EPA-830). Also at NBC-TV studio, Burbank, California on 27 June 1968 (released in 1968 on LP *Elvis TV Special*, RCA-Victor LPM-4088) and at Mid-South Coliseum, Memphis on 20 March 1974 (released in 1974 on LP *Elvis – Recorded Live On Stage In Memphis*, RCA-Victor CPL1-0606).

MOLLY DARLING *(Hays)*
C&W hit in 1948 for Eddy Arnold (RCA-Victor 2489).

✱ Original by Eddy Arnold (RCA-Victor 2489) 1947.
◆ *Elvis' source:* Eddy Arnold (RCA-Victor 2489) 1947.

MONA LISA *(Livingstone/Evans)*
From the 1950 film, 'Capt. Carey, USA'. Crossover (pop and R&B) hit in 1950 for Nat 'King' Cole (Capitol 1010). Pop hit in 1950 for Dennis Day (RCA-Victor 3753), Ralph Flanagan (RCA-Victor 3888), Harry James (Columbia 38768), Art Lund (MGM 10689), Charlie Spivak (London 619) and Victor Young (Decca 27048). C&W hit in 1950 for Moon Mullican (King 886) and Jimmy Wakely (Capitol 1151).

✱ Original by Nat 'King' Cole (Capitol 1010) 1950.
◆ *Elvis' sources:* Nat 'King' Cole (Capitol 1010) 1950.
                Dennis Day (RCA-Victor 3753) 1950.
                Ralph Flanagan (RCA-Victor 3888) 1950.
                Harry James – Voc. Dick Williams (Columbia 38768) 1950.
                Art Lund (MGM 10689) 1950.
                Moon Mullican (King 886) 1950.
                Charlie Spivak (London 619) 1950.
                Jimmy Wakely (Capitol 1151) 1950.
                Victor Young – Voc. Don Cherry (Decca 27048) 1950.
◉ Elvis later made a private recording of this title at his army house at 14 Goethestrasse, Bad Nauheim, West Germany in April 1959 (released in 1983 on LP *Elvis: A Legendary Performer (Volume 4)*, RCA-Victor CPL1-4848).

MY HAPPINESS *(Peterson/Bergantine)*
Crossover (pop and R&B) hit in 1948 for Ella Fitzgerald (Decca 24446). Pop hit in 1948 John Laurenz (Mercury 5144), the Marlin Sisters (Columbia 38217), Pied Pipers (Capitol 15094) and Jon & Sandra Steele (Damon 11133), and in 1953 for the Mulcays (Cardinal 1014).

✱ Original by Jon & Sandra Steele (Damon 11133) 1948.
◆ *Elvis' sources:* Ella Fitzgerald (Decca 24446) 1948.
                John Laurenz (Mercury 5144) 1948.
                Marlin Sisters (Columbia 38217) 1948.
                Pied Pipers (Capitol 15094) 1948.
                Jon & Sandra Steele (Damon 11133) 1948.
◉ Elvis made a private recording of this title at Memphis Recording Service (Sun Studio) on 18 July 1953 [see **4.2** for details].

RIDERS IN THE SKY [GHOST RIDERS IN THE SKY] *(Jones)*
Composed by Stan Jones. From the 1949 film, 'Riders In The Sky'. Crossover (pop and C&W) hit in 1949 for Burl Ives (Columbia 38445) and Vaughn Monroe (RCA-Victor 2902). Pop hit in 1949 for Bing Crosby (Decca 24618) and Peggy Lee (Capitol 608).

✱ Original by the Sons Of The Pioneers (RCA-Victor 0060) 1949.
◆ *Elvis' sources:* Bing Crosby (Decca 24618) 1949.
                Burl Ives (Columbia 38445) 1949.
                Peggy Lee (Capitol 608) 1949.
                Vaughn Monroe (RCA-Victor 2902) 1949.
                Sons Of The Pioneers (RCA-Victor 0060) 1949.
◉ Jam recorded at MGM Soundstage, Hollywood on 15 July 1970. First released in 1997 on bootleg CD *Electrifying* (Bilko 5100). Officially released in 2001 on CD *The Way It Was*, BMG/Follow That Dream 74321 84216-2).

SHAKE A HAND *(Morris)*

Crossover (pop and R&B) hit in 1953 for Faye Adams (Herald 416). Pop hit in 1953 for Savannah Churchill (Decca 28836). C&W hit in 1953 for Red Foley (Decca 28839).

✶ Original by Faye Adams (Herald 416) 1953.
◆ *Elvis' sources:* Faye Adams (Herald 416) 1953.
                 Savannah Churchill (Decca 28836) 1953.
                 Red Foley (Decca 28839) 1953.
○ Elvis later recorded this title at RCA Studio C, Hollywood on 12 March 1975 (released in 1975. on LP *Today*, RCA-Victor APL1-1039).

TAKE YOUR HANDS OFF IT [BIRTHDAY CAKE] *(Hughes)*

Like **KEEP YOUR HANDS OFF HER** [see **4.5**]*, based on a popular double entendre song originating in the 1890s. Many variants. Mary Stafford's* **TAKE YOUR FINGER OFF IT** *(Paramount 7502) from 1926 is one of the earliest recorded examples of this theme.*

✶ Original **TAKE YOUR HANDS OFF IT** by Billy Hughes' Buckaroos (Fargo 1119) 1947.
◆ *Elvis' sources:* **KEEP YOUR HANDS OFF IT** by Billy Hughes' Buckaroos (4 Star 1202) 1947
                        (reissue of Fargo 1119).
                        BIRTHDAY CAKE by Billy Hughes' Buckaroos (4 Star 1559) 1951 (*second reissue of Fargo 1119).*
                        BIRTHDAY CAKE by Randy Hughes (Tennessee 787) 1951.
                        BIRTHDAY CAKE by Skeets McDonald (Fortune 165) 1952.

TENNESSEE WALTZ *(Stewart/King)*

Crossover (pop and C&W) hit in 1948 for Pee Wee King (RCA-Victor 0407) and in 1950-51 for Patti Page (Mercury 5534). C&W hit in 1948 for Roy Acuff (Columbia 20551) and Cowboy Copas (King 696), and in 1951 again for Pee Wee King (RCA-Victor 0407). R&B hit in 1950 for Erskine Hawkins (Coral 60313) and in 1951 for Stick McGhee (Atlantic 926). Pop hit in 1951 for the Fontane Sisters (RCA-Victor 3979), Spike Jones (RCA-Victor 4011), Guy Lombardo (Decca 27336), Anita O'Day (London 867), Les Paul & Mary Ford (Capitol 1316) and Jo Stafford (Columbia 39129).

✶ Original by Cowboy Copas (King 696) 1948.
◆ *Elvis' sources:* Roy Acuff (Columbia 20551) 1948.
                      Cowboy Copas (King 696) 1948.
                      Pee Wee King (RCA-Victor 2680) 1948.
                      Pee Wee King (Bluebird 58-0070) 1949.
                      Erskine Hawkins (Coral 60313) 1950.
                      Spike Jones (RCA-Victor 4011) 1950.
                      Sammy Kaye (Columbia 39113) 1950.
                      Patti Page (Mercury 5534) 1950.
                      Les Paul & Mary Ford (Capitol 1316) 1950.
                      Fontane Sisters (RCA-Victor 3979) 1951.
                      Pee Wee King (RCA-Victor 0407) 1951.
                      Guy Lombardo (Decca 27336) 1951.
                      Claude McLin (Chess 1446) 1951.
                      TENNESSEE WALTZ BLUES by Stick McGhee (Atlantic 926) 1951.
                      Anita O'Day (London 867) 1951.
                      Jo Stafford (Columbia 39129) 1951.
○ Elvis later made a private recording of this title at Rocca Place, Hollywood, California between February 1966 and early 1967 (released in 1997 on 4-CD *Platinum – A Life In Music*, BMG/RCA 67489-2).

THAT'S ALL RIGHT *(Crudup)*

★ Original by Arthur 'Big Boy' Crudup (RCA-Victor 20-2205) 1947.
◆ *Elvis' sources:*   Arthur 'Big Boy' Crudup (RCA-Victor 2205) 1947.
                          Arthur 'Big Boy' Crudup (RCA-Victor 50-0000) 1949.
〇 Elvis recorded this title at Sun Studio, Memphis on 5 July 1954 (Sun 209, 1954) [see **4.6** for details].

TOMORROW NIGHT *(Coslow/Grosz)*
A hit in 1939 for Horace Heidt (Columbia 35203). Crossover (pop and R&B) hit in 1948 for Lonnie Johnson (King 4201). Not to be confused with Louis Armstrong's 1933 recording 'Tomorrow Night (After Tonight)' (RCA-Victor 68-0774) or Junior Wells' 'Tomorrow Night' (States 143) 1954.

★ Original by Horace Heidt (Columbia 35203) 1939.
◆ *Elvis' sources:*   Horace Heidt (Columbia 35203) 1939.
                          Lonnie Johnson (King 4201) 1948.
                          Lonnie Johnson (Paradise 11) 1948.
〇 Elvis recorded this title at Sun Studio, Memphis on 19 August and 8 December 1954 [see **4.8** and **4.12** for details]. Second version unissued/lost.

Humes High Annual Minstrel Show
L.C. Humes High School, 659 North Manassas Street, Memphis, Tennessee
Thursday, 9 April 1953 (8.00 pm)

TILL I WALTZ AGAIN WITH YOU *(Prosen)*
Pop hit in 1953 for Teresa Brewer (Coral 60873), the Harmonicats (Mercury 70069), Russ Morgan (Decca 28539) and Dick Todd (Decca 28506). C&W hit in 1953 for Tommy Sosebea (Coral 60916).

★ Original by Teresa Brewer (Coral 60873) 1952.
◆ *Elvis' sources:*   Teresa Brewer (Coral 60873) 1952.
                          Russ Morgan (Decca 28539) 1953.
                          Tommy Sosebea (Coral 60916) 1953.
                          Dick Todd (Decca 28506) 1953.

Elvis sang the following song as an encore:

KEEP THEM COLD ICY FINGERS OFF OF ME *(Lair)*

★ Original by Fairley Holden (King 612) 1947.
◆ *Elvis' source:* Fairley Holden (King 612) 1947.

3.5

Memphis, between 1949 and 1954 (exact dates unknown)

Marcus Van Story, who later played double-bass at Sun, met Elvis in late 1948 or early 1949 and recalled singing the following songs with him.

GREAT BIG EYES *(Gross)*

★ Original by Archibald (Imperial 5212) 1952.
◆ *Elvis' source:* Archibald (Imperial 5212) 1952.

I NEED YOU SO *(Hunter)*
R&B hit in 1950 for Ivory Joe Hunter (MGM 10663). Pop hit in 1950 for Hugo Winterhalter (RCA-Victor 3884).

★ Original by Ivory Joe Hunter (MGM 10663) 1950.
◆ *Elvis' sources:* Ivory Joe Hunter (MGM 10663) 1950.
　　　　　　　　　Orioles (Jubilee 5037) 1950.
　　　　　　　　　Hugo Winterhalter – Voc. Don Cornell (RCA-Victor 3884) 1950.
O Elvis later recorded this title at Radio Recorders, Hollywood on 23 February 1957 (released in 1957 on EP *Just For You*, RCA-Victor EPA-4041).

KEEP THEM COLD ICY FINGERS OFF OF ME *(Lair)*

★ Original by Fairley Holden (King 612) 1947.
◆ *Elvis' source:* Fairley Holden (King 612) 1947.

LAWDY MISS CLAWDY *(Price)*
R&B hit in 1952 for Lloyd Price (Specialty 428).

★ Original by Lloyd Price (Specialty 428) 1952.
◆ *Elvis' source:* Lloyd Price (Specialty 428) 1952.
O Elvis later recorded this title at RCA, New York on 3 February 1956 (released in 1956 on EP *Elvis Presley*, RCA-Victor EPA-830). Also at NBC-TV studio, Burbank, California on 27 June 1968 (released in 1968 on LP *Elvis TV Special*, RCA-Victor LPM-4088) and at Mid-South Coliseum, Memphis on 20 March 1974 (released in 1974 on LP *Elvis – Recorded Live On Stage In Memphis*, RCA-Victor CPL1-0606).

LITTLE WHITE CHURCH *(Christian)*

★ Original by Mac Wiseman (Dot 1075) 1951.
◆ *Elvis' source:* Mac Wiseman (Dot 1075) 1951.

3.6

Crown Electric Company Inc, 353 Poplar Avenue, Memphis, Tennessee
Tuesday, 20 April–mid-October 1954 (exact date unknown)

James R. Tipler (owner of Crown Electric, where Elvis was employed as a stock clerk and then a local delivery driver) recalled him singing the following songs at work. Of course, he also sang many others.

BABY PLEASE DON'T GO *(Willams)*
R&B hit in 1951 for the Orioles (Jubilee 5065).

★ Original by Big Joe Williams (Bluebird 6200) 1935.
◆ *Elvis' sources:* Big Joe Williams (Bluebird 8969) 1942.
　　　　　　　　　Leroy Dallas (Sittin' In With 537) 1949.
　　　　　　　　　Orioles (Jubilee 5065) 1951.
　　　　　　　　　KEEP YOUR LAMP DOWN LOW by Billy Wright (Savoy 827) 1951.
　　　　　　　　　TURN YOUR LAMP DOWN LOW by Muddy Waters (Chess 1542) 1953.

IT'S TOO SOON TO KNOW *(Chessler)*
Crossover (pop and R&B) hit in 1948 for the Orioles (It's A Natural 5000). R&B hit in 1948 for Ella Fitzgerald (Decca 24497), the Ravens (National 9056) and Dinah Washington (Mercury 8107).

★ Original by the Orioles (It's A Natural 5000) 1948.
◆ *Elvis' sources:* Deep River Boys (RCA-Victor 3203) 1948.
　　　　　　　　　Ella Fitzgerald (Decca 24497) 1948.
　　　　　　　　　Ravens (National 9056) 1948.
　　　　　　　　　Dinah Washington (Mercury 8107) 1948.

TILL I WALTZ AGAIN WITH YOU *(Prosen)*
Pop hit in 1953 for Teresa Brewer (Coral 60873), the Harmonicats (Mercury 70069), Russ Morgan (Decca 28539) and Dick Todd (Decca 28506). C&W hit in 1953 for Tommy Sosebea (Coral 60916).

★ Original by Teresa Brewer (Coral 60873) 1952.
◆ *Elvis' sources:* Teresa Brewer (Coral 60873) 1952.
　　　　　　　　　Russ Morgan (Decca 28539) 1953.
　　　　　　　　　Tommy Sosebea (Coral 60916) 1953.
　　　　　　　　　Dick Todd (Decca 28506) 1953.

WORK WITH ME ANNIE *(Ballard)*
Crossover (pop and R&B) hit in 1954 for the Midnighters (Federal 12169).

★ Original by the Midnighters (Federal 12169) 1954.
◆ *Elvis' source:* Midnighters (Federal 12169) 1954.

◆ SECTION 4 ◆

The Sun Sessions 1953-55

The recordings that Elvis made at the Sun studio in Memphis are of immense historical interest. Not only are they supreme examples of the nascent rockabilly style, they also chart Elvis' musical development over what were without doubt the most innovative and important years of his entire career. Having lain dormant on file for many years, the full details of these groundbreaking sessions are revealed here for the first time.

🕐 = Timed on professional CD player, started at the first music note.

4.1

Sun Studio, 706 Union Avenue, Memphis, Tennessee
Monday, 1 June 1953 (Session: 10.30 am–8.30 pm)
Prisonaires   Vocal group
William Stewart   Acoustic guitar

---

*The Prisonaires (Johnny Bragg, John Drue, Marcell Saunders, William Stewart and Ed Thurman) were a group of black inmates from the Tennessee State Penitentiary in Nashville, who were given permission to travel to Memphis to record at Sun as part of their rehabilitation programme. In later years, lead singer Bragg claimed that Elvis happened by the studio that day and helped him with his phrasing on what was to become their most famous song, **JUST WALKIN' IN THE RAIN**:*
'I was having problems phrasing some of the words. Sam was ready to give up on it, and here come this guy out of nowhere, wearing raggedy blue jeans. He said: "I believe I can help him pronounce the words." Sam got mad. He said: "Didn't I tell you to stay outta here? These men are prisoners. We're likely to be sued. I said: "If he thinks he can help me phrase this thing, give him a chance." Sam said: "OK, let him try", so we took a break, and Elvis worked with me on my diction. He didn't know too much about what he was doing, but he worked with me on it, and when we went back, we got it on the first cut.'
This version of events, from Escott & Hawkins' 'Good Rockin' Tonight' (1991) is retold in greater detail in Jay Warner's 'Just Walkin' In The Rain' (2001). However, opinion is divided as to whether this event actually occurred.
There is strong evidence (like Marion Keisker's reaction on 18 July 1953, when Elvis went down to the Memphis Recording Service to cut his first acetate) to suggest that he wasn't known at Sun prior to that date. Furthermore, it's likely that he didn't meet Sam Phillips until some time later, as only Marian was in the office that day. How, then, is it possible that Elvis, who was not known to either Marion or Sam, who had never made a record or been inside a studio in his life,

simply ambled into the Sun studio and was permitted to go anywhere near the recording?
Escott & Hawkins are also dubious: 'Bragg may have telescoped the time frame, confusing the first Prisonaires session with a later one; certainly, there is no mention of Presley in the article about the session that appeared in the Memphis Press Scimitar *the following day.' Something does not quite stack up about his story, but in the absence of any firm evidence I have decided to give him the benefit of the doubt.*

JUST WALKIN' IN THE RAIN *(Riley/Bragg/Killen)*

✱ Original by the Prisonaires (Sun 186) 1953.
◆ *Elvis' source:* Prisonaires (Sun 186) 1953.

Memphis Recording Service [Sun Studio]
706 Union Avenue, Memphis, Tennessee
Saturday, 18 July 1953 (2.30 pm–3.20 pm)
Elvis Presley   Vocal and acoustic guitar (old Martin D-18)
Marion Keisker   Producer and sound engineer

Private direct-to-disc recordings onto a 10-inch 78 rpm acetate. Elvis reputedly cut these sides as a present for his mother. It certainly wasn't a birthday present, as has been claimed in some books, unless it was very late: Gladys Presley's birthday was 25 April.
Sam Phillips was not in the office that day, so Marion Keisker engineered the recording. According to her files, Marion talked with Elvis from 2.30 until 2.50 and asked him various questions including — famously — who he sounded like. 'I don't sound like nobody' came the now equally famous reply. He recorded between 2.50 and 3.05, chatting with her in between songs, and they talked again from 3.05 until 3.20 while Elvis paid for his session and prepared to leave. Impressed with what she'd heard, Marion noted for future reference: 'Good ballad singer. Hold.'

MY HAPPINESS *(Peterson/Bergantine)* 2.32 ⏱
Crossover (pop and R&B) hit in 1948 for Ella Fitzgerald (Decca 24446). Pop hit in 1948 John Laurenz (Mercury 5144), the Marlin Sisters (Columbia 38217), Pied Pipers (Capitol 15094) and Jon & Sandra Steele (Damon 11133), and in 1953 for the Mulcays (Cardinal 1014).

✱ Original by Jon & Sandra Steele (Damon 11133) 1948.
◆ *Elvis' sources:* Ella Fitzgerald (Decca 24446) 1948.
                John Laurenz (Mercury 5144) 1948.
                Marlin Sisters (Columbia 38217) 1948.
                Pied Pipers (Capitol 15094) 1948.
                Jon & Sandra Steele (Damon 11133) 1948.

RCA master WPA5-2531 allocated in 1990.
First issued in 1990 on LP/CD *The Great Performances* (RCA-Victor 2227-1-R / 2227-2-R).
Reissued in 1999 on 2-CD *Sunrise* (BMG/RCA 07863 67675-2).

THAT'S WHEN YOUR HEARTACHES BEGIN *(Raskin/Brown/Fisher)* 2.47 ⏱

✱ Original by the Ink Spots (Decca 3720) 1941.
◆ *Elvis' sources:* Ink Spots (Decca 3720) 1941.
                Billy Bunn (RCA-Victor 4657) 1952.

RCA master WPA5-2532 allocated in 1990.
First issued in 1992 on 5-CD box set *The King Of Rock'n'Roll: The Complete 50s Masters* (BMG/RCA 07863 66050-2).

Memphis Recording Service [Sun Studio]
706 Union Avenue, Memphis, Tennessee
Monday, 4 January 1954 (between 7.00 pm and 9.00 pm, exact time unknown)
Elvis Presley   Vocal and acoustic guitar (old Martin D-18)
Sam Phillips   Producer and sound engineer

Private direct-to-disc recordings onto a 10-inch 78 rpm acetate. Marion Keisker was not present on this occasion. Also on this day, Earl Peterson cut 'Boogie Blues' b/w 'In The Dark' (Sun 197).

I'LL NEVER STAND IN YOUR WAY *(Heath/Rose)* 2.01 🕐
Pop hit in 1953 for Joni James (MGM 11606).

★ Original by Joni James (MGM 11606) 1953.
◆ *Elvis' source:* Joni James (MGM 11606) 1953.

RCA master CPA5-5101 allocated in 1997.
First issued in 1997 on 4-CD *Platinum – A Life In Music* (BMG/RCA 67489-2).

IT WOULDN'T BE THE SAME WITHOUT YOU *(Wakely/Rose)* 2.04 🕐

★ Original by Al Rogers (MGM 10709) 1950.
◆ *Elvis' source:* Al Rogers (MGM 10709) 1950.

RCA master CPA5-5102 allocated in 1997.
First issued in 1999 on 2-CD *Sunrise* (BMG/RCA 07863 67675-2).

Memphis Recording Service [Sun Studio]
706 Union Avenue, Memphis, Tennessee
Saturday, 5 June 1954 (2.15 pm–2.50 pm)
Elvis Presley   Vocal and acoustic guitar (old Martin D-18)
Sam Phillips   Producer and sound engineer

Private direct-to-disc recordings onto a 10-inch 78 rpm acetate. Master nos. 0914.A and 0914.B. It is not known which number referred to which side. Presumed lost.

CASUAL LOVE AFFAIR *(Composer unknown)*
This song is a mystery. It is not known who composed it, or whether it has ever been recorded commercially. It not listed in BMI, ASCAP or Library of Congress catalogues.

CARELESS LOVE (BLUES) *(Handy/Williams/Koenig)*

Composition by W.C. Handy, Spencer Williams and Martha Koenig based on a traditional Irish ballad. A hit in 1925 for Bessie Smith (Columbia 14083).

★ Original by Bessie Smith (Columbia 14083) 1925.
◆ *Elvis' sources:* Bessie Smith (Columbia 14083) 1925.
　　　　　　　　　 Lonnie Johnson (OKeh 8635) 1928.
　　　　　　　　　 Riley Puckett (Columbia 15747) 1932.
　　　　　　　　　 Riley Puckett (Bluebird 5532) 1934.
　　　　　　　　　 Delmore Brothers (Bluebird 7436) 1938.
　　　　　　　　　 Four Tunes (RCA-Victor 0008) 1949.
　　　　　　　　　 Ravens (National 9085) 1949.
　　　　　　　　　 Fats Domino (Imperial 5145) 1951.

Sun Studio, 706 Union Avenue, Memphis, Tennessee
Saturday, 26 June 1954 (rehearsal, 2.30 pm–4.00 pm)
Elvis Presley　　　Vocal and acoustic guitar (old Martin D-18)
Sam Phillips　　　 Producer and sound engineer

WITHOUT YOU *(Composer unknown)*

While in Nashville for a Prisonaires recording session on 8 May 1954, Sam Phillips acquired an acetate of this song from local music publisher Red Wortham. It appears never to have been published or copyrighted, but is thought to have been written by another inmate of the Tennessee State Penitentiary — possibly a white short-termer (Wortham's uncle worked there as a guard, hence the connection). Apparently, Sam was keen to record the song, but couldn't find the singer who had made the demo, whereupon Marion Keisker suggested Elvis. Elvis attempted it seven times, but Phillips was dissatisfied with the results. A subsequent attempt to record it with Scotty Moore and Bill Black on Monday, 5 July 1954 (see next session), likewise did not produce a satisfactory result.

RAG MOP *(Anderson/Wills)*

Crossover (pop and R&B) hit in 1950 for Lionel Hampton (Decca 24855). Crossover hit (pop and C&W) for Johnnie Lee Wills (Bullet 696). Pop hit in 1950 for the Ames Brothers (Coral 60140), Jimmy Dorsey (Columbia 38710), Eddy Howard (Mercury 5371), Ralph Flanagan (RCA-Victor 3688) and the Starlighters (Capitol 844). R&B hit in 1950 for Doc Sausage (Regal 3251) and Joe Liggins (Specialty 350).

★ Original by Johnnie Lee Wills (Bullet 696) 1949.
◆ *Elvis' sources:* Johnnie Lee Wills (Bullet 696) 1949.
　　　　　　　　　 Ames Brothers (Coral 60140) 1950.
　　　　　　　　　 Jimmy Dorsey – Voc. Claire Hogan (Columbia 38710) 1950.
　　　　　　　　　 Ralph Flanagan (RCA-Victor 3688) 1950.
　　　　　　　　　 Lionel Hampton (Decca 24855) 1950.
　　　　　　　　　 Eddy Howard (Mercury 5371) 1950.
　　　　　　　　　 Joe Liggins (Specialty 350) 1950.
　　　　　　　　　 Joe Lutcher (Modern 20-736) 1950.
　　　　　　　　　 Doc Sausage (Regal 3251) 1950.
　　　　　　　　　 Starlighters (Capitol 844) 1950.

*Only the previous two songs were tried out all the way through. The songs listed below (not in chronological order) were also attempted, though mostly only for the first couple of lines or so. (As Elvis told Press-Scimitar reporter Bob Johnson in 1956: 'I sang everything I knew. Pop stuff, spirituals, just a few words of anything I remembered...'.) During the session, he chatted with Sam Phillips between songs. Only one title — **CASUAL LOVE AFFAIR** — was recorded.*

BE MY LOVE *(Cahn/Brodszky)*
Song from the 1950 film, 'The Toast Of New Orleans'. Pop hit in 1950 for Ray Anthony (Capitol 1352), Billy Eckstine (MGM 10799) and Mario Lanza (RCA-Victor 1353).

★ Original by Mario Lanza (RCA-Victor 1353) 1950.
◆ *Elvis' sources:*   Ray Anthony (Capitol 1352) 1950.
                      Mario Lanza (RCA-Victor 1353) 1950.
                      Billy Eckstine (MGM 10799) 1951.
O Elvis made a home recording of this title at Rocca Place, Hollywood circa 1966-67 (unissued).

BLUE MOON *(Rodgers/Hart)*
A hit in 1935 for Al Bowlly (Victor 24849), Glen Gray (Decca 312) and Benny Goodman (Columbia 3003). Featured in the 1948 film, 'Words And Music'. Crossover (pop and R&B) hit in 1949 for Billy Eckstine (MGM 10311) and a pop hit for Mel Torme (Capitol 15428).

★ Original by Frankie Trumbauer (Victor 24812) 1934.
◆ *Elvis' sources:*   Billy Eckstine (MGM 10311) 1948.
                      Mel Torme (Capitol 15428) 1949.
                      Ivory Joe Hunter (MGM 11132) 1951.
O Elvis subsequently recorded this title on 19 August 1954 [see **4.8** for details].

BLUES STAY AWAY FROM ME *(Delmore/Delmore/Raney/Glover)*
C&W hit in 1949 for Eddie Crosby (Decca 46180), and in 1950 for the Delmore Brothers (King 803). Crossover hit (pop and C&W) in 1949-50 for the Owen Bradley Quintet (Coral 60107).

★ Original by the Delmore Brothers (King 803) 1949.
◆ *Elvis' sources:*   Owen Bradley Quintet (Coral 60107) 1949.
                      Eddie Crosby (Decca 46180) 1949.
                      Delmore Brothers (King 803) 1949.
                      Lonnie Johnson (King 4336) 1949.

BORN TO LOSE *(Brown)*
Crossover hit (pop and C&W) in 1943-44 for Ted Daffan's Texans (OKeh 6706).

★ Original by Ted Daffan's Texans (OKeh 6706) 1943.
◆ *Elvis' source:* Ted Daffan's Texans (OKeh 6706) 1943.

CANDY KISSES *(Morgan)*
C&W hit in 1949 for Elton Britt (RCA-Victor 0006), Cowboy Copas (King 777), Red Foley (Decca 46151), Bud Hobbs (MGM 10366), Eddie Kirk (Capitol 15391) and George Morgan (Columbia 20547). Pop hit in 1949 for Eddy Howard (Mercury 5272).

★ Original by George Morgan (Columbia 20547) 1949.
◆ *Elvis' sources:*   Elton Britt (RCA-Victor 0006) 1949.
                      Cowboy Copas (King 777) 1949.
                      Red Foley (Decca 46151) 1949.
                      Bud Hobbs (MGM 10366) 1949.

Eddy Howard (Mercury 5272) 1949.
Eddie Kirk (Capitol 15391) 1949.
George Morgan (Columbia 20547) 1949.
Roy Rogers in the 1949 film, *Down Dakota Way*.

CASUAL LOVE AFFAIR *(Composer unknown)*
This song is a mystery. It is not known who composed it, or whether it has ever been recorded commercially. It not listed in BMI, ASCAP or Library of Congress catalogues.

This was the only title was recorded at this session. Short of tape as usual, Sam Phillips used an old leftover to make a test recording. Tape lost.

CRYING IN THE CHAPEL *(Glenn)*
Crossover (pop and C&W) hit in 1953 for Rex Allen (Decca 28758) and Darrell Glenn (Valley 105). Crossover (pop and R&B) hit in 1953 for the Orioles (Jubilee 5122). Pop hit in 1953 for Ella Fitzgerald (Decca 26762), Art Lund (Coral 61018) and June Valli (RCA-Victor 5368).

✱ Original by Darrell Glenn (Valley 105) 1953.
◆ *Elvis' sources:*   Rex Allen (Decca 28758) 1953.
                      Ella Fitzgerald (Decca 26762) 1953.
                      Four Kings Of Harmony Of Miami, Fla. (Gotham 741) 1953.
                      Darrell Glenn (Valley 105) 1953.
                      Art Lund (Coral 61018) 1953.
                      Orioles (Jubilee 5122) 1953.
                      Statesmen Quartet (Statesmen 1031/1032) 1953.
                      Sister Rosetta Tharpe (Decca 48302) 1953.
                      June Valli (RCA-Victor 5368) 1953.
◉ Elvis later recorded this title at RCA Studio B, Nashville on 31 October 1960 (released in 1965 on single RCA-Victor 447-0643).

DANIEL SAW THE STONE *(Traditional)*
Negro spiritual. Heard in black churches in the South from circa 1865; in white churches from ?

✱ Original recording on cylinder by the Standard Quartette (*no details*) 1893.
  Original recording on 78 rpm by the Davis Bible Singers (Columbia 14525) 1929.
◆ *Elvis' source:* Golden Gate Quartet (OKeh 6204) 1941.

DO SOMETHING FOR ME *(Ward/Marks)*
R&B hit in 1950 for the Dominoes (Federal 12001).

✱ Original by the Dominoes (Federal 12001) 1950.
◆ *Elvis' sources:*   Dominoes (Federal 12001) 1950.
                      Ink Spots (Decca 27493) 1951.

HAND ME DOWN MY WALKING CANE *(Crudup)*

✱ Original by Arthur 'Big Boy' Crudup (RCA-Victor 0100) 1949.
◆ *Elvis' source:* Arthur 'Big Boy' Crudup (RCA-Victor 0100) 1949.

HARBOR LIGHTS *(Kennedy/Williams)*
A hit in 1937 for Frances Langford (Decca 1441) and Claude Thornhill (Vocalion 03595), and in 1950 for Ray Anthony (Capitol 1190), Jerry Byrd & Jerry Murad's Harmonicats (Mercury 5461), Bing Crosby (Decca 27219), Ralph Flanagan (RCA-Victor 3911), Ken Griffin (Columbia 38889), Sammy Kaye (Columbia 38953) and Guy Lombardo (Decca 27208). R&B hit in 1951 for Dinah Washington (Mercury 5488).

✱ Original **HARBOUR LIGHTS** by Roy Fox – Voc. Barry Gray
(His Master's Voice BD-5173) 1937, UK.
  US Original **HARBOR LIGHTS** by Rudy Vallee (Bluebird 7067) 1937.
◆ *Elvis' sources:* Ray Anthony – Voc. Ronnie Deauville (Capitol 1190) 1950.
                     Bing Crosby (Decca 27219) 1950.
                     Ken Griffin (Columbia 38889) 1950.
                     Sammy Kaye (Columbia 38953) 1950.
                     Guy Lombardo (Decca 27208) 1950.
                     Billy Ward & His Dominoes (Federal 12010) 1951.
                     Dinah Washington (Mercury 5488) 1951.
❍ Elvis subsequently recorded this title on 5 July 1954 [see **4.6** for details].

HOW COULD I KNOW *(Capano/Beck/Berman)*

✱ Original by the Ravens (National 9059) 1948.
◆ *Elvis' source:* Ravens (National 9059) 1948.

I ALMOST LOST MY MIND *(Hunter)*
Crossover (pop and R&B) hit in 1950 for Nat 'King' Cole (Capitol 889), and a R&B hit for Ivory Joe Hunter (MGM 8011 and 10578).

✱ Original by Ivory Joe Hunter (MGM 8011 and 10578) 1949.
◆ *Elvis' sources:* Nat 'King' Cole (Capitol 889) 1949.
                     Ivory Joe Hunter (MGM 8011 and 10578) 1949.
                     Lionel Hampton – Voc. Sonny Parker (Decca 24864) 1950.
❍ Elvis subsequently recorded this title in August 1955 (rehearsal take, erased) [see **4.24** for details].

I APOLOGIZE *(Hoffman/Goodhart/Nelson)*
A hit in 1931 for Bing Crosby (Brunswick 6179) and Nat Shilkret (Victor 22781). Crossover (pop and R&B) hit in 1951 for Billy Eckstine (MGM 10903), and a pop hit for Champ Butler (Columbia 39189) and Tony Martin (RCA-Victor 4056).

✱ Original by Bing Crosby (Brunswick 6179) 1931.
◆ *Elvis' sources:* Champ Butler (Columbia 39189) 1951.
                     Billy Eckstine (MGM 10903) 1951.
                     Tony Martin (RCA-Victor 4056) 1951.
                     Dinah Washington (Mercury 8209) 1951.
❍ Elvis sang a few lines of this song prior to recording **BEYOND THE BEND** at Radio Recorders, Hollywood on 22 September 1962. This snippet was released in 1991 on 3-CD *Collectors' Gold* (BMG/RCA 3114-2-R). Elvis was in the studio recording tracks for the MGM film, *It Happened At The World's Fair* (released 1963).

IF I DIDN'T CARE *(Lawrence)*
Pop hit in 1939 for the Ink Spots (Decca 2286) and in 1954 for the Hilltoppers (Dot 15220).

✱ Original by the Ink Spots (Decca 2286) 1939.
◆ *Elvis' sources:*   Ink Spots (Decca 2286) 1939.
                   Hilltoppers (Dot 15220) 1954.

I'LL NEVER SMILE AGAIN *(Lowe)*
Pop hit in 1940 for Tommy Dorsey (Victor 26628) and Glenn Miller (Bluebird 10673), and in 1953 for the Four Aces (Decca 28391).

✱ Original by Tommy Dorsey – Voc. Frank Sinatra & The Pied Pipers (Victor 26628) 1940.
◆ *Elvis' sources:*   Tommy Dorsey – Voc. Frank Sinatra & The Pied Pipers (Victor 26628) 1940.
                   Ink Spots (Decca 3346) 1940.
                   Glenn Miller (Bluebird 10673) 1940.
                   Scamps (Modern 20-561) 1947.
                   James Von Streeter (Savoy 712) 1949.
                   John 'Schoolboy' Porter (Chance 1101) 1951.
                   Four Aces (Decca 28391) 1953.

I'M SO LONESOME I COULD CRY *(Williams)*
Flip of **MY BUCKET'S GOT A HOLE IN IT**, *a C&W hit in 1949 for Hank Williams (MGM 10560).*

✱ Original by Hank Williams (MGM 10560) 1949.
◆ *Elvis' source:* Hank Williams (MGM 10560) 1949.
❍ Elvis later recorded this title at the Honolulu International Center Arena, Hawaii on 14 January 1973 (released in 1973 on 2-LP *Aloha From Hawaii*, RCA-Victor VPSX-6089). Another version recorded on 12 January 1973 was released in 1988 on LP/CD *The Alternate Aloha* (BMG/RCA 6985-1-R / 6985-2-R).

I NEED YOU SO *(Hunter)*
R&B hit in 1950 for Ivory Joe Hunter (MGM 10663) and a pop hit for Hugo Winterhalter (RCA-Victor 3884).

✱ Original by Ivory Joe Hunter (MGM 10663) 1950.
◆ *Elvis' sources:*   Ivory Joe Hunter (MGM 10663) 1950.
                   Orioles (Jubilee 5037) 1950.
                   Hugo Winterhalter – Voc. Don Cornell (RCA-Victor 3884) 1950.
❍ Elvis later recorded this title at Radio Recorders, Hollywood on 23 February 1957 (released in 1957 on EP *Just For You*, RCA-Victor EPA-4041).

I REALLY DON'T WANT TO KNOW *(Barnes/Robertson)*
C&W hit in 1954 for Eddy Arnold (RCA-Victor 5525). Pop hit in 1954 for Les Paul & Mary Ford (Capitol 2735).

✱ Original by Eddy Arnold (RCA-Victor 5525) 1953.
◆ *Elvis' sources:*   Eddy Arnold (RCA-Victor 5525) 1953.
                   Dominoes (King 1368) 1954.
                   Les Paul & Mary Ford (Capitol 2735) 1954.
❍ Elvis later recorded this title at RCA Studio B, Nashville on 7 June 1970 (released in 1971 on LP *Elvis Country*, RCA-Victor LSP-4460).

IT'S TOO SOON TO KNOW *(Chessler)*
Crossover (pop and R&B) hit in 1948 for the Orioles (It's A Natural 5000). R&B hit in 1948 for Ella Fitzgerald (Decca 24497), the Ravens (National 9056) and Dinah Washington (Mercury 8107).

✱ Original by the Orioles (It's A Natural 5000) 1948.
◆ *Elvis' sources:*   Deep River Boys (RCA-Victor 3203) 1948.
Ella Fitzgerald (Decca 24497) 1948.
Ravens (National 9056) 1948.
Dinah Washington (Mercury 8107) 1948.

JUST WALKIN' IN THE RAIN *(Riley/Bragg/Killen)*

✱ Original by the Prisonaires (Sun 186) 1953.
◆ *Elvis' source:* Prisonaires (Sun 186) 1953.

KEEP YOUR HANDS OFF HER *(Broonzy)*
Like **TAKE YOUR HANDS OFF IT** *aka* **BIRTHDAY CAKE** [see **3.3**], *based on a popular double entendre song originating in the 1890s. Many variants.* **KEEP YOUR HANDS OFF THAT** *by Sam Manning & His Blue Hot Syncopators (OKeh 8302, 1926) is one of the earliest recorded examples of this theme. Another version,* **HANDS OFF***, was a No. 1 R&B hit in 1955 for Jay McShann – Voc. Priscilla Bowman (Vee-Jay 155).*

✱ Original by Big Bill Broonzy (Bluebird 6188) 1935.
◆ *Elvis' sources:*   Big Bill Broonzy (Bluebird 6188) 1935.
Leadbelly (Asch AA 1/2) 1944.
○ Elvis later recorded this title at RCA Studio B, Nashville on 5 June 1970 as part of a medley with **GOT MY MOJO WORKING** (released in 1971 on LP *Love Letters From Elvis*, RCA-Victor LSP-4530). He also made a private recording of it at his home on Monovale Drive, Hollywood in the autumn of 1960 (released in 1999 on CD *The Home Recordings*, BMG/RCA 07863 67676-2).

LILACS IN THE RAIN *(DeRose/Parish)*
A hit in 1939 for Bob Crosby (Decca 2763) and Charlie Barnet (Bluebird 10439).

✱ Original by Bob Crosby (Decca 2763) 1938.
◆ *Elvis' source:* Ravens (National 9148) 1951.

MEAN OL' FRISCO *(Crudup)*

✱ Original by Arthur 'Big Boy' Crudup (Bluebird 34-0704) 1942.
◆ *Elvis' sources:*   Arthur 'Big Boy' Crudup (Bluebird 34-0704) 1942.
Brownie McGhee (Alert 401) 1946.
Jack Dupree Trio (Continental 6066) 1948.

MY HAPPINESS *(Peterson/Bergantine)*

Crossover (pop and R&B) hit in 1948 for Ella Fitzgerald (Decca 24446). Pop hit in 1948 John Laurenz (Mercury 5144), the Marlin Sisters (Columbia 38217), Pied Pipers (Capitol 15094) and Jon & Sandra Steele (Damon 11133), and in 1953 for the Mulcays (Cardinal 1014).

✱ Original by Jon & Sandra Steele (Damon 11133) 1948.
◆ *Elvis' sources:* Ella Fitzgerald (Decca 24446) 1948.
      John Laurenz (Mercury 5144) 1948.
      Marlin Sisters (Columbia 38217) 1948.
      Pied Pipers (Capitol 15094) 1948.
      Jon & Sandra Steele (Damon 11133) 1948.
○ Elvis made a private recording of this title at Memphis Recording Service (Sun Studio) on 18 July 1953 [see **4.2** for details].

OLD SHEP *(Foley/Arthur)*

✱ Original by Red Foley (Decca 5944) 1941.
◆ *Elvis' source:* Red Foley (Decca 5944) 1941.
○ Elvis later recorded this title at Radio Recorders, Hollywood on 2 September 1956 (released in 1956 on LP *Elvis*, RCA-Victor LPM-1382).

PAPER DOLL *(Black)*

Pop hit in 1942 for the Mills Brothers (Decca 18318), which became a crossover (pop and R&B) hit in 1943.

✱ Original by the Mills Brothers (Decca 18318) 1942.
◆ *Elvis' source:* Mills Brothers (Decca 18318) 1942.

PLAY A SIMPLE MELODY *(Berlin)*

Composed in 1914 by Irving Berlin for the Broadway musical, 'Watch Your Step'. A hit in 1915 for Walter Van Brunt & Mary Carson (Edison Amberol 2607), in 1916 for Billy Murray & Edna Brown [Elsie Baker] (Victor 18051), and in 1950 for Bing & Gary Crosby (Decca 27112), Georgia Gibbs (Coral 60227), Phil Harris (RCA-Victor 3781) and Jo Stafford (Capitol 1039).

✱ Original by Walter Van Brunt & Mary Carson (Edison Amberol 2607) 1915.
◆ *Elvis' sources:* Bing & Gary Crosby (Decca 27112) 1950.
      Georgia Gibbs (Coral 60227) 1950.
      Phil Harris (RCA-Victor 3781) 1950.
      Jo Stafford (Capitol 1039) 1950.

PRISONER OF LOVE *(Robin/Columbo/Gaskill)*

A hit in 1932 for Russ Columbo (Victor 22867). Crossover (pop and R&B) hit in 1946 for Billy Eckstine (National 9017) and the Ink Spots (Decca 18864), and a pop hit that same year for Perry Como (RCA-Victor 1814).

✱ Original by Russ Columbo (Victor 22867) 1932.
◆ *Elvis' sources:* Perry Como (RCA-Victor 1814) 1946.
      Billy Eckstine (National 9017) 1946.
      Ink Spots (Decca 18864) 1946.

RAGS TO RICHES *(Adler/Ross)*
Pop hit in 1953 for Tony Bennett (Columbia 40048). R&B hit in 1953 for Billy Ward & His Dominoes (King 1280).

✱ Original by Tony Bennett (Columbia 40048) 1953.
◆ *Elvis' sources:* Tony Bennett (Columbia 40048) 1953.
        Billy Ward & His Dominoes (King 1280) 1953.
❍ Elvis later recorded this title at RCA Studio B, Nashville on 22 September 1970 (released in 1971 as the flip side of single **WHERE DID THEY GO LORD**, RCA-Victor 9980).

THAT LUCKY OLD SUN *(Gillespie/Smith)*
Crossover (pop and R&B) hit in 1949 for Louis Armstrong (Decca 24752). Pop hit in 1949 for Bob Houston (MGM 10509), Frankie Laine (Mercury 5316), Vaughn Monroe (RCA-Victor 3531), Frank Sinatra (Columbia 38608) and Sarah Vaughan (Columbia 38559). R&B hit in 1949 for Herb Lance & The Classics (Sittin' In With 524).

✱ Original by Frankie Laine (Mercury 5316) 1949.
◆ *Elvis' sources:* Louis Armstrong (Decca 24752) 1949.
        Ebonaires (Modern 20-711) 1949.
        Bob Houston (MGM 10509) 1949.
        Frankie Laine (Mercury 5316) 1949.
        Vaughn Monroe (RCA-Victor 3531) 1949.
        Herb Lance & The Classics (Sittin' In With 524) 1949.
        Frank Sinatra (Columbia 38608) 1949.
        Sarah Vaughan (Columbia 38559) 1949.

THAT'S AMORE *(Warren/Brooks)*
Pop hit in 1953 for Dean Martin (Capitol 2589).

✱ Original by Dean Martin (Capitol 2589) 1953.
◆ *Elvis' source:* Dean Martin (Capitol 2589) 1953.
❍ Elvis sang a few lines of this song during a concert in Las Vegas on 29 March 1975 (Dinner Show). An audience recording of this concert was available for a time on the bootleg circuit.

THAT'S MY DESIRE *(Kresa/Loveday)*
Crossover (pop and R&B) hit in 1947 for Frankie Laine (Mercury 5007). Pop hit in 1947 for Woody Herman (Columbia 37329), Sammy Kaye (RCA-Victor 2251), and Martha Tilton (Capitol 395). R&B hit in 1947 for Hadda Brooks (Modern Music 147) and Ella Fitzgerald (Decca 28993).

✱ Original by Frankie Laine (Mercury 5007) 1946.
◆ *Elvis' sources:* Frankie Laine (Mercury 5007) 1946.
        Hadda Brooks (Modern Music 147) 1947.
        Cats & The Fiddle (Manor 1064) 1947.
        Ella Fitzgerald (Decca 28993) 1947.
        Five Scamps (Modern 516) 1947.
        Woody Herman (Columbia 37329) 1947.
        Sammy Kaye (RCA-Victor 2251) 1947.
        Martha Tilton (Capitol 395) 1947.
        Flamingos (Chance 1140) 1953.

THERE IS SOMETHING WITHIN ME *(Nubin/Tharpe)*

✱ Original by Rosetta Tharpe (Decca 8548) 1941.
◆ *Elvis' source:* Rosetta Tharpe (Decca 8548) 1941.

TOMORROW NEVER COMES *(Tubb/Bond)*
C&W hit in 1945 for Ernest Tubb (Decca 6106).

✱ Original by Ernest Tubb (Decca 6106) 1945.
◆ *Elvis' source:* Ernest Tubb (Decca 6106) 1945.
○ Elvis later recorded this title at RCA Studio B, Nashville on 7 June 1970 (released in 1971 on LP *Elvis Country*, RCA-Victor LSP-4460).

TOMORROW NIGHT *(Coslow/Grosz)*
A hit in 1939 for Horace Heidt (Columbia 35203). Crossover (pop and R&B) hit in 1948 for Lonnie Johnson (King 4201). Not to be confused with Louis Armstrong's 1933 recording 'Tomorrow Night (After Tonight)' (RCA-Victor 68-0774) or Junior Wells' 'Tomorrow Night' (States 143) 1954.

✱ Original by Horace Heidt (Columbia 35203) 1939.
◆ *Elvis' sources:*   Horace Heidt (Columbia 35203) 1939.
                     Lonnie Johnson (King 4201) 1948.
                     Lonnie Johnson (Paradise 11) 1948.
○ Elvis subsequently recorded this title on 19 August and 8 December 1954 [see **4.8** and **4.12** for details]. Second version unissued/lost.

WORKING ON THE BUILDING *(Hoyle/Bowles)*
Gospel song composed in 1934 by W.O. Hoyle and Lillian Bowles. Heard in white churches in the South from 1934; in black churches from ?

✱ Original by the Blackwood Brothers (*no details, possibly released on own label*) 1934.
◆ *Elvis' radio sources:*   Carter Family (Bluebird 5716) 1934.
                          J.E. Mainer's Mountaineers (King 543) 1946.
                          Five Blind Boys Of Mississippi (Coleman 5968) 1948.
                          Soul Comforters (DeLuxe 1157) 1948.
                          Soul Stirrers (Aladdin 2020) 1948.
                          Swan's Silvertone Singers (King 4248) 1948.
○ Elvis later recorded this title at RCA Studio B, Nashville on 31 October 1960 (released in 1960 on LP *His Hand In Mine*, RCA LPM/LSP-2328). *[Also see introductory note to this section.]*

YOU BELONG TO ME *(King/Stewart/Price)*
Pop hit in 1952 for Dean Martin (Capitol 2165), Patti Page (Mercury 5899) and Jo Stafford (Columbia 39811).

✱ Original by Joni James (MGM 11295) 1952.
◆ *Elvis' sources:*   Tamara Hayes (RCA-Victor 4943) 1952.
                     Joni James (MGM 11295) 1952.
                     Annie Laurie (OKeh 6915) 1952.
                     Buddy Lucas (Jubilee 5094) 1952.
                     Dean Martin (Capitol 2165) 1952.
                     Orioles (Jubilee 5102) 1952.
                     Patti Page (Mercury 5899) 1952.
                     Tab Smith (United 131) 1952.
                     Jo Stafford (Columbia 39811) 1952.

4.6

Sun Studio, 706 Union Avenue, Memphis, Tennessee
Monday, 5 July 1954 (Doors open: 7.05pm. Session 7.20 pm–0.30 am Tuesday)

Elvis Presley	Vocal and acoustic guitar (old Martin D-18)
Scotty Moore	Lead guitar (Gibson ES-295)
Bill Black	Double bass
Sam Phillips	Producer and sound engineer

WITHOUT YOU *(Composer unknown)*
An unpublished song which Sam Phillips acquired in Nashville (see previous session for full details). Attempted ten times without result 7.20–7.50 pm. Not recorded.

▶ *Elvis' interpretation:* pop ballad.

> Dialogue
> Test 1 *(incomplete)*
> Test 2 *(incomplete)*
> Test 3 *(incomplete)*
> Elvis irritated
> Test 4 *(incomplete)*
> Break – 10 minutes
> Dialogue
> Test 5 *(incomplete)*
> Test 6 *(incomplete)*
> Test 7 *(incomplete)*
> Elvis irritated
> Test 8 *(incomplete)*
> Dialogue
> Test 9 *(incomplete)*
> Elvis irritated
> Test 10 *(incomplete)*
> Break until 8.15 pm

HARBOR LIGHTS *(Kennedy/Williams)*
A hit in 1937 for Frances Langford (Decca 1441) and Claude Thornhill (Vocalion 03595), and in 1950 for Ray Anthony (Capitol 1190), Jerry Byrd & Jerry Murad's Harmonicats (Mercury 5461), Bing Crosby (Decca 27219), Ralph Flanagan (RCA-Victor 3911), Ken Griffin (Columbia 38889), Sammy Kaye (Columbia 38953) and Guy Lombardo (Decca 27208). R&B hit in 1951 for Dinah Washington (Mercury 5488).

★ Original **HARBOUR LIGHTS** by Roy Fox – Voc. Barry Gray
(His Master's Voice BD-5173) 1937, UK.
US Original **HARBOR LIGHTS** by Rudy Vallee (Bluebird 7067) 1937.
◆ *Elvis' sources:* Ray Anthony – Voc. Ronnie Deauville (Capitol 1190) 1950.
Bing Crosby (Decca 27219) 1950.
Ken Griffin (Columbia 38889) 1950.
Sammy Kaye (Columbia 38953) 1950.
Guy Lombardo (Decca 27208) 1950.
Billy Ward & His Dominoes (Federal 12010) 1951.
Dinah Washington (Mercury 5488) 1951.

▶ *Elvis' interpretation:* pop ballad.

Take 1 *(false start)*	?
Take 2	2.36 🕐
Take 3	2.28 🕐
Take 4 *(false start)*	?
Take 5	2.20
Take 6 *(false start)*	?
Break	

Supplied to RCA on Sun tape No. 15 [see *Appendix C*].
RCA master EPA3-2742 allocated in 1976 to Take 2.
Take 1 unissued.
Take 2 first issued in 1976 on LP *Elvis: A Legendary Performer (Volume 2)* (RCA-Victor CPL1-1349). Reissued in 1999 on 2-CD *Sunrise* (BMG/RCA 07863 67675-2).
Take 3 first issued in 2002 on 4-CD *Today, Tomorrow And Forever* (BMG/RCA 07863 65115-2).
Takes 4, 5 and 6 unissued.

I LOVE YOU BECAUSE *(Payne)*
C&W hit in 1950 for Leon Payne (Capitol 40238), Clyde Moody (King 837) and Ernest Tubb (Decca 46213).

✱ Original by Leon Payne (Capitol 40238) 1949.
◆ *Elvis' sources:*   Leon Payne (Capitol 40238) 1949.
                  Gene Autry (Columbia 20709) 1950.
                  Clyde Moody (King 837) 1950.
                  Ernest Tubb (Decca 46213) 1950.

▶ *Elvis' interpretation:* country ballad.

Take 1 *(false start)*	0.18 🕐
Take 2	3.29 🕐
Take 3	3.33
Take 4 *(false start)*	0.32
Take 5	3.27

Supplied to RCA on Sun tape No. 13 [see *Appendix C*].
RCA master G2WB-1086 allocated in mid-January 1956 to spliced version of Takes 3 and 5.
Take 1 first issued in 1999 on 2-CD *Sunrise* (BMG/RCA 07863 67675-2).
Take 2 first issued in 1974 on LP *Elvis: A Legendary Performer (Volume 1)* (RCA-Victor CPL1-0341). Reissued in 1999 on 2-CD *Sunrise* (BMG/RCA 07863 67675-2).
Takes 3, 4 and 5 first issued in 1987 on 2-LP/CD *The Complete Sun Sessions* (BMG/RCA 6414-1-R / 6414-2-R).
Takes 3 and 5 (spliced, timed at 2.44) first issued in 1956 on LP *Elvis Presley* (RCA-Victor LPM-1254). Reissued in 1999 on 2-CD *Sunrise* (BMG/RCA 07863 67675-2).

So far, the session had failed to produce the magic spark of originality that Sam Phillips was looking for. During the break, Elvis suddenly launched into **THAT'S ALL RIGHT***, heralding the arrival of a new era.*

THAT'S ALL RIGHT *(Crudup)*
✱ Original by Arthur 'Big Boy' Crudup (RCA-Victor 20-2205) 1947.
◆ *Elvis' sources:* Arthur 'Big Boy' Crudup (RCA-Victor 2205) 1947.
                  Arthur 'Big Boy' Crudup (RCA-Victor 50-0000) 1949.

▶ *Elvis' interpretation:* rockabilly.

Take 1 *(false start)*	0.04 🕐
Take 2 *(false start)*	0.07 🕐
Take 3	1.55 🕐
Take 4 *(incomplete)*	?
Take 5 *(incomplete)*	?
Take 6 *(incomplete)*	?
Take 7	1.56 🕐
Take 8 *(incomplete)*	?
Take 9 *(incomplete)*	?

Supplied to RCA on Sun tape Nos. 2 and 13 [see *Appendix C*].
RCA master F2WW-8040 (per Sun tape box No. 2) or F2WB-8040 (per Sun tape box No. 13) allocated in 1955 to Take 7.
Takes 1, 2 and 3 issued in 1999 (with renumbered master OPA1-4849) on 2-CD *Sunrise* (BMG/RCA 07863 67675-2).
Takes 4, 5 and 6 were only a few seconds long and contained studio chatter etc. Erased.
Take 7 (Sun matrix U-128) recorded after midnight on Tuesday, 6 July 1954, issued on Sun 209 on Monday, 19 July 1954. Reissued in 1999 on 2-CD *Sunrise* (BMG/RCA 07863 67675-2).
Takes 8 and 9 were only a few seconds long and contained studio chatter etc. Erased.

TIGER MAN (KING OF THE JUNGLE) *(Louis/Burns)*
Song written by Joe Hill Louis and Sam Burns (the latter a pseudonym for Sam Phillips). Louis was also the first to cut it (in the spring of 1953), but it was not released at the time. It was subsequently recorded by Rufus Thomas. During one of his August 1970 shows in Las Vegas, Elvis performed **TIGER MAN***, after which he explained to the audience: 'This is my second record, but not too many people got to heard it.' The flip side of the* **TIGER MAN** *single was to have been* **BLUE MOON***, recorded on 19 August 1954* [see **4.8**].

✱ Original by Rufus Thomas (Sun 188) 1953.
◆ *Elvis' source:* Rufus Thomas (Sun 188) 1953.
◎ Elvis later recorded this title at NBC-TV studio, Burbank, CA on 27 June 1968 (released in 1968 on LP *Singer Presents Elvis Singing Flaming Star And Others*, PRS 279). Another version dates from a midnight show at the International Hotel, Las Vegas on 25 August 1969 (released in 1969 on 2-LP *Elvis In Person (From Memphis To Vegas/From Vegas To Memphis)*, RCA-Victor LSP-6020).

▶ *Elvis' interpretation:* raw rockabilly.

Take 1	2.17

Tape lost.

COOL DISPOSITION *(Crudup)*

✱ Original by Arthur 'Big Boy' Crudup (Bluebird 34-0738) 1945.
◆ *Elvis' source:* Arthur 'Big Boy' Crudup (Bluebird 34-0738) 1945.

▶ *Elvis' interpretation:* raw rockabilly.

Take 1	1.55

Tape lost.

HEY MAMA, EVERYTHING'S ALL RIGHT *(Crudup)*

✱ Original by Arthur 'Big Boy' Crudup (RCA-Victor 3261) 1948.
◆ *Elvis' source:* Arthur 'Big Boy' Crudup (RCA-Victor 3261) 1948.

▶ *Elvis' interpretation:* raw rockabilly.

Take 1 *(incomplete)*   0.30

Tape lost.

ROCK ME MAMMA *(Crudup)*
R&B hit in 1945 for Arthur 'Big Boy' Crudup (Bluebird 34-0725).

✱ Original by Arthur 'Big Boy' Crudup (Bluebird 34-0725) 1945.
◆ *Elvis' sources:* Arthur 'Big Boy' Crudup (Bluebird 34-0725) 1945.
        ROCKIN' AND ROLLIN' by Lil' Son Jackson (Imperial 5113) 1951.
        ALL NIGHT LONG by Muddy Waters (Chess 1509) 1952.

▶ *Elvis' interpretation:* raw rockabilly.

Take 1 *(incomplete)*   0.24

Tape lost.

Sun Studio, 706 Union Avenue, Memphis, Tennessee
Tuesday, 6 July 1954 (Doors open: 7.15 pm. Session: 7.40 pm–0.15 am Wed.)
Elvis Presley   Vocal and acoustic guitar (old Martin D-18)
Scotty Moore   Lead guitar (Gibson ES-295)
Bill Black   Double bass
Sam Phillips   Producer and sound engineer

The first nine songs were tried out but not recorded.

BLUE EYES CRYING IN THE RAIN *(Rose)*

✱ Original by Roy Acuff (Columbia 37822) 1947.
◆ *Elvis' sources:* Roy Acuff (Columbia 37822) 1947.
        Roy Acuff (Columbia 20357) 1948.
❍ Elvis later recorded this title at Graceland, Memphis on 7 February 1976 (released in 1976 on LP *From Elvis Presley Boulevard*, RCA-Victor APL1-1506).

▶ *Elvis' interpretation:* country ballad.

BLUE MOON *(Rodgers/Hart)*
A hit in 1935 for Al Bowlly (Victor 24849), Glen Gray (Decca 312) and Benny Goodman (Columbia 3003). Featured in the 1948 film, 'Words And Music'. Crossover (pop and R&B) hit in 1949 for Billy Eckstine (MGM 10311) and a pop hit for Mel Torme (Capitol 15428).

✱ Original by Frankie Trumbauer (Victor 24812) 1934.
◆ *Elvis' sources:*   Billy Eckstine (MGM 10311) 1948.
                     Mel Torme (Capitol 15428) 1949.
                     Ivory Joe Hunter (MGM 11132) 1951.
◐ Elvis subsequently recorded this title on 19 August 1954 [see **4.8** for details].

▶ *Elvis' interpretation:* pop ballad.

DARK AS A DUNGEON *(Travis)*

✱ Original by Merle Travis (78 rpm 4-disc album *Folk Songs Of The Hills*, Capitol AD-50) 1947.
◆ *Elvis' source:* Merle Travis (78 rpm 4-disc album *Folk Songs Of The Hills*, Capitol AD-50) 1947.

▶ *Elvis' interpretation:* country ballad.

GONE *(Rogers)*
Song composed by Smokey Rogers. Not to be confused with the Drifters' **GONE** *(Atlantic 1055) 1955.*

✱ Original by Terry Preston *[Ferlin Husky]* (Capitol 2298) 1952.
◆ *Elvis' source:* Terry Preston (Capitol 2298) 1952.

▶ *Elvis' interpretation:* pop ballad.

I DON'T HURT ANYMORE *(Robertson/Rollins)*
C&W hit in 1954 for Hank Snow (RCA-Victor 5698).

✱ Original by Hank Snow (RCA-Victor 5698) 1954.
◆ *Elvis' source:* Hank Snow (RCA-Victor 5698) 1954.

▶ *Elvis' interpretation:* country blues.

LONG, LONG JOURNEY *(Feathers)*
Flip of **I'M IN THE MOOD FOR LOVE**, *a pop hit in 1946 for Billy Eckstine (National 9016). Elvis called this song* **LONG JOURNEY**.

✱ Original by Billy Eckstine (National 9016) 1945.
◆ *Elvis' source:* Billy Eckstine (National 9016) 1945.

▶ *Elvis' interpretation:* blues.

RAGS TO RICHES *(Adler/Ross)*
Pop hit in 1953 for Tony Bennett (Columbia 40048). R&B hit in 1953 for Billy Ward & His Dominoes (King 1280).

✱ Original by Tony Bennett (Columbia 40048) 1953.
◆ *Elvis' sources:* Tony Bennett (Columbia 40048) 1953.
　　　　　　　　　　 Billy Ward & His Dominoes (King 1280) 1953.
◯ Elvis later recorded this title at RCA Studio B, Nashville on 22 September 1970 (released in 1971 as the flip side of single **WHERE DID THEY GO LORD**, RCA-Victor 9980).

▶ *Elvis' interpretation:* pop ballad.

SUNSHINE *(Berlin)*
A hit in 1928 for Paul Whiteman (Victor 21240) and Nick Lucas (Brunswick 3850). Not to be confused with Al Dexter's **SUNSHINE** *(Vocalion 04988)* [see **5.10**].

✱ Original by Paul Whiteman – Voc. Bing Crosby (Victor 21240) 1928.
◆ *Elvis' source:* Paul Whiteman – Voc. Bing Crosby (Victor 21240) 1928.

▶ *Elvis' interpretation:* bluesy ballad.

TOMORROW NEVER COMES *(Tubb/Bond)*
C&W hit in 1945 for Ernest Tubb (Decca 6106).

✱ Original by Ernest Tubb (Decca 6106) 1945.
◆ *Elvis' source:* Ernest Tubb (Decca 6106) 1945.
◯ Elvis later recorded this title at RCA Studio B, Nashville on 7 June 1970 (released in 1971 on LP *Elvis Country*, RCA-Victor LSP-4460).

▶ *Elvis' interpretation:* country ballad.

During one of the breaks, Elvis messed around with the following two songs:

THE LOVEBUG ITCH *(Carson/Botkin)*
C&W hit in 1950 for Eddy Arnold (RCA-Victor 0382).

✱ Original by Eddy Arnold (RCA-Victor 2128) 1947.
◆ *Elvis' sources:* Eddy Arnold (RCA-Victor 2128) 1947.
　　　　　　　　　　 Eddy Arnold (RCA-Victor 0382) 1950.
　　　　　　　　　　 Red Foley, Ernest Tubb & Minnie Pearl (Decca 46278) 1950.

▶ *Elvis' interpretation:* comic country.

CATTLE CALL *(Owens)*

✱ Original by Tex Owens (Decca 5015) 1934.
◆ *Elvis' sources:* Jimmy Wakely (Decca 5880) 1940.
　　　　　　　　　　 Eddy Arnold (Bluebird 33-0527) 1945.
◯ Informal jam at MGM Soundstage, Hollywood on 29 July 1970 during rehearsals for the August season in Las Vegas. Released in 1992 on video *The Lost Performances* and in in 1997 on 4-CD *Platinum – A Life In Music* (BMG/RCA 67489-2). Another version, from stage rehearsals at the International Hotel, Las Vegas on 4 August 1970, was included in the remastered film/video *Elvis – That's The Way It Is: Special Edition* and on CD *One Night In Vegas* (Follow

That Dream/BMG 74321-81234-2), both released in 2001. A third version was sung during rehearsals at RCA Studio A, Hollywood on 31 March 1972. It was filmed by MGM for *Elvis On Tour* but wasn't included in the final edit. Released in 1989 on bootleg CD *The Complete On Tour Sessions (Volume 1)* (Vicky 0211).

▶ *Elvis' interpretation:* comic country.

During this last break around 11.45 pm, Bill Black started messing around and sang a jokey version of **BLUE MOON OF KENTUCKY**. *Elvis and Scotty joined in, Sam Phillips started his two Ampex 350 recorders and got his 'B' side for* **THAT'S ALL RIGHT**:

BLUE MOON OF KENTUCKY *(Monroe)*
This number started life as a slow country ballad, but developed into something quite different. After Take 3 Sam Phillips remarked: 'Fine, man. Hell that's different! That's a pop song now, nearly 'bout.' Then, Elvis, Scotty and Bill decided to speed it up, and the rest is history. Take 5 was recorded after midnight on Wednesday, 7 July 1954. (Several sources have claimed that this was actually cut at a third informal session held on 7 July 1954 (time unknown), but Marion Keisker's notes do not mention a third session.)

✱ Original by Bill Monroe (Columbia 37888) 1947.
◆ *Elvis' source:* Bill Monroe (Columbia 37888) 1947.

▶ *Elvis' interpretation:* rockabilly.

Take 1	2.02	
Take 2	2.02	
Take 3	1.04	⏱
Take 4	?	
Take 5	2.03	⏱
Take 6	1.55	

Supplied to RCA on Sun tape No. 14 [see *Appendix C*].
RCA master F2WB-8041 allocated in 1955 to Take 5.
Takes 1 and 2 unissued.
Take 3 first issued in 1999 (with renumbered master OPA1-4194) on 2-CD *Sunrise* (BMG/RCA 07863 67675-2).
Take 4 lost.
Take 5 (Sun matrix U-129) issued on Sun 209 on Monday, 19 July 1954. Reissued in 1999 on 2-CD *Sunrise* (BMG/RCA 07863 67675-2).
Take 6 lost.

4.8

Sun Studio, 706 Union Avenue, Memphis, Tennessee
Thursday, 19 August 1954 (evening, exact time unknown)

Elvis Presley	Vocal and acoustic guitar (new Martin D-18)
Scotty Moore	Lead guitar (Gibson ES-295)
Bill Black	Double bass
Unknown	Bongos *(it was impossible to determine from Marion Keisker's files whether it was Elvis or Buddy Cunningham who played bongos on* **BLUE MOON***)*
Sam Phillips	Producer and sound engineer

BLUE MOON *(Rodgers/Hart)*

A hit in 1935 for Al Bowlly (Victor 24849), Glen Gray (Decca 312) and Benny Goodman (Columbia 3003). Featured in the 1948 film, 'Words And Music'. Crossover (pop and R&B) hit in 1949 for Billy Eckstine (MGM 10311) and a pop hit for Mel Torme (Capitol 15428).

★ Original by Frankie Trumbauer (Victor 24812) 1934.
◆ *Elvis' sources:* Billy Eckstine (MGM 10311) 1948.
Mel Torme (Capitol 15428) 1949.
Ivory Joe Hunter (MGM 11132) 1951.

This cut was scheduled along with **TIGER MAN [4.6]** *to be Elvis' second single. In the event, however, it was cancelled and replaced with* **GOOD ROCKIN' TONIGHT** *b/w* **I DON'T CARE IF THE SUN DON'T SHINE** *(Sun 210).*

▶ *Elvis' interpretation:* pop ballad.

Take 1	2.56 🕐
Take 2	3.14 🕐
Take 3 *(false start)*	0.11 🕐
Take 4 *(false start)*	0.21 🕐
Take 5	2.25 🕐
Take 6	2.41 🕐

Supplied to RCA on Sun tape No. 8 [see *Appendix C*]. *[The Sun tape reel bears a sticker inscribed '8/19 Wed. nite'. This is misleading: 19 August 1954 was a Thursday.]*
RCA master F2WB-8117 allocated in 1955.
Take 1 first issued in 1992 on 5-CD box set *The King Of Rock'n'Roll: The Complete 50s Masters* (BMG/RCA 07863 66050-2).
Take 2 first issued in 1997 on 4-CD *Platinum – A Life In Music* (BMG/RCA 67489-2).
Takes 3, 4 and 5 first issued in 1999 on 2-CD *Sunrise* (BMG/RCA 07863 67675-2).
Take 6 first issued in 1956 on LP *Elvis Presley* (RCA-Victor LPM-1254). Reissued in 1999 on 2-CD *Sunrise* (BMG/RCA 07863 67675-2).

TOMORROW NIGHT *(Coslow/Grosz)*

A hit in 1939 for Horace Heidt (Columbia 35203). Crossover (pop and R&B) hit in 1948 for Lonnie Johnson (King 4201). Not to be confused with Louis Armstrong's 1933 recording 'Tomorrow Night (After Tonight)' (RCA-Victor 68-0774) or Junior Wells' 'Tomorrow Night' (States 143) 1954.

✦ Original by Horace Heidt (Columbia 35203) 1939.
◆ *Elvis' sources:*   Horace Heidt (Columbia 35203) 1939.
                        Lonnie Johnson (King 4201) 1948.
                        Lonnie Johnson (Paradise 11) 1948.

First version. Second version recorded on 8 December 1954 [see **4.12**].

▶ *Elvis' interpretation:* pop ballad.

Take 1	?
Take 2	?
Take 3	?
Take 4	?
Take 5	?
Take 6	?
Take 7	2.59 🕒

Supplied to RCA on Sun tape No. 7 [see *Appendix C*].
RCA master F2WB-8115 allocated in 1955 to Take 7.
Takes 1, 2, 3, 4, 5 and 6 lost.
Take 7 originally issued in 1965 in edited form with overdubs on LP *Elvis For Everyone!* (RCA-Victor LPM/LSP-3450). The overdubs (guitars, drums, bass, harmonica and backing vocals) were added by Chet Atkins at RCA Studio B, Nashville on 18 March 1965. An edited version without overdubs was issued in 1987 on 2-LP/CD *The Complete Sun Sessions* (BMG/RCA 6414-1-R / 6414-2-R). The complete and unedited version without overdubs was first issued in 1992 on 5-CD box set *The King Of Rock'n'Roll: The Complete 50s Masters* (BMG/RCA 66050-2). Reissued in 1999 on 2-CD *Sunrise* (BMG/RCA 07863 67675-2).

I'LL NEVER LET YOU GO (LITTLE DARLIN') *(Wakely)*

✦ Original by Jimmy Wakely (Decca 5973) 1941.
◆ *Elvis' sources:*   Gene Autry (OKeh 06360) 1941.
                        Jimmy Wakely (Decca 5973) 1941.
                        Jimmy Liggins (Specialty 470) 1953.

First version. Second version recorded on 10 September 1954 [see **4.9**].

▶ *Elvis' interpretation:* country pop.

Take 1	?
Take 2	?
Take 3	?
Take 4	?
Take 5	2.25 🕒

Supplied to RCA on Sun tape Nos. 7, 9 and 12 [see *Appendix C*].
RCA master F2WB-8116 allocated in 1955.
Takes 1, 2, 3 and 4 lost or erased.
Take 5 first issued in 1956 on LP *Elvis Presley* (RCA-Victor LPM-1254). Reissued in 1999 on 2-CD *Sunrise* (BMG/RCA 07863 67675-2).

Sun Studio, 706 Union Avenue, Memphis, Tennessee
Friday, 10 September 1954 (Session: 10.40 pm–0.10 am Saturday)
Elvis Presley   Vocal and acoustic guitar (new Martin D-18)
Scotty Moore   Lead guitar (Gibson ES-295)
Bill Black   Double bass
Sam Phillips   Producer and sound engineer

This session took place immediately after Elvis' shows at the Eagle's Nest [see **5.11**].

SATISFIED *(Carson)*

✱ Original by Martha Carson (Capitol 1900) 1951.
◆ *Elvis' sources:* Martha Carson (Capitol 1900) 1951.
                  Johnnie Ray (Columbia 40006) 1953.

▶ *Elvis' interpretation:* raw rockabilly.

Elvis missed out a verse of about one minute on Take 4.

          Dialogue
          Take 1 *(incomplete)*   0.40
          Take 2 *(false start)*   0.15
          Take 3 *(incomplete)*   1.05
          Take 4 *(incomplete)*   1.15
          Break until 11.15 pm

Take 4 supplied to RCA on Sun tape No. 12 [see *Appendix C*].
Takes 1, 2 and 3 were erased in 1954.
Take 4 lost.

I'LL NEVER LET YOU GO (LITTLE DARLIN') *(Wakely)*

✱ Original by Jimmy Wakely (Decca 5973) 1941.
◆ *Elvis' sources:* Gene Autry (OKeh 06360) 1941.
                  Jimmy Wakely (Decca 5973) 1941.
                  Jimmy Liggins (Specialty 470) 1953.

Second version. First version recorded on 19 August 1954 [see **4.8**].

▶ *Elvis' interpretation:* country pop.

          Take 1   ?
          Take 2   ?
          Take 3   ?
          Take 4   ?
          Break until 11.45 pm

Supplied to RCA on Sun tape No. 9 [see *Appendix C*].
RCA master F2WB-8116 erroneously allocated in 1955.
Unknown incomplete take (1.04 ⏱, RCA master renumbered OPA1-4197) issued in 1999 – with dialogue – on 2-CD *Sunrise* (BMG/RCA 07863 67675-2).
Other takes lost.

After the break, the following two songs were tried out but not recorded:

YOU ARE MY SUNSHINE *(Davis/Mitchell)*
A hit in 1941 for Gene Autry (OKeh 06274), Bing Crosby (Decca 3952) and Wayne King (Victor 26767).

★ Original by the Pine Ridge Boys (Bluebird 8263) 1939.
◆ *Elvis' sources:*   Jimmie Davis (Decca 5813) 1940.
                    Gene Autry (OKeh 06274) 1941.
                    Bing Crosby (Decca 3952) 1941.
                    Wayne King (Victor 26767) 1941.
                    Gene Autry (Columbia 20047) 1947.

▶ *Elvis' interpretation:* country ballad.

WABASH CANNONBALL *(Kindt)*
Song composed in 1905 by William Kindt, based on **THE GREAT ROCK ISLAND ROUTE** *by J.A. Rolfe, 1882. A hit in 1939 for Roy Acuff (Vocalion 04466).*

★ Original by Hugh Cross (Columbia 15439) 1929.
◆ *Elvis' sources:*   Carter Family (Victor 23731) 1933.
                    Roy Acuff (Vocalion 04466) 1938.
                    Roy Acuff (Conqueror 9121) 1938.
                    Bill Carlisle's Kentucky Boys (Decca 5713) 1939.
                    Carter Family (Bluebird 8350) 1939.
                    Roy Acuff (Columbia 37008) 1946.
                    Roy Acuff (Columbia 20034) 1947.
                    Roy Acuff (Columbia 20197) 1948.

▶ *Elvis' interpretation:* raw rockabilly.

Sun Studio, 706 Union Avenue, Memphis, Tennessee
Wednesday, 15 September 1954 (afternoon, exact time unknown)

Elvis Presley	Vocal and acoustic guitar (new Martin D-18)
Scotty Moore	Lead guitar (Gibson ES-295)
Bill Black	Double bass
Sam Phillips	Producer and sound engineer

I DON'T CARE IF THE SUN DON'T SHINE *(David)*
Pop hit in 1950 for Patti Page (Mercury 5396).

★ Original by Patti Page (Mercury 5396) 1950.
◆ *Elvis' sources:*   Dean Martin (Capitol 981) 1950.
                    Patti Page (Mercury 5396) 1950.

▶ *Elvis' interpretation:* rockabilly.

Note   *There are no bongos on this cut: the drumming effect was created by Elvis patting the back of his guitar.*

Take 1 *(incomplete)*   0.41 ⏱
Take 2 *(false start)*   0.20 ⏱
Take 3   2.31 ⏱
Take 4   2.28 ⏱

RCA master F2WB-8042 allocated in 1955 to Take 4.
Takes 1, 2 and 3 first issued in 1984 on 6-LP box set *Elvis: A Golden Celebration* (RCA-Victor CPM6-5172). Reissued in 1999 on 2-CD *Sunrise* (BMG/RCA 07863 67675-2).
Take 4 (Sun matrix U-130) issued on Sun 210 on Monday, 27 September 1954. Reissued in 1984 on 6-LP box set *Elvis: A Golden Celebration* (RCA-Victor CPM6-5172) and in 1999 on 2-CD *Sunrise* (BMG/RCA 07863 67675-2).

JUST BECAUSE *(Shelton/Shelton/Robin)*
Crossover (pop and C&W) hit in 1948 for Frankie Yankovic (Columbia 12359), and a pop hit for Eddy Howard (Majestic 1231).

★ Original by the Lone Star Cowboys *[Shelton Brothers – Bob and Joe]* (Bluebird 6052) 1933.
◆ *Elvis' sources:*   Dick Stabile (Decca 716) 1937.
                   Shelton Brothers *[Bob and Joe]* (Decca 5872) 1942.
                   Eddy Howard (Majestic 1231) 1948.
                   Frankie Yankovic (Columbia 12359) 1948.

▶ *Elvis' interpretation:* This song was given fast (rockabilly) and slow (blues) treatments and was recorded in seventeen takes including false starts and incomplete cuts [no details].

Take 1   ?
Take 2   ?
Take 3   ?
Take 4   ?
Take 5   ?
Take 6   ?
Take 7   ?
Take 8   ?
Take 9   ?
Take 10   ?
Take 11   ?
Take 12   ?
Take 13   ?
Take 14   ?
Take 15   ?
Take 16   ?
Take 17   ?

Supplied to RCA on Sun tape Nos. 3, 9 and 10 [see *Appendix C*].
RCA master F2WB-8118 allocated in 1955 to unknown take.
Unknown take (2.34 ⏱) first issued in 1956 on LP *Elvis Presley* (RCA-Victor LPM-1254). Reissued in 1999 on 2-CD *Sunrise* (BMG/RCA 07863 67675-2).
Three unknown takes (incomplete 'blues' versions) were erased in 1954.

GOOD ROCKIN' TONIGHT *(Brown)*
R&B hit in 1948 and 1949 for Roy Brown (DeLuxe 1093), and in 1948 for Wynonie Harris (King 4210).

★ Original by Roy Brown (DeLuxe 1093) 1947.
◆ *Elvis' sources:*   Roy Brown (DeLuxe 1093) 1947.
                    Wynonie Harris (King 4210) 1948.

▶ *Elvis' interpretation:* rockabilly.

Take 1	?
Take 2	2.13 🕐
Take 3 *(incomplete)*	?
Take 4 *(incomplete)*	?

Supplied to RCA on Sun tape Nos. 3 and 10 [see *Appendix C*].
RCA master F2WW-8043 (per Sun tape box No. 3) or F2WB-8043 (per Sun tape boxes Nos. 9 and 10) allocated in 1955.
Take 1 unissued.
Take 2 (Sun matrix U-131) issued on Sun 210 on Monday, 27 September 1954. Reissued in 1999 on 2-CD *Sunrise* (BMG/RCA 07863 67675-2).
Takes 3 and 4 were only a few seconds long and were erased in 1954.

Note 1   *Future Sun rockabilly singer Ray Harris (a friend of Bill Black's) was in the studio during the recording of* **GOOD ROCKIN' TONIGHT**.

Note 2   *In the booklet to CD 'The Prisonaires' (Bear Family BCD-15523, 1990), Colin Escott notes: 'Short of tape as usual, Phillips pulled a reel of Elvis Presley's out-takes of* **GOOD ROCKIN' TONIGHT** *and recorded over the top. Little tastes of "We're gonna rock, rock, rock..." can be heard between the Prisonaires' cuts.' Sadly, much of Elvis' unissued Sun material met the same fate.*

4.11

Sun Studio, 706 Union Avenue, Memphis, Tennessee
Monday, 15 November 1954 (Session 4.00 pm–5.15 pm)

Elvis Presley	Vocal and acoustic guitar (new Martin D-18)
Scotty Moore	Lead guitar (Gibson ES-295)
Bill Black	Double bass
Sam Phillips	Producer and sound engineer

MY BABY'S GONE *(Kesler/Taylor)*

★ Original by Elvis.

This was Elvis' first attempt at the Stan Kesler-Bill Taylor composition, **YOU'RE RIGHT, I'M LEFT, SHE'S GONE,** *popularly known as the 'slow' or 'blues' version. The version which appeared on Sun 217 was recorded on 6 March 1955 [see* **4.16**].

▶ *Elvis' interpretation:* bluesy.

69

Take 1	2.47 🕐
Take 2	?
Take 3	?
Take 4 *(false start)*	?
Take 5	2.42 🕐
Take 6	?
Take 7	?
Take 8 *(incomplete)*	?
Take 9 *(incomplete)*	?
Break until 4.45 pm	

This song was supplied to RCA on Sun tape No. 6, but was initially not allocated a RCA master number. Confusingly, it was later allocated the same number as **I'M LEFT, YOU'RE RIGHT, SHE'S GONE** — a later version of this song recorded on 6 March 1955 which was included on Sun tape No. 5 [see **4.16** for details].

Take 1 first issued in 1987 on 2-LP/CD *The Complete Sun Sessions* (BMG/RCA 6414-1-R / 6414-2-R). Reissued in 1999 on 2-CD *Sunrise* (BMG/RCA 07863 67675-2).
Takes 2, 3 and 4 first issued in 1987 on 2-LP/CD *The Complete Sun Sessions* 2-LP (BMG/RCA 6414-1-R / 6414-2-R).
Take 5 was used to produce a 10-inch 78 rpm acetate for radio station WHBQ in November or December 1954. The label of this acetate states 'Blues' and Elvis' surname is mis-spelt 'Pressley'. First commercial release in 1987 on 2-LP/CD *The Complete Sun Sessions* (BMG/RCA 6414-1-R / 6414-2-R). Reissued in 1999 on 2-CD *Sunrise* (BMG/RCA 07863 67675-2).
Takes 6 and 7 first issued in 1987 on 2-LP/CD *The Complete Sun Sessions* 2-LP (BMG/RCA 6414-1-R / 6414-2-R).
Takes 8 and 9 contained predominantly studio chatter and were erased in 1954.

NIGHT TRAIN TO MEMPHIS *(Hughes/Bradley/Smith)*

✱ Original by Roy Acuff (OKeh 6693) 1943.
◆ *Elvis' sources:*   Roy Acuff (OKeh 6693) 1943.
                              Roy Acuff (Columbia 37029) 1946.
                              Roy Acuff (Columbia 20054) 1947.

▶ *Elvis' interpretation:* raw rockabilly.

Take 1 *(incomplete)*	1.35
Take 2	2.10
Take 3	2.15
Take 4	2.20
Break until 5.00 pm	

Tape lost. During the Seventies, several collectors claimed that Sam Phillips' brother, Jud, had some takes of **NIGHT TRAIN TO MEMPHIS** and **TENNESSEE SATURDAY NIGHT** in his possession.

TENNESSEE SATURDAY NIGHT *(Hughes)*
C&W hit in 1949 for Johnny Bond (Columbia 20545) and Red Foley (Decca 46136).

✱ Original by Red Foley (Decca 46136) 1948.
◆ *Elvis' sources:*   Red Foley (Decca 46136) 1948.
                              Johnny Bond (Columbia 20545) 1949.
                              Ella Mae Morse (Capitol 1903) 1951.

▶ *Elvis' interpretation:* raw rockabilly.

Take 1	2.40
Take 2	2.44
Take 3	2.36

Tape lost. During the Seventies, several collectors claimed that Sam Phillips' brother, Jud, had some takes of **NIGHT TRAIN TO MEMPHIS** and **TENNESSEE SATURDAY NIGHT** in his possession.

4.12

Sun Studio, 706 Union Avenue, Memphis, Tennessee
Wednesday, 8 December 1954 (Session: 7.00 pm–8.00 pm)

Elvis Presley	Vocal and acoustic guitar (new Martin D-18)
Scotty Moore	Lead guitar (Gibson ES-295)
Bill Black	Double bass
Sam Phillips	Producer and sound engineer

UNCLE PEN *(Monroe)*
Song written by Bill Monroe after his uncle, Pendleton Vandiver.

★ Original by Bill Monroe – Voc. Bill Monroe & Jimmy Martin (Decca 46283) 1951.
◆ *Elvis' source:* Bill Monroe – Voc. Bill Monroe & Jimmy Martin (Decca 46283) 1951.

▶ *Elvis' interpretation:* raw rockabilly.

Take 1 *(incomplete)*	1.55
Take 2	2.20
Take 3	2.25
Break	

Tape lost.

OAKIE BOOGIE *(Tyler)*
C&W hit in 1947 for Jack Guthrie (Capitol 341). Pop hit in 1952 for Ella Mae Morse (Capitol 2072).

★ Original by Johnny Tyler (Stanchel 101) 1946.
◆ *Elvis' sources:* Luderin Darbonne (DeLuxe 5029) 1947.
    Jack Guthrie (Capitol 341) 1947.
    Ella Mae Morse (Capitol 2072) 1952.
    Jack Guthrie (Capitol 2128) 1952.

▶ *Elvis' interpretation:* raw rockabilly.

Take 1	2.15
Take 2	2.10
Take 3	2.00
Take 4 *(false start)*	0.50
Take 5	2.17
Break	

Tape lost.

TOMORROW NIGHT *(Coslow/Grosz)*
A hit in 1939 for Horace Heidt (Columbia 35203). Crossover (pop and R&B) hit in 1948 for Lonnie Johnson (King 4201). Not to be confused with Louis Armstrong's 1933 recording 'Tomorrow Night (After Tonight)' (RCA-Victor 68-0774) or Junior Wells' 'Tomorrow Night' (States 143) 1954.

✱ Original by Horace Heidt (Columbia 35203) 1939.
◆ *Elvis' sources:*   Horace Heidt (Columbia 35203) 1939.
                      Lonnie Johnson (King 4201) 1948.
                      Lonnie Johnson (Paradise 11) 1948.

Second version. First version recorded on 19 August 1954 [see **4.8**]. *On Take 3, Elvis changed some of the words.*

▶ *Elvis' interpretation:* bluesy pop ballad.

Take 1	3.00
Take 2	2.56
Take 3	2.50
Break	

Tape lost.

JUANITA *(Norton)*
Composition by Caroline Norton. Not to be confused with Big Joe Williams' 1951 recording of the same name (Trumpet 170), which was based on Sleepy John Estes' **VERNITA BLUES** *(Decca 7342) from 1937; or Chuck Willis' 1956 waxing (Atlantic 1112), later covered by Charlie Rich on his 1960 album, 'Lonely Weekends' (Phillips International PLP-1970).*

✱ Original by Rufus Thomas (Chess 1517) 1952.
◆ *Elvis' source:* Rufus Thomas (Chess 1517) 1952.

Elvis' interpretation (Take 1): bluesy.
Elvis' interpretation (Take 2): raw rockabilly.

Take 1	2.08
Take 2	2.14

Tape lost.

4.13

Sun Studio, 706 Union Avenue, Memphis, Tennessee
Monday, 13 December 1954 (Session 8.00 pm–8.45 pm)

Elvis Presley	Vocal and acoustic guitar (new Martin D-18)
Scotty Moore	Lead guitar (Gibson ES-295)
Bill Black	Double bass
Sam Phillips	Producer and sound engineer

NINE POUND HAMMER *(Traditional)*
Traditional folk-song from circa 1890.

★ Original **THE NINE POUND HAMMER** by Al Hopkins (Brunswick 177) 1927.
◆ *Elvis' sources:* **NINE POUND HAMMER IS TOO HEAVY** by the Monroe Brothers
(Bluebird 6422) 1936.
Merle Travis (78 rpm 4-disc album *Folk Songs Of The Hills*, Capitol AD-50) 1947.

▶ *Elvis' interpretation:* raw rockabilly.

Take 1	1.55
Take 2	1.50

Tape lost.

*Short break, during which Elvis sang the following two songs. It is not known whether he sang
them all the way through, or whether they were captured on tape.*

BLUES STAY AWAY FROM ME *(Delmore/Delmore/Raney/Glover)*
*C&W hit in 1949 for Eddie Crosby (Decca 46180), and in 1950 for the Delmore Brothers (King
803). Crossover hit (pop and C&W) in 1949-50 for the Owen Bradley Quintet (Coral 60107).*

★ Original by the Delmore Brothers (King 803) 1949.
◆ *Elvis' sources:* Owen Bradley Quintet (Coral 60107) 1949.
Eddie Crosby (Decca 46180) 1949.
Delmore Brothers (King 803) 1949.
Lonnie Johnson (King 4336) 1949.

▶ *Elvis' interpretation:* bluesy.

JUST WALKIN' IN THE RAIN *(Riley/Bragg/Killen)*

★ Original by the Prisonaires (Sun 186) 1953.
◆ *Elvis' source:* Prisonaires (Sun 186) 1953.

▶ *Elvis' interpretation:* bluesy ballad.

Session resumed.

THUNDERBOLT BOOGIE *(Stephens)*

★ Original by Todd Rhodes – Voc. LaVern Baker (King 4601) 1953.
◆ *Elvis' source:* Todd Rhodes – Voc. LaVern Baker (King 4601) 1953.

▶ *Elvis' interpretation:* raw rockabilly.

73

Take 1 *(incomplete)*	0.48
Take 2 *(incomplete)*	1.56
Take 3 *(false start)*	0.12
Take 4	2.10

Tape lost.

Sun Studio, 706 Union Avenue, Memphis, Tennessee
Monday, 20 December 1954 (Session 8.00 pm–8.40 pm)
Elvis Presley   Vocal and acoustic guitar (new Martin D-18)
Scotty Moore   Lead guitar (Gibson ES-295)
Bill Black   Double bass
Sam Phillips   Producer and sound engineer

MILKCOW BLUES BOOGIE *(Arnold)*
The '**BOOGIE**' *was probably added by Elvis or Sam Phillips.*

✱ Original **MILK COW BLUES** by Freddie Spruell (OKeh 8422) 1926. [Incidentally, this record
was issued under the same catalogue number with two different 'B' sides.]
Sleepy John Estes recorded his variation on the theme (Victor 38614) in 1930.
Kokomo Arnold subsequently reworked the theme in five different versions:
MILK COW BLUES (Decca 7026) 1934.
MILK COW BLUES No. 2 (Decca 7059) 1935.
MILK COW BLUES No. 3 (Decca 7116) 1935.
MILK COW BLUES No. 4 (Decca 7163) 1936.
MILK COW BLUES No. 5 (Decca, unissued), recorded 1936.
◆ *Elvis' sources:*   Kokomo Arnold (Decca 7026) 1934.
               Johnny Lee Wills (Decca 5985) 1941.
               Jimmy Wakely (Capitol 40107) 1948.

▶ *Elvis' interpretation:* rockabilly.

Take 1	2.30
Take 2	2.27
Take 3	2.39 🕐

RCA master F2WB-8044 allocated in 1955 to Take 3.
Takes 1 and 2 lost.
Take 3 (Sun matrix U-140) issued on Sun 215 on Tuesday, 28 December 1954 (not 8 January
1955, as has erroneously been reported for decades). Reissued in 1999 on 2-CD *Sunrise*
(BMG/RCA 07863 67675-2). Original Sun tape lost. RCA dubbed this side from a Sun 78.

YOU'RE A HEARTBREAKER *(Sallee)*
Composition by Jack Sallee. Flip of **WILD HORSES**, *a pop hit in 1953 for Ray Anthony (Capitol
2349). This is not the same song as Jimmy Heap's* **(YOU'RE A) HEARTBREAKER** *(Capitol
2294) 1952.*

✱ Original by Ray Anthony —- Voc. Jo Ann Greer (Capitol 2349) 1953.
◆ *Elvis' source:* Ray Anthony —- Voc. Jo Ann Greer (Capitol 2349) 1953.

First version. Second version recorded on 6 March 1955 [see **4.16**].

▶ *Elvis' interpretation:* rockabilly/country.

Take 1	2.06
Take 2	2.00
Take 3 *(false start)*	0.23
Take 4	2.12

RCA master F2WB-8045 allocated in 1955 to Take 4.
Takes 1, 2 and 3 lost.
Take 4 (Sun matrix U-141) issued on Sun 215 on Tuesday, 28 December 1954 (not 8 January 1955, as has erroneously been reported for decades). Reissued in 1999 on 2-CD *Sunrise* (BMG/RCA 07863 67675-2). Original Sun tape lost. RCA dubbed this side from a Sun 78.

At the end of the session, there was an informal jam during which Elvis sang jokey versions of the following two songs. It is not known whether he sang them all the way through, or whether they were captured on tape.

BEAR CAT (THE ANSWER TO HOUND DOG *(Phillips)*
Composition by Sam Phillips based on Big Mama Thornton's **HOUND DOG** *(Peacock 1612) 1953. R&B hit in 1953 for Rufus Thomas (Sun 181).*

✱ Original by Rufus Thomas (Sun 181) 1953.
◆ *Elvis' source:* Rufus Thomas (Sun 181) 1953.

▶ *Elvis' interpretation:* comic raw rockabilly.

WE ALL GOTTA GO SOMETIME *(Louis)*

✱ Original by Joe Hill Louis (Sun 178) 1953.
◆ *Elvis' source:* Joe Hill Louis (Sun 178) 1953.

▶ *Elvis' interpretation:* comic blues.

4.15

Sun Studio, 706 Union Avenue, Memphis, Tennessee
Thursday, 3 February 1955 (exact time unknown)

Elvis Presley	Vocal and acoustic guitar (original Martin D-28)
Scotty Moore	Lead guitar (Gibson ES-295)
Bill Black	Double bass
Sam Phillips	Producer and sound engineer

I GOT A WOMAN *(Charles)*
R&B hit in 1955 for Ray Charles (Atlantic 1050).

✱ Original by Ray Charles (Atlantic 1050) 1955.
◆ *Elvis' source:* Ray Charles (Atlantic 1050) 1955.
O Elvis later recorded this title at RCA, Nashville on 10 January 1956 (released in 1956 on LP *Elvis Presley*, RCA-Victor LPM-1254).

▶ *Elvis' interpretation:* rockabilly.

Take 1	?
Take 2	?

Supplied to RCA on Sun tape No. 4 [see *Appendix C*].

TRYIN' TO GET TO YOU *(McCoy/Singleton)*

✱ Original by the Eagles (Mercury 70391) 1954.
◆ *Elvis' source:* Eagles (Mercury 70391) 1954.

First version. Second version recorded on 11 July 1955 [see **4.20**].

▶ *Elvis' interpretation:* bluesy.

Take 1	?
Take 2 *(incomplete)*	?
Take 3 *(incomplete)*	?

Take 1 supplied to RCA on Sun tape No. 4 [see *Appendix C*].
Takes 2 and 3 erased in 1955.

BABY LET'S PLAY HOUSE *(Gunter)*

1955 R&B hit for Arthur Gunter (Excello 2047) based on Eddy Arnold's **I WANNA PLAY HOUSE WITH YOU** *(RCA-Victor 0476) 1951. Elvis memorably replaced Gunter's lyric 'You may have religion' with 'You may drive a pink Cadillac'.*

✱ Original by Arthur Gunter (Excello 2047) 1954.
◆ *Elvis' source:* Arthur Gunter (Excello 2047) 1954.

▶ *Elvis' interpretation:* rockabilly.

Take 1	?
Take 2	2.16 🕐

Supplied to RCA on Sun tape No. 4 [see *Appendix C*].
RCA master F2WW-8046 allocated in 1955 to Take 2.
Take 1 lost.
Take 2 (Sun matrix U-143) issued on Sun 217 on Monday, 25 April 1955. (According to Marion Keisker, Sun 217 was originally to have been released on 1 April 1955, but was delayed until Monday, 25 April. The first reviews of the record appeared in *Billboard* and *Cash Box* some three weeks later in mid-May.) Reissued in 1999 on 2-CD *Sunrise* (BMG/RCA 07863 67675-2).

4.16

Sun Studio, 706 Union Avenue, Memphis, Tennessee
Sunday, 6 March 1955 (evening, exact time unknown)

Elvis Presley	Vocal and acoustic guitar (original Martin D-28)
Scotty Moore	Lead guitar (Gibson ES-295)
Bill Black	Double bass
Jimmie Lott	Drums
Sam Phillips	Producer and sound engineer

Drummer Jimmie Lott was only 15 or 16 at the time of this recording.

✱ Original by Elvis.

I'M LEFT, YOU'RE RIGHT, SHE'S GONE *(Kesler/Taylor)*
Second attempt at the the Stan Kesler–Bill Taylor composition, **YOU'RE RIGHT, I'M LEFT, SHE'S GONE**, *first recorded in November 1954 as* **MY BABY'S GONE** [see 4.11].

▶ *Elvis' interpretation:* rockabilly/country.

Take 1	?
Take 2	?
Take 3	?
Take 4	?
Take 5	?
Take 6	2.37 🕐

Supplied to RCA on Sun tape No. 5 [see *Appendix C*].
RCA master F2WW-8047 allocated in 1955 to Take 6.
Takes 1 to 5 lost.
Take 6 (Sun matrix U-142) issued on Sun 217, Monday, 25 April 1955. (According to Marion Keisker, Sun 217 was originally to have been released on 1 April 1955, but was delayed until Monday, 25 April. The first reviews of the record appeared in *Billboard* and *Cash Box* some three weeks later in mid-May.) Reissued in 1999 on 2-CD *Sunrise* (BMG/RCA 07863 67675-2).

YOU'RE A HEARTBREAKER *(Sallee)*
Composition by Jack Sallee. Flip of **WILD HORSES***, a pop hit in 1953 for Ray Anthony (Capitol 2349). This is not the same song as Jimmy Heap's* **(YOU'RE A) HEARTBREAKER** *(Capitol 2294) 1952.*

★ Original by Ray Anthony — Voc. Jo Ann Greer (Capitol 2349) 1953.
◆ *Elvis' source:* Ray Anthony — Voc. Jo Ann Greer (Capitol 2349) 1953.

Second version. First version recorded on 20 December 1954 [see **4.14**].

▶ *Elvis' interpretation:* rockabilly/country.

Take 1	?
Take 2	?
Take 3	?

Tape lost.

HOW DO YOU THINK I FEEL *(Walker/Pierce)*

★ Original by Red Sovine (Decca 29068) early 1954.
◆ *Elvis' source:* Jimmie Rodgers Snow (RCA-Victor 5900) 1954.
○ Elvis later recorded this title at Radio Recorders, Hollywood on 1 September 1956 (released in 1956 on LP *Elvis*, RCA-Victor LPM-1382).

▶ *Elvis' interpretation:* rhumba and blues versions.

Number of takes unknown. Tape lost.

An extract of this song was included on the mid-1990s bootleg CD, *When All Was Kool* (Mystery Train CD-2001). All that can be heard is Scotty's guitar and the drums, with Elvis singing faintly in the background. It has the feel of a rehearsal.

4.17

Sun Studio, 706 Union Avenue, Memphis, Tennessee
Tuesday, 15 March 1955 (Session 8.00 pm–8.30 pm)

Elvis Presley	Vocal and acoustic guitar (original Martin D-28)
Scotty Moore	Lead guitar (Gibson ES-295)
Bill Black	Double bass
Sam Phillips	Producer and sound engineer

TENNESSEE PARTNER *(Traditional)*

Another mystery song, annotated in Marion Keisker's files simply as 'Country Trad.'. However, it seems strange that apparently no-one else — not even the Carter Family — has recorded it. Perhaps it was an adaptation of Jimmy Work's **TENNESSEE BORDER** *(Alben 501, released late 1948), a massive C&W hit in 1949 for Bob Atcher, Red Foley, Tennessee Ernie Ford and Jimmie Skinner, or* **TENNESSEE BORDER #2**, *a C&W hit that same year for Homer & Jethro and Ernest Tubb & Red Foley. We shall probably never know.*

★ Original by ?

▶ *Elvis' interpretation:* raw rockabilly.

According to Marion's notes, Elvis omitted a verse of approximately one minute's duration.

Take 1	1.52
Take 2	1.59

Tape lost.

ROCKIN' LITTLE SALLY *(Gordon)*
Song written for Elvis by Rosco Gordon.

★ Original by Elvis.

▶ *Elvis' interpretation:* raw rockabilly.

Take 1	2.13

Tape lost.

BREAKIN' THE RULES *(Blasingame/Gray/Thompson)*
C&W hit in 1954 for Hank Thompson (Capitol 2758).

★ Original by Hank Thompson (Capitol 2758) 1954.
◆ *Elvis' source:* Hank Thompson (Capitol 2758) 1954.

▶ *Elvis' interpretation:* no data.

Take 1	2.07

Tape lost.

4.18

Sun Studio, 706 Union Avenue, Memphis, Tennessee
March 1955 (rehearsal, exact date unknown)
Elvis Presley   Vocal and acoustic guitar (original Martin D-28)
Scotty Moore   Lead guitar (Gibson ES-295)
Bill Black   Double bass
Sam Phillips   Producer and sound engineer

NIGHTMARE *(Leiber/Stoller/Otis)*
Flip of **HOUND DOG***, a R&B hit in 1953 for Big Mama Thornton (Peacock 1612).*

✱ Original by Willie Mae 'Big Mama' Thornton (Peacock 1612) 1953.
◆ *Elvis' source:* Willie Mae 'Big Mama' Thornton (Peacock 1612) 1953.

▶ *Elvis' interpretation:* blues.

Tape erased.

I PLAYED THE FOOL *(Alexis)*
R&B hit in 1953 for the Clovers (Atlantic 977).

✱ Original by the Clovers (Atlantic 977) 1952.
◆ *Elvis' source:* Clovers (Atlantic 977) 1952.

▶ *Elvis' interpretation:* bluesy.

Tape erased.

UNKNOWN TITLES

Tape erased.

4.19

Sun Studio, 706 Union Avenue, Memphis, Tennessee
April 1955 (rehearsal, exact date unknown)
Elvis Presley   Vocal and acoustic guitar (original Martin D-28)
Scotty Moore   Lead guitar (Gibson ES-295)
Bill Black   Double bass
Sam Phillips   Producer and sound engineer

MEXICAN JOE *(Torok)*
C&W hit in 1953 for Jim Reeves (Abbott 116).

✱ Original by Jim Reeves (Abbott 116) 1953.
◆ *Elvis' source:* Jim Reeves (Abbott 116) 1953.

▶ *Elvis' interpretation:* raw rockabilly.

Tape erased.

JUST IN CASE *(Cushing/Crudup)*
Song based on the melody of **THAT'S ALL RIGHT**. *Written for Elvis by Roy Cushing, a nineteen year old fan from Gilmer, Texas, who gave it to him after a show there on 26 January 1955.*

✱ Original by Elvis.

▶ *Elvis' interpretation:* raw rockabilly.

Tape erased.

UNKNOWN TITLES

Tape erased.

Sun Studio, 706 Union Avenue, Memphis, Tennessee
Monday, 11 July 1955 (early afternoon, exact time unknown)

Elvis Presley	Vocal and acoustic guitar (new Martin D-28)
Scotty Moore	Lead guitar (Gibson L5)
Bill Black	Double bass
Johnny Bernero	Drums *(except* **MYSTERY TRAIN***)*
Unknown	Piano *(it was impossible to determine from Marion Keisker's files whether Elvis played piano on* **TRYIN' TO GET TO YOU***)*
Sam Phillips	Producer and sound engineer.

I FORGOT TO REMEMBER TO FORGET *(Kesler/Feathers)*
Song written by Stan Kesler, who recorded a demo of it at the Sun studio on Saturday, 25 June 1955 between 3.00 and 3.30 pm, with himself on fiddle and Charlie Feathers on vocal and acoustic guitar. Feathers subsequently claimed that he had finished off the song and that he should be credited as co-composer. They also recorded a demo of **WE'RE GETTING CLOSER TO BEING APART** *at the same session. In 1973, Feathers cut a new version of* **I FORGOT TO REMEMBER TO FORGET** *for his 'Living Legend' LP (Redita 107, Netherlands).*

✱ Original by Elvis.

▶ *Elvis' interpretation:* slow country.

Take ?   2.30 ◷

Supplied to RCA on Sun tape No. 1 [see *Appendix C*].
RCA master F2WW-8000 allocated in 1955 to unknown take.
Unknown take (Sun matrix U-157) issued on Sun 223 on Monday, 1 August 1955. Reissued in 1999 on 2-CD *Sunrise* (BMG/RCA 07863 67675-2).
Other takes lost.

MYSTERY TRAIN *(Parker/Phillips)*

Elvis' recording is a combination of two Little Junior Parker tunes — the lyrics of **MYSTERY TRAIN** *and the* **LOVE MY BABY** *guitar riff — which were issued back-to-back on Sun 192. Parker's* **MYSTERY TRAIN** *itself was based on the Carter Family's* **WORRIED MAN BLUES** *(Bluebird 6020) 1930.*

✱ Original by Little Junior's Blue Flames (Sun 192) 1953.
◆ *Elvis' source:* Little Junior's Blue Flames (Sun 192) 1953.

▶ *Elvis' interpretation:* rockabilly.

Take ?   2.25 🕐

Supplied to RCA on Sun tape No. 1 [see *Appendix C*].
RCA master F2WW-8001 allocated in 1955 to unknown take.
Unknown take (Sun matrix U-156) issued on Sun 223 on Monday, 1 August 1955. Reissued in 1999 on 2-CD *Sunrise* (BMG/RCA 07863 67675-2).
Other takes lost.

Note   *Sun rockabilly singer Jack Earls was in the studio during the recording of* **MYSTERY TRAIN***, when a dispute reportedly arose as to precisely how many coaches it had: Elvis sang 'fifteen coaches long', but Sam Phillips thought it should be sixteen. Earls mentioned that he had the record at home and was duly despatched to fetch it so that Elvis could learn the words.*

TRYIN' TO GET TO YOU *(McCoy/Singleton)*

✱ Original by the Eagles (Mercury 70391) 1954.
◆ *Elvis' source:* Eagles (Mercury 70391) 1954.

Second version. First version recorded on 3 February 1955 [see **4.15**].

▶ *Elvis' interpretation:* bluesy.

Take ?   2.32 🕐

Supplied to RCA on Sun tape No. 1 [see *Appendix C*].
RCA master F2WW-8039 allocated in 1955.
Unknown take first issued in 1956 on LP *Elvis Presley* (RCA-Victor LPM-1254). Reissued in 1999 on 2-CD *Sunrise* (BMG/RCA 07863 67675-2).
Other takes lost.

At the next session that afternoon, Carl Perkins recorded 'Gone, Gone, Gone' (Sun 224).

Sun Studio, 706 Union Avenue, Memphis, Tennessee
July 1955 (rehearsal, exact date unknown)
Elvis Presley   Vocal and acoustic guitar (new Martin D-28)
Scotty Moore   Lead guitar (Gibson L5)
Bill Black   Double bass
Sam Phillips   Producer and sound engineer

DOWN THE LINE *(Holly/Montgomery)*
Rockabilly number written by Buddy Holly and Bob Montgomery. Holly sang it to Elvis on Friday, 3 June 1955. Buddy & Bob recorded a demo of it at the Nesman Studio in Wichita Falls, Texas on Tuesday, 7 June 1955 along with **BABY LET'S PLAY HOUSE***.*

▶ *Elvis' interpretation:* raw rockabilly.

Tape erased.

UNKNOWN TITLES

Tape erased.

Sun Studio, 706 Union Avenue, Memphis, Tennessee
August 1955 (rehearsal, exact date unknown)
Elvis Presley   Vocal and acoustic guitar (new Martin D-28)
Scotty Moore   Lead guitar (Gibson L5)
Bill Black   Double bass
Sam Phillips   Producer and sound engineer

MAYBELLENE *(Berry)*
Crossover (pop and R&B) hit in 1955 for Chuck Berry (Chess 1604). R&B hit in 1955 for Jim Lowe (Dot 15407). C&W hit in 1955 for Marty Robbins (Columbia 21446).

✱ Original by Chuck Berry (Chess 1604) 1955.
◆ *Elvis' source:* Chuck Berry (Chess 1604) 1955.

▶ *Elvis' interpretation:* raw rockabilly.

Tape erased.

UNKNOWN TITLES

Tape erased.

Sun Studio, 706 Union Avenue, Memphis, Tennessee
August 1955 (rehearsal, exact date unknown)
Elvis Presley   Vocal and acoustic guitar (new Martin D-28)
Scotty Moore   Lead guitar (Gibson L5)
Bill Black   Double bass
Sam Phillips   Producer and sound engineer

UNKNOWN TITLES

Tape erased.

4.24

Sun Studio, 706 Union Avenue, Memphis, Tennessee
August 1955 (rehearsal, exact date unknown)
Elvis Presley   Vocal and acoustic guitar (new Martin D-28)
Scotty Moore   Lead guitar (Gibson L5)
Bill Black   Double bass
Sam Phillips   Producer and sound engineer

CRYIN' HEART BLUES *(Brown)*
C&W hit in 1951 for Johnnie & Jack (RCA-Victor 0478). This song was later retitled **MEAN HEART BLUES** *by Elvis* [see **5.64**].

✱ Original by Johnnie & Jack (RCA-Victor 0478) 1951.
◆ *Elvis' source:* Johnnie & Jack (RCA-Victor 0478) 1951.

▶ *Elvis' interpretation:* raw rockabilly.

Tape erased.

I ALMOST LOST MY MIND *(Hunter)*
Crossover (pop and R&B) hit in 1950 for Nat 'King' Cole (Capitol 889), and a R&B hit for Ivory Joe Hunter (MGM 8011 and 10578).

✱ Original by Ivory Joe Hunter (MGM 8011 and 10578) 1949.
◆ *Elvis' sources:* Nat 'King' Cole (Capitol 889) 1949.
                Ivory Joe Hunter (MGM 8011 and 10578) 1949.
                Lionel Hampton – Voc. Sonny Parker (Decca 24864) 1950.

▶ *Elvis' interpretation:* bluesy.

Tape erased.

SOMETHIN' BLUES *(Gordon)*
Song written for Elvis by Rosco Gordon.

★ Original by Elvis.

▶ *Elvis' interpretation:* blues.

Tape erased.

Sun Studio, 706 Union Avenue, Memphis, Tennessee
1954 or 1955 (exact date and time unknown)
Elvis Presley   Vocal and acoustic guitar?
Jones Brothers   Vocal group
Charles Bishop?   Guitar?
Sam Phillips?   Producer and sound engineer

Sometime during 1954 or 1955, Elvis cut a 'direct-to-disc' session at Sun with a black gospel group called the Jones Brothers (William Gresham, Eddie Hollins, Charles Jones, Jake McIntosh, John Prye and James Rayford). The following unissued titles might be the cuts in question.

DO YOU KNOW THE MAN *(Composer unknown)*

Presumed lost.

SOMEWHERE IN GLORY *(Composer unknown)*

Presumed lost.

*Note   Elvis also tried out **NOAH** and **YOU'LL NEVER WALK ALONE** at this session, but neither of these songs was recorded.*

4.26

Sun Studio, 706 Union Avenue, Memphis, Tennessee
Thursday, 3 November 1955 (evening, exact time unknown)

Elvis Presley	Vocal and acoustic guitar (new Martin D-28)
Scotty Moore	Lead guitar (Gibson L5)
Bill Black	Double bass
Johnny Bernero	Drums
Sam Phillips	Producer and sound engineer

This was Elvis' last Sun session. Carl Perkins was also present in the studio.

WHEN IT RAINS IT REALLY POURS *(Emerson)*

✱ Original by Billy 'The Kid' Emerson (Sun 214) 1954.
◆ *Elvis' source:* Billy 'The Kid' Emerson (Sun 214) 1954.
○ Elvis re-recorded this title at Radio Recorders, Hollywood on 24 February 1957 (released in 1965 on LP *Elvis For Everyone!* RCA-Victor LPM/LSP-3450).

▶ *Elvis' interpretation:* bluesy.

Take 1	?	
Take 2	?	
Take 3	?	
Take 4	?	
Take 5	?	
Take 6	?	
Take 7 *(incomplete)*	4.03 ○	(0.36 excluding dialogue)
Take 8	?	
Take 9 *(incomplete)*	3.05 ○	(0.11 excluding dialogue)
Take 10	?	
Take 11	2.01 ○	
Take 12 *(studio chatter)*	?	
Take 13 *(studio chatter)*	?	

Supplied to RCA on Sun tape No. 11 [see *Appendix C*].
RCA master NPA5-5826 allocated in 1983 to Takes 7, 9 and 11.
Takes 1-6 unissued.
Take 7 first issued in 1983 on LP *Elvis: A Legendary Performer (Volume 4)* (RCA-Victor CPL1-4848).
Take 8 unissued.
Take 9 first issued in 1983 on LP *Elvis: A Legendary Performer (Volume 4)* (RCA-Victor CPL1-4848).
Take 10 unissued.
Take 11 first issued in 1983 on LP *Elvis: A Legendary Performer (Volume 4)* (RCA-Victor CPL1-4848). Reissued in 1999 on 2-CD *Sunrise* (BMG/RCA 07863 67675-2).
Takes 12 and 13 were not proper 'takes', in that they consisted of studio chatter with music in the background. Both were erased in 1955.

Short break during which Elvis sang humorous and straight versions of the following two songs. Neither of these was recorded. [See **6.13** for details of other songs sung informally by Elvis at Sun Studio during 1955.]

LONG TALL MAMA *(Edwards)*
Song composed by Bernice Edwards in December 1927. R&B hit for Smokey Hogg in 1948 (Modern 574). Not to be confused with Big Bill Broonzy's eponymous 1932 recording (Banner 33085), or with Jimmie Rodgers' LONG TALL MAMA BLUES (Victor 23766) from 1933, which are both completely different songs.

✱ Original by Moanin' Bernice Edwards (Paramount 12633) 1928.
◆ *Elvis' source:* Smokey Hogg (Modern 574) 1948.

▶ *Elvis' interpretation:* comic raw rockabilly.

GONE, GONE, GONE *(Perkins)*
Short jam with Carl Perkins.

✱ Original by Carl Perkins (Sun 224) 1955.
◆ *Elvis' source:* Carl Perkins (Sun 224) 1955.

▶ *Elvis' interpretation:* comic raw rockabilly.

Session resumed.

WE'RE GETTING CLOSER TO BEING APART *(Kesler/Feathers)*
Song written by Stan Kesler and Charlie Feathers. They recorded a demo of it at Sun on Saturday, 25 June 1955 between 3.00 and 3.30 pm, with Kesler on fiddle and Feathers on vocal and acoustic guitar. They also recorded a demo of I FORGOT TO REMEMBER TO FORGET at the same session. The demo of WE'RE GETTING CLOSER TO BEING APART was issued in the 1980s on 'The Sun Country Years 1950-59' box set (Bear Family BFX-15211, West Germany). A remake by Feathers was issued as a single in 1976 (Vetco 922).

✱ Original by Elvis.

▶ *Elvis' interpretation:* country blues.

Take 1	?
Take 2	?
Take 3	?
Take 4	?
Take 5	?
Take 6	?
Take 7	?

The cut was timed around 2.25–2.30. The seven takes listed above include false starts and incomplete takes (no details). Tape lost.

According to Marion Keisker, WHEN IT RAINS IT REALLY POURS b/w WE'RE GETTING CLOSER TO BEING APART *were intended to be Elvis' sixth Sun release (all of Elvis' Sun discs had a blues/R&B side and a country/pop side). Some sources claim that the sides were to have been* WHEN IT RAINS IT REALLY POURS b/w TRYIN' TO GET TO YOU, *but both of these are R&B numbers and this combination would have been contrary to Sam Phillips' release policy for Elvis of one 'black' side and one 'white' side. The single was due to be released in December 1955 as Sun 229, but never appeared because Elvis signed with RCA on 21 November. The catalogue number was subsequently reassigned to Maggie Sue Wimberly.*

◆ SECTION 5 ◆

Personal Appearances 1954-55

This section contains a listing of some of Elvis' shows of 1954 and 1955 compiled by Graham Metson from public performance copyright records. For greater clarity, and to avoid repetition, only songs of particular interest have been listed. For example, if there are six instances of Elvis singing **BLUE GUITAR** live during 1954 and 1955, only the earliest performance of that number has been listed. For those researchers who require them, the complete playlists for these shows appear in *Appendix D*.

During the course of his investigations, Graham also uncovered details of some low-key personal appearances by Elvis on flatbed trucks and in small honky tonks. These are listed separately in *Appendix A*.

Finally, Graham also compiled some information about amateur films and recordings of Elvis' stage performances. This is presented in *Appendix E*.

On his personal appearances during 1954 and 1955, Elvis performed all his covers of blues, R&B, hillbilly and western swing material in a rockabilly style. The only exception was pop ballads such as **MY HAPPINESS**, **I APOLOGIZE**, **THAT'S AMORE**, **ONLY YOU**, etc, which he sang 'straight'.

Bon Air Club, 4862 Summer Avenue, Memphis, Tennessee
Saturday, 17 July 1954 (evening, exact time unknown)

Elvis Presley	Vocal and acoustic guitar (old Martin D-18)
Scotty Moore	Lead guitar (Gibson ES-295)
Bill Black	Double bass

This was the professional live debut of Elvis Presley & The Blue Moon Boys. They performed the only two songs they knew well enough to play in front of an audience. Sun 209 was issued two days later on Monday, 19 July 1954.

THAT'S ALL RIGHT *(Crudup)*

✱ Original by Arthur 'Big Boy' Crudup (RCA-Victor 20-2205) 1947.
◆ *Elvis' sources:* Arthur 'Big Boy' Crudup (RCA-Victor 2205) 1947.
                Arthur 'Big Boy' Crudup (RCA-Victor 50-0000) 1949.
⊙ Elvis recorded this title at Sun Studio, Memphis on 5 July 1954 (Sun 209, 1954) [see **4.6** for details].

BLUE MOON OF KENTUCKY *(Monroe)*
This number started life as a slow country ballad, but developed into something quite different when Elvis, Scotty and Bill decided to speed it up.

★ Original by Bill Monroe (Columbia 37888) 1947.
◆ *Elvis' source:* Bill Monroe (Columbia 37888) 1947.
O Elvis recorded this title at Sun Studio, Memphis on 6 July 1954 (Sun 209, 1954) [see **4.7** for details].

Bon Air Club, 4862 Summer Avenue, Memphis, Tennessee
Saturday, 24 July 1954 (9.00 pm)
Elvis Presley   Vocal and acoustic guitar (old or new Martin D-18)
Scotty Moore   Lead guitar (Gibson ES-295)
Bill Black   Double bass

Notable song(s) performed:

I APOLOGIZE *(Hoffman/Goodhart/Nelson)*
A hit in 1931 for Bing Crosby (Brunswick 6179) and Nat Shilkret (Victor 22781). Crossover (pop and R&B) hit in 1951 for Billy Eckstine (MGM 10903), and a pop hit for Champ Butler (Columbia 39189) and Tony Martin (RCA-Victor 4056).

★ Original by Bing Crosby (Brunswick 6179) 1931.
◆ *Elvis' sources:* Champ Butler (Columbia 39189) 1951.
                    Billy Eckstine (MGM 10903) 1951.
                    Tony Martin (RCA-Victor 4056) 1951.
                    Dinah Washington (Mercury 8209) 1951.

Bel Air Club, 1850 South Bellevue Boulevard, Memphis, Tennessee
Saturday, 24 July 1954 (Two sets at 10.00 pm and 10.45 pm)
Elvis Presley   Vocal and acoustic guitar (old or new Martin D-18)
Scotty Moore   Lead guitar (Gibson ES-295)
Bill Black   Double bass

Notable song(s) performed:

CRY OF THE WILD GOOSE *(Gilkyson)*
Crossover (pop and C&W) hit in 1950 for Tennessee Ernie Ford (Capitol 40280), and a pop hit that same year for Frankie Laine (Mercury 5363). Elvis would surely also have been tickled by the humour of Cactus Pryor's **CRY OF THE DYING DUCK IN A THUNDER-STORM** *(4 Star 1459), a C&W hit in 1950.*

★ Original by Terry Gilkyson (4 Star 1430) 1950.
◆ *Elvis' sources:* Tennessee Ernie Ford (Capitol 40280) 1950.
                    Terry Gilkyson (4 Star 1430) 1950.
                    Frankie Laine (Mercury 5363) 1950.
                    Merv Shiner (Decca 46220) 1950.

Bon Air Club, 4862 Summer Avenue, Memphis, Tennessee
Saturday, 31 July 1954 (Two sets at 9.00 pm and 9.45 pm)
Elvis Presley   Vocal and acoustic guitar (old or new Martin D-18)
Scotty Moore   Lead guitar (Gibson ES-295)
Bill Black   Double bass

Notable song(s) performed:

SITTING ON TOP OF THE WORLD *(Vincson/Chatmon)*
Composition by Walter Vincson and Bo Chatmon/Chatman/Carter. Not to be confused with Frank Crumit's **I'M SITTING ON TOP OF THE WORLD (JUST ROLLING ALONG, JUST ROLLING ALONG)** *(Victor 19928) 1926.*

✱ Original by the Mississippi Sheiks (OKeh 8784) 1930.
◆ *Elvis' sources:* Mississippi Sheiks (OKeh 8784) 1930.
                    Bob Wills (Vocalion 03139) 1935.

5.5

Eagle's Nest Club, corner of Lamar Avenue and Winchester Road, Memphis, Tenn.
Saturday, 7 August 1954 (Two sets at 9.00 pm and 10.00 pm)
Elvis Presley   Vocal and acoustic guitar (new Martin D-18)
Scotty Moore   Lead guitar (Gibson ES-295)
Bill Black   Double bass

Notable song(s) performed:

TIGER MAN (KING OF THE JUNGLE) *(Louis/Burns)*
Song written by Joe Hill Louis and Sam Burns (the latter a pseudonym for Sam Phillips). Louis was also the first to cut it (in the spring of 1953), but it was not released at the time. It was subsequently recorded by Rufus Thomas. During one of his August 1970 shows in Las Vegas, Elvis performed **TIGER MAN**, *after which he explained to the audience: 'This is my second record, but not too many people got to heard it.' The flip side of the* **TIGER MAN** *single was to have been* **BLUE MOON**, *recorded on 19 August 1954* [see **4.8**].

✱ Original by Rufus Thomas (Sun 188) 1953.
◆ *Elvis' source:* Rufus Thomas (Sun 188) 1953.
○ Elvis recorded this title at Sun Studio, Memphis on 5 July 1954 (unissued) [see **4.6** for details]. He re-recorded at NBC-TV studio, Burbank, CA on 27 June 1968 (released in 1968 on LP *Singer Presents Elvis Singing Flaming Star And Others*, PRS 279). Another version dates from a midnight show at the International Hotel, Las Vegas on 25 August 1969 (released in 1969 on 2-LP *Elvis In Person (From Memphis To Vegas/From Vegas To Memphis)*, RCA-Victor LSP-6020).

5.6

Roy Brown open air concert, Tupelo, Mississippi
Sunday, 15 August 1954 (3.00 pm)
Elvis Presley   Vocal and acoustic guitar (new Martin D-18)

Elvis made an impromptu solo appearance during the first part of this show (arranged through Brown's guitarist, Edgar Blanchard) and also at another Roy Brown concert in Indianola, Mississippi (date unknown), at which he performed **THAT'S ALL RIGHT***. He performed the song below as a country blues, based on Kokomo Arnold's* **OLD ORIGINAL KOKOMO BLUES** *(Decca 7026) 1926.*

Notable song(s) performed:

KOKOMO BLUES *(Blackwell/Arnold)*

✱ Original by Scrapper Blackwell (Vocalion 1192) 1928.
◆ *Elvis' sources:*   Scrapper Blackwell (Vocalion 1192) 1928.
          OLD ORIGINAL KOKOMO BLUES by Kokomo Arnold (Decca 7026) 1934.

5.7

Eagle's Nest Club, corner of Lamar Avenue and Winchester Road, Memphis, Tenn.
Monday,16 August 1954 (Two sets at 8.45 pm and 9.30 pm)
Elvis Presley   Vocal and acoustic guitar (new Martin D-18)
Scotty Moore   Lead guitar (Gibson ES-295)
Bill Black   Double bass

Notable song(s) performed:

ICE COLD LOVE *(Swift)*

✱ Original by Jimmy Grissom (Miltone 230) 1948.
◆ *Elvis' source:* Jimmy Grissom (Miltone 230) 1948.

Note   Elvis also featured **ICE COLD LOVE** *in his live act during 1955, this time inspired by Benny Martin's version (Mercury 70560) 1955.*

5.8

Bel Air Club, 1850 South Bellevue Boulevard, Memphis, Tennessee
Monday, 16 August 1954 (10.30 pm)

Elvis Presley	Vocal and acoustic guitar (new Martin D-18)
Scotty Moore	Lead guitar (Gibson ES-295)
Bill Black	Double bass

Notable song(s) performed:

RAG MOP *(Anderson/Wills)*
Crossover (pop and R&B) hit in 1950 for Lionel Hampton (Decca 24855). Crossover hit (pop and C&W) for Johnnie Lee Wills (Bullet 696). Pop hit in 1950 for the Ames Brothers (Coral 60140), Jimmy Dorsey (Columbia 38710), Eddy Howard (Mercury 5371), Ralph Flanagan (RCA-Victor 3688) and the Starlighters (Capitol 844). R&B hit in 1950 for Doc Sausage (Regal 3251) and Joe Liggins (Specialty 350).

✱ Original by Johnnie Lee Wills (Bullet 696) 1949.
◆ *Elvis' sources:* Johnnie Lee Wills (Bullet 696) 1949.
Ames Brothers (Coral 60140) 1950.
Jimmy Dorsey – Voc. Claire Hogan (Columbia 38710) 1950.
Ralph Flanagan (RCA-Victor 3688) 1950.
Lionel Hampton (Decca 24855) 1950.
Eddy Howard (Mercury 5371) 1950.
Joe Liggins (Specialty 350) 1950.
Joe Lutcher (Modern 20-736) 1950.
Doc Sausage (Regal 3251) 1950.
Starlighters (Capitol 844) 1950.

5.9

Bel Air Club, 1850 South Bellevue Boulevard, Memphis, Tennessee
Saturday, 21 August 1954 (Two sets at 9.00 pm and 9.45 pm)

Elvis Presley	Vocal and acoustic guitar (new Martin D-18)
Scotty Moore	Lead guitar (Gibson ES-295)
Bill Black	Double bass

Notable song(s) performed:

JOHN HENRY *(Traditional)*
Folk-song of black origin dating back to the 1880s. Often said to have originated during the construction of the Big Bend Tunnel on the Chesapeake & Ohio Railroad. In reality, however, its subject was one John Henry Dabney, who died in 1887 just outside the east portal of Oak Mountain Tunnel, Dunnavant, Alabama, after beating a steam drill. A hit in 1924 for Fiddlin' John Carson (OKeh 7004) and in 1927 for Gid Tanner & Riley Puckett (Columbia 15019).

✱ Original **JOHN HENRY BLUES** by Fiddlin' John Carson (OKeh 7004) 1924.
◆ *Elvis' sources:* **JOHN HENRY BLUES** by Fiddlin' John Carson (OKeh 7004) 1924.
Gid Tanner & Riley Puckett (Columbia 15019) 1925.
DEATH OF JOHN HENRY by Uncle Dave Macon (Brunswick 112) 1927.
Gid Tanner (Columbia 15142) 1927.
Henry Thomas (Vocalion 1094) 1927.

DeFord Bailey (Victor 23336) 1928.
DEATH OF JOHN HENRY by Uncle Dave Macon (Vocalion 05096) 1939.
Leadbelly (Asch 343-3) 1943.
J.E. Mainer's Mountaineeers (King 550) 1946.
Merle Travis (78 rpm 4-disc album *Folk Songs Of The Hills*, Capitol AD-50) 1947.

5.10

Eagle's Nest Club, corner of Lamar Avenue and Winchester Road, Memphis, Tenn.
Friday, 27 August 1954 (Three sets at 8.45 pm, 9.40 pm and 10.15 pm)

Elvis Presley	Vocal and acoustic guitar (new Martin D-18)
Scotty Moore	Lead guitar (Gibson ES-295)
Bill Black	Double bass

Notable song(s) performed:

TOO LATE TO WORRY, TOO BLUE TO CRY *(Dexter)*
Crossover (pop and C&W) hit in 1944 for Al Dexter (OKeh 6718), and a C&W hit that same year
for Texas Jim Lewis (Decca 6099).

✱ Al Dexter (OKeh 6718) 1944.
◆ *Elvis' sources:* Al Dexter (OKeh 6718) 1944.
　　　　　　　　　　Texas Jim Lewis (Decca 6099) 1944.

Note　*Elvis also performed Al Dexter's* **SUNSHINE** *(Vocalion 04988) at an Eagle's Nest Show*
　　　between 27 August and 10 December 1954 — date not stated in files. Not to be confused
　　　with Paul Whiteman's **SUNSHINE** *(Victor 21240)* [see **4.7**].

UNCLE JOSH *(Presley/Monroe)*
Humorous song based on Bill Monroe's **UNCLE PEN** *with new lyrics by Elvis. Almost certainly*
inspired by Uncle Josh Weathersby, the rustic comic character created by Cal Stewart, whose
hilarious escapades provided him with 42 best-selling records between 1898 and 1921.

✱ Original **UNCLE PEN** by Bill Monroe – Voc. Bill Monroe & Jimmy Martin (Decca 46283) 1951.
◆ *Elvis' source:* **UNCLE PEN** by Bill Monroe – Voc. Bill Monroe & Jimmy Martin
　　　　　　　　　　　　　(Decca 46283) 1951.
◯ Elvis recorded **UNCLE PEN** at Sun Studio, Memphis on 8 December 1954 (unissued) [see
4.12 for details].

5.11

Eagle's Nest Club, corner of Lamar Avenue and Winchester Road, Memphis, Tenn.
Friday, 10 September 1954 (Two sets at 9.00 pm and 9.50 pm)
Elvis Presley   Vocal and acoustic guitar (new Martin D-18)
Scotty Moore   Lead guitar (Gibson ES-295)
Bill Black   Double bass

Notable song(s) performed:

GOOD ROCKIN' TONIGHT *(Brown)*
R&B hit in 1948 and 1949 for Roy Brown (DeLuxe 1093), and in 1948 for Wynonie Harris (King 4210).

✱ Original by Roy Brown (DeLuxe 1093) 1947.
◆ *Elvis' sources:* Roy Brown (DeLuxe 1093) 1947.
                          Wynonie Harris (King 4210) 1948.
○ Elvis recorded this title at Sun Studio, Memphis on 15 September 1954 (Sun 210, 1954) [see **4.10** for details].

5.12

Eagle's Nest Club, corner of Lamar Avenue and Winchester Road, Memphis, Tenn.
Friday, 24 September 1954 (Two sets at 9.00 pm and 9.40 pm)
Elvis Presley   Vocal and acoustic guitar (new Martin D-18)
Scotty Moore   Lead guitar (Gibson ES-295)
Bill Black   Double bass

Notable song(s) performed:

MILKCOW BLUES BOOGIE *(Arnold)*
*The '**BOOGIE**' was probably added by Elvis or Sam Phillips.*

✱ Original **MILK COW BLUES** by Freddie Spruell (OKeh 8422) 1926. [Incidentally, this record was issued under the same catalogue number with two different 'B' sides.]
Sleepy John Estes recorded his variation on the theme (Victor 386l4) in 1930.
Kokomo Arnold subsequently reworked the theme in five different versions:
MILK COW BLUES (Decca 7026) 1934.
MILK COW BLUES No. 2 (Decca 7059) 1935.
MILK COW BLUES No. 3 (Decca 7116) 1935.
MILK COW BLUES No. 4 (Decca 7163) 1936.
MILK COW BLUES No. 5 (Decca, unissued), recorded 1936.
◆ *Elvis' sources:* Kokomo Arnold (Decca 7026) 1934.
                          Johnny Lee Wills (Decca 5985) 1941.
                          Jimmy Wakely (Capitol 40107) 1948.
○ Elvis recorded this title at Sun Studio, Memphis on 20 December 1954 (Sun 215, 1954) [see **4.14** for details].

5.13

Bel Air Club, 1850 South Bellevue Boulevard, Memphis, Tennessee
Friday, 24 September 1954 (10.45 pm)
Elvis Presley   Vocal and acoustic guitar (new Martin D-18)
Scotty Moore   Lead guitar (Gibson ES-295)
Bill Black   Double bass

Notable song(s) performed:

BLUE GUITAR *(Wooley)*

✱ Original by Sheb Wooley (MGM 11717) 1954.
◆ *Elvis' source:* Sheb Wooley (MGM 11717) 1954.

5.14

Eagle's Nest Club, corner of Lamar Avenue and Winchester Road, Memphis, Tenn.
Saturday, 25 September 1954 (Three sets at 9.00 pm, 9.45 pm and 10.30 pm)
Elvis Presley   Vocal and acoustic guitar (new Martin D-18)
Scotty Moore   Lead guitar (Gibson ES-295)
Bill Black   Double bass

Notable song(s) performed:

BLUES STAY AWAY FROM ME *(Delmore/Delmore/Raney/Glover)*
C&W hit in 1949 for Eddie Crosby (Decca 46180), and in 1950 for the Delmore Brothers (King 803). Crossover hit (pop and C&W) in 1949-50 for the Owen Bradley Quintet (Coral 60107).

✱ Original by the Delmore Brothers (King 803) 1949.
◆ *Elvis' sources:* Owen Bradley Quintet (Coral 60107) 1949.
                Eddie Crosby (Decca 46180) 1949.
                Delmore Brothers (King 803) 1949.
                Lonnie Johnson (King 4336) 1949.

5.15

Eagle's Nest Club, corner of Lamar Avenue and Winchester Road, Memphis, Tenn.
Wednesday, 6 October 1954 (Two sets at 9.15 pm and 10.00 pm)

Elvis Presley	Vocal and acoustic guitar (new Martin D-18)
Scotty Moore	Lead guitar (Gibson ES-295)
Bill Black	Double bass

Notable song(s) performed:

THAT'S AMORE *(Warren/Brooks)*
Pop hit in 1953 for Dean Martin (Capitol 2589).

✱ Original by Dean Martin (Capitol 2589) 1953.
◆ *Elvis' source:* Dean Martin (Capitol 2589) 1953.

LAST TRAIN TO MEMPHIS *(Presley/Hughes/Bradley/Smith)*
Actually **NIGHT TRAIN TO MEMPHIS** *with new lyrics by Elvis.*

✱ Original **NIGHT TRAIN TO MEMPHIS** by Roy Acuff (OKeh 6693) 1943.
◆ *Elvis' sources:* **NIGHT TRAIN TO MEMPHIS** by Roy Acuff (OKeh 6693) 1943.
　　　　　　　　　NIGHT TRAIN TO MEMPHIS by Roy Acuff (Columbia 37029) 1946.
　　　　　　　　　NIGHT TRAIN TO MEMPHIS by Roy Acuff (Columbia 20054) 1947.
○ Elvis recorded **NIGHT TRAIN TO MEMPHIS** at Sun Studio, Memphis on 15 November 1954 (unissued) [see **4.11** for details].

5.16

The Silver Slipper Club, Highway 42, Atlanta, Georgia
Friday, 8 October 1954 (Two sets at 8.30 pm and 10.30 pm)

Elvis Presley	Vocal and acoustic guitar (new Martin D-18)
Scotty Moore	Lead guitar (Gibson ES-295)
Bill Black	Double bass
Unknown	Pedal steel guitar

This was the first time that Felton Jarvis saw Elvis on stage. The owner of the Silver Slipper Club was deejay Texas Bill Strength.

Notable song(s) performed:

GIVE ME MORE, MORE, MORE (OF YOUR KISSES) *(Price/Frizzell/Beck)*
C&W hit in 1952 for Lefty Frizzell (Columbia 20885).

✱ Original by Lefty Frizzell (Columbia 20885) 1951.
◆ *Elvis' source:* Lefty Frizzell (Columbia 20885) 1951.

5.17

Eagle's Nest Club, corner of Lamar Avenue and Winchester Road, Memphis, Tenn.
Wednesday, 13 October 1954 (Three sets at 9.00 pm, 9.35 pm and 10.20 pm)
Elvis Presley   Vocal and acoustic guitar (new Martin D-18)
Scotty Moore   Lead guitar (Gibson ES-295)
Bill Black   Double bass

Notable song(s) performed:

DARK AS A DUNGEON *(Travis)*

✱ Original by Merle Travis (78 rpm 4-disc album *Folk Songs Of The Hills*, Capitol AD-50) 1947.
◆ *Elvis' source:* Merle Travis (78 rpm 4-disc album *Folk Songs Of The Hills*, Capitol AD-50) 1947.

5.18

Eagle's Nest Club, corner of Lamar Avenue and Winchester Road, Memphis, Tenn.
Friday, 29 October 1954 (Two sets at 9.00 pm and 9.50 pm)
Elvis Presley   Vocal and acoustic guitar (new Martin D-18)
Scotty Moore   Lead guitar (Gibson ES-295)
Bill Black   Double bass

Notable song(s) performed:

BORN TO LOSE *(Brown)*
Crossover hit (pop and C&W) in 1943-44 for Ted Daffan's Texans (OKeh 6706).

✱ Original by Ted Daffan's Texans (OKeh 6706) 1943.
◆ *Elvis' source:* Ted Daffan's Texans (OKeh 6706) 1943.

JUST BECAUSE *(Shelton/Shelton/Robin)*
Crossover (pop and C&W) hit in 1948 for Frankie Yankovic (Columbia 12359), and a pop hit for Eddy Howard (Majestic 1231).

✱ Original by the Lone Star Cowboys *[Shelton Brothers – Bob and Joe]* (Bluebird 6052) 1933.
◆ *Elvis' sources:*   Dick Stabile (Decca 716) 1937.
               Shelton Brothers *[Bob and Joe]* (Decca 5872) 1942.
               Eddy Howard (Majestic 1231) 1948.
               Frankie Yankovic (Columbia 12359) 1948.
◎ Elvis recorded this title at Sun Studio, Memphis on 15 September 1954 [see **4.10** for details].

5.19

Bel Air Club, 1850 South Bellevue Boulevard, Memphis, Tennessee
Monday, 15 November 1954 (9.00 pm)

Elvis Presley	Vocal and acoustic guitar (new Martin D-18)
Scotty Moore	Lead guitar (Gibson ES-295)
Bill Black	Double bass

Notable song(s) performed:

TOMORROW NIGHT *(Coslow/Grosz)*
A hit in 1939 for Horace Heidt (Columbia 35203).   Crossover (pop and R&B) hit in 1948 for Lonnie Johnson (King 4201).   Not to be confused with Louis Armstrong's 1933 recording 'Tomorrow Night (After Tonight)' (RCA-Victor 68-0774) or Junior Wells' 'Tomorrow Night' (States 143) 1954.

✱ Original by Horace Heidt (Columbia 35203) 1939.
◆ *Elvis' sources:*   Horace Heidt (Columbia 35203) 1939.
                          Lonnie Johnson (King 4201) 1948.
                          Lonnie Johnson (Paradise 11) 1948.
◐ Elvis recorded this title at Sun Studio, Memphis on 19 August and 8 December 1954 [see **4.8** and **4.12** for details]. Second version unissued/lost.

5.20

Magnolia Gardens, Houston, Texas
Sunday, 21 November 1954 (exact time unknown)

Elvis Presley	Vocal and acoustic guitar (new Martin D-18)
Scotty Moore	Lead guitar (Gibson ES-295)
Bill Black	Double bass
Unknown	Pedal steel guitar

Notable song(s) performed:

MY HAPPINESS *(Peterson/Bergantine)*
Crossover (pop and R&B) hit in 1948 for Ella Fitzgerald (Decca 24446). Pop hit in 1948 John Laurenz (Mercury 5144), the Marlin Sisters (Columbia 38217), Pied Pipers (Capitol 15094) and Jon & Sandra Steele (Damon 11133), and in 1953 for the Mulcays (Cardinal 1014).

✱ Original by Jon & Sandra Steele (Damon 11133) 1948.
◆ *Elvis' sources:*   Ella Fitzgerald (Decca 24446) 1948.
                          John Laurenz (Mercury 5144) 1948.
                          Marlin Sisters (Columbia 38217) 1948.
                          Pied Pipers (Capitol 15094) 1948.
                          Jon & Sandra Steele (Damon 11133) 1948.
◐ Elvis made a private recording of this title at Memphis Recording Service (Sun Studio) on 18 July 1953 [see **4.2** for details].

5.21

Cook's Hoedown Club, Houston, Texas
Sunday, 21 November 1954 (exact time unknown)
Elvis Presley   Vocal and acoustic guitar (new Martin D-18)
Scotty Moore   Lead guitar (Gibson ES-295)
Bill Black   Double bass
Unknown   Pedal steel guitar

Notable song(s) performed:

OAKIE BOOGIE *(Tyler)*
C&W hit in 1947 for Jack Guthrie (Capitol 341). Pop hit in 1952 for Ella Mae Morse (Capitol 2072).

✱ Original by Johnny Tyler (Stanchel 101) 1946.
◆ *Elvis' sources:*   Luderin Darbonne (DeLuxe 5029) 1947.
                   Jack Guthrie (Capitol 341) 1947.
                   Ella Mae Morse (Capitol 2072) 1952.
                   Jack Guthrie (Capitol 2128) 1952.
○ Elvis recorded this title at Sun Studio, Memphis on 8 December 1954 (unissued) [see **4.12** for details].

FOOL, FOOL, FOOL *(Nugetre)*
Composed by Atlantic's Ahmet Ertegun ('Nugetre' is 'Ertegun' backwards). R&B hit in 1951 for the Clovers (Atlantic 944). Pop hit in 1952 for Kay Starr (Capitol 2151).

✱ Original by the Clovers (Atlantic 944) 1951.
◆ *Elvis' sources:*   Clovers (Atlantic 944) 1951.
                   Kay Starr (Capitol 2151) 1952.

5.22

Catholic Club, Helena, Arkansas
Thursday, 2 December 1954 (exact time unknown)
Elvis Presley   Vocal and acoustic guitar (new Martin D-18)
Scotty Moore   Lead guitar (Gibson ES-295)
Bill Black   Double bass

Notable song(s) performed:

TENNESSEE SATURDAY NIGHT *(Hughes)*
C&W hit in 1949 for Johnny Bond (Columbia 20545) and Red Foley (Decca 46136).

✱ Original by Red Foley (Decca 46136) 1948.
◆ *Elvis' sources:*   Red Foley (Decca 46136) 1948.
                   Johnny Bond (Columbia 20545) 1949.
                   Ella Mae Morse (Capitol 1903) 1951.
○ Elvis recorded this title at Sun Studio, Memphis on 15 November 1954 (unissued) [see **4.11** for details].

I'M GONNA SIT RIGHT DOWN AND CRY (OVER YOU) *(Thomas/Biggs)*
Flip of **YOU'LL NEVER WALK ALONE***, a crossover (pop and R&B) hit in 1954 for Roy Hamilton (Epic 5-9015). Composed by Joe Thomas and Howard Biggs. (NB. This Joe Thomas is not the saxophonist/vocalist Joe Thomas who gained fame with Lunceford's band and went on to record for King, but the brother of Walter 'Foots' Thomas, former musician-turned-agent. He and Biggs, ex-pianist/arranger with Luis Russell and the Ravens, held A&R positions with Victor in the early 1950s, then OKeh, then Decca/Coral. Their other big song was* **GOT YOU ON MY MIND** *(RCA-Victor 4348), a R&B hit in 1951 for Big John Greer, former vocalist/tenor saxophonist with Lucky Millinder.)*

★ Original by Roy Hamilton (Epic 5-9015) 1954.
◆ *Elvis' source:* Roy Hamilton (Epic 5-9015) 1954.
⦿ Elvis later recorded this title at RCA, New York on 31 January 1956 (released in 1956 on LP *Elvis Presley*, RCA-Victor LPM-1254).

5.23

Municipal Auditorium, Texarkana, Arkansas
Friday, 3 December 1954 (exact time unknown)
Elvis Presley   Vocal and acoustic guitar (new Martin D-18)
Scotty Moore   Lead guitar (Gibson ES-295)
Bill Black   Double bass

Notable song(s) performed:

SHAKE, RATTLE AND ROLL *(Calhoun)*
Crossover (pop and R&B) hit in 1954 for Joe Turner (Atlantic 1026). Pop hit in 1954 for Bill Haley (Decca 29124).

★ Original by Joe Turner (Atlantic 1026) 1954.
◆ *Elvis' sources:* Bill Haley (Decca 29124) 1954.
                  Joe Turner (Atlantic 1026) 1954.
⦿ Elvis later recorded this title at CBS-TV studio, New York on 28 January 1956 for the Dorsey brothers' *Stage Show* in medley with **FLIP, FLOP AND FLY** (released in 1984 on 6-LP box set *Elvis: A Golden Celebration*, RCA-Victor CPM6-5172) and subsequently at RCA, New York on 3 February 1956 (released in 1956 on EP *Elvis Presley*, RCA-Victor EPA-830).

5.24

Eagle's Nest Club, corner of Lamar Avenue and Winchester Road, Memphis, Tenn.
Friday, 10 December 1954 (Three sets at 9.00 pm, 9.45 pm and 10.30 pm)
Elvis Presley   Vocal and acoustic guitar (new Martin D-18)
Scotty Moore   Lead guitar (Gibson ES-295)
Bill Black   Double bass

This was Elvis' final performance at the Eagle's Nest.

Notable song(s) performed:

MONEY HONEY *(Stone)*
R&B hit in 1953 for the Drifters (Atlantic 1006).

★ Original by the Drifters (Atlantic 1006) 1953.

◆ *Elvis' source:* Drifters (Atlantic 1006) 1953.

○ Elvis later recorded this title at RCA, Nashville on 10 January 1956 (released in 1956 on EP *Heartbreak Hotel*, RCA-Victor EPA-821).

HEARTS OF STONE *(Ray/Jackson)*
R&B hit in 1954 for Otis Williams & His Charms (DeLuxe 6062).

★ Original by the Jewels (R&B 1301) 1954.

◆ *Elvis' sources:* Fontane Sisters (Dot 15265) 1954.
Jewels (R&B 1301) 1954.
McGuire Sisters (Coral 61335) 1954.
Otis Williams & His Charms (DeLuxe 6062) 1954.

Cook's Hoedown Club, Houston, Texas
Tuesday, 28 December 1954 (exact time unknown)
Elvis Presley   Vocal and acoustic guitar (new Martin D-18)
Scotty Moore   Lead guitar (Gibson ES-295)
Bill Black   Double bass

Notable song(s) performed:

HARBOR LIGHTS *(Kennedy/Williams)*
A hit in 1937 for Frances Langford (Decca 1441) and Claude Thornhill (Vocalion 03595), and in 1950 for Ray Anthony (Capitol 1190), Jerry Byrd & Jerry Murad's Harmonicats (Mercury 5461), Bing Crosby (Decca 27219), Ralph Flanagan (RCA-Victor 3911), Ken Griffin (Columbia 38889), Sammy Kaye (Columbia 38953) and Guy Lombardo (Decca 27208). R&B hit in 1951 for Dinah Washington (Mercury 5488).

★ Original **HARBOUR LIGHTS** by Roy Fox – Voc. Barry Gray
(His Master's Voice BD-5173) 1937, UK.
  US Original **HARBOR LIGHTS** by Rudy Vallee (Bluebird 7067) 1937.

◆ *Elvis' sources:* Ray Anthony – Voc. Ronnie Deauville (Capitol 1190) 1950.
Bing Crosby (Decca 27219) 1950.
Ken Griffin (Columbia 38889) 1950.
Sammy Kaye (Columbia 38953) 1950.
Guy Lombardo (Decca 27208) 1950.
Billy Ward & His Dominoes (Federal 12010) 1951.
Dinah Washington (Mercury 5488) 1951.

○ Elvis recorded this title at Sun Studio, Memphis on 5 July 1954 [see **4.6** for details].

5.26

Eagles Hall, Houston, Texas
Friday, 31 December 1954 (exact time unknown)
Elvis Presley   Vocal and acoustic guitar (new Martin D-18)
Scotty Moore   Lead guitar (Gibson ES-295)
Bill Black   Double bass

Notable song(s) performed:

LITTLE MAMA *(Taylor/Carroll/Ertegun/Wexler)*
R&B hit in 1954 for the Clovers (Atlantic 1022). Not to be confused with the Onie Wheeler song of the same title (OKeh 18049) 1954.

★ Original by the Clovers (Atlantic 1022) 1954.
◆ *Elvis' source:* Clovers (Atlantic 1022) 1954.

THE TEXAS SPECIAL *(Hughes)*

★ Original by Luke Wills (RCA-Victor 3081) 1948.
◆ *Elvis' source:* Luke Wills (RCA-Victor 3081) 1948.

5.27

City Auditorium, Clarksdale, Mississippi
Wednesday, 12 January 1955 (8.00 pm)
Elvis Presley   Vocal and acoustic guitar (model unknown)
Scotty Moore   Lead guitar (Gibson ES-295)
Bill Black   Double bass
Leon Post   Piano
Sonny Trammell   Pedal steel guitar

Notable song(s) performed:

I DON'T CARE IF THE SUN DON'T SHINE *(David)*
Pop hit in 1950 for Patti Page (Mercury 5396).

★ Original by Patti Page (Mercury 5396) 1950.
◆ *Elvis' sources:* Dean Martin (Capitol 981) 1950.
             Patti Page (Mercury 5396) 1950.
◉ Elvis recorded this title at Sun Studio, Memphis on 15 September 1954 (Sun 210, 1954) [see **4.10** for details].

Junior College Auditorium, Booneville, Mississippi
Monday, 17 January 1955 (8.00 pm)
Elvis Presley   Vocal and acoustic guitar (model unknown)
Scotty Moore   Lead guitar (Gibson ES-295)
Bill Black   Double bass
Leon Post   Piano
Sonny Trammell   Pedal steel guitar

Notable song(s) performed:

TWEEDLE DEE *(Scott)*
Crossover (pop and R&B) hit in 1954-55 for LaVern Baker (Atlantic 1047). Pop hit in 1955 for Georgia Gibbs (Mercury 70517).

✱ Original by LaVern Baker (Atlantic 1047) 1954.
◆ *Elvis' sources:* LaVern Baker (Atlantic 1047) 1954.
              Georgia Gibbs (Mercury 70517) 1955.

5.29

Community Center, Sheffield, Alabama
Wednesday, 19 January 1955 (8.00 pm)
Elvis Presley   Vocal and acoustic guitar (model unknown)
Scotty Moore   Lead guitar (Gibson ES-295)
Bill Black   Double bass
Leon Post   Piano
Sonny Trammell   Pedal steel guitar

Notable song(s) performed:

I GOT A WOMAN *(Charles)*
R&B hit in 1955 for Ray Charles (Atlantic 1050).

✱ Original by Ray Charles (Atlantic 1050) 1955.
◆ *Elvis' source:* Ray Charles (Atlantic 1050) 1955.
○ Elvis recorded this title at Sun Studio, Memphis on 3 February 1955 (unissued) [see **4.15** for details]. He re-recorded it at RCA, Nashville on 10 January 1956 (released in 1956 on LP *Elvis Presley*, RCA-Victor LPM-1254).

5.30

National Guard Armory, Sikeston, Missouri
Friday, 21 January 1955 (8.00 pm)
Elvis Presley   Vocal and acoustic guitar (model unknown)
Scotty Moore   Lead guitar (Gibson ES-295)
Bill Black   Double bass
Leon Post   Piano
Sonny Trammell   Pedal steel guitar

Notable song(s) performed:

YOU'RE A HEARTBREAKER *(Sallee)*
Composition by Jack Sallee. Flip of **WILD HORSES***, a pop hit in 1953 for Ray Anthony (Capitol 2349). This is not the same song as Jimmy Heap's* **(YOU'RE A) HEARTBREAKER** *(Capitol 2294) 1952.*

★ Original by Ray Anthony –– Voc. Jo Ann Greer (Capitol 2349) 1953.
◆ *Elvis' source:* Ray Anthony –– Voc. Jo Ann Greer (Capitol 2349) 1953.
○ Elvis recorded this title at Sun Studio, Memphis on 20 December 1954 (Sun 215, 1954) [see **4.14** for details]. He re-recorded it on 6 March 1955 (unissued) [see **4.16** for details].

5.31

Humble Oil Camp, Hawkins, Texas
Monday, 24 January 1955 (8.00 pm)
Elvis Presley   Vocal and acoustic guitar (model unknown)
Scotty Moore   Lead guitar (Gibson ES-295)
Bill Black   Double bass
Leon Post   Piano
Sonny Trammell   Pedal steel guitar

Notable song(s) performed:

NINE POUND HAMMER *(Traditional)*
Traditional folk-song from circa 1890.

★ Original **THE NINE POUND HAMMER** by Al Hopkins (Brunswick 177) 1927.
◆ *Elvis' sources:* **NINE POUND HAMMER IS TOO HEAVY** by the Monroe Brothers (Bluebird 6422) 1936.
Merle Travis (78 rpm 4-disc album *Folk Songs Of The Hills*, Capitol AD-50) 1947.
○ Elvis recorded this title at Sun Studio, Memphis on 13 December 1954 (unissued) [see **4.13** for details].

5.32

Rural Electric Administration Building, Gilmer, Texas
Wednesday, 26 January 1955 (7.30 pm)

Elvis Presley	Vocal and acoustic guitar (model unknown)
Scotty Moore	Lead guitar (Gibson ES-295)
Bill Black	Double bass
Leon Post	Piano
Sonny Trammell	Pedal steel guitar

Notable song(s) performed:

SATISFIED *(Carson)*

✱ Original by Martha Carson (Capitol 1900) 1951.
◆ *Elvis' sources:* Martha Carson (Capitol 1900) 1951.
　　　　　　　　Johnnie Ray (Columbia 40006) 1953.
○ Elvis recorded this title at Sun Studio, Memphis on 10 September 1954 [see **4.9** for details].

5.33

High School Auditorium, Gaston, Texas
Friday, 28 January 1955 (8.00 pm)

Elvis Presley	Vocal and acoustic guitar (model unknown)
Scotty Moore	Lead guitar (Gibson ES-295)
Bill Black	Double bass
Leon Post	Piano
Sonny Trammell	Pedal steel guitar

Notable song(s) performed:

FIREBALL MAIL *(Jenkins)*

✱ Original by Roy Acuff (OKeh 6685) 1943.
◆ *Elvis' sources:* Roy Acuff (OKeh 6685) 1943.
　　　　　　　　Roy Acuff (Columbia 37028) 1946.

5.34

High School Auditorium, Randolph, Mississippi
Tuesday, 1 February 1955 (evening, exact time unknown)
Elvis Presley   Vocal and acoustic guitar (model unknown)
Scotty Moore   Lead guitar (Gibson ES-295)
Bill Black   Double bass

Notable song(s) performed:

OAKIE BOOGIE *(Tyler)*
C&W hit in 1947 for Jack Guthrie (Capitol 341). Pop hit in 1952 for Ella Mae Morse (Capitol 2072).

✱ Original by Johnny Tyler (Stanchel 101) 1946.
◆ *Elvis' sources:*   Luderin Darbonne (DeLuxe 5029) 1947.
                    Jack Guthrie (Capitol 341) 1947.
                    Ella Mae Morse (Capitol 2072) 1952.
                    Jack Guthrie (Capitol 2128) 1952.
○ Elvis recorded this title at Sun Studio, Memphis on 8 December 1954 (unissued) [see **4.12** for details].

Note: Elvis changed one lyric.

5.35

Ripley High School Gymnasium, Ripley, Mississippi
Monday, 7 February 1955 (8.00 pm)
Elvis Presley   Vocal and acoustic guitar (original Martin D-28)
Scotty Moore   Lead guitar (Gibson ES-295)
Bill Black   Double bass

Notable song(s) performed:

MEXICAN JOE *(Torok)*
C&W hit in 1953 for Jim Reeves (Abbott 116).

✱ Original by Jim Reeves (Abbott 116) 1953.
◆ *Elvis' source:* Jim Reeves (Abbott 116) 1953.
○ Elvis recorded this title at Sun Studio, Memphis in April 1955 (rehearsal take, erased) [see **4.19** for details].

Sport Arena, Carlsbad, New Mexico
Friday, 11 February 1955 (4.00 pm)
Elvis Presley   Vocal and acoustic guitar (original Martin D-28)
Scotty Moore   Lead guitar (Gibson ES-295)
Bill Black   Double bass

In the evening, Elvis played another show at Hobbs, New Mexico.

Notable song(s) performed:

BABY LET'S PLAY HOUSE *(Gunter)*
1955 R&B hit for Arthur Gunter (Excello 2047) based on Eddy Arnold's **I WANNA PLAY HOUSE WITH YOU** *(RCA-Victor 0476) 1951. Elvis memorably replaced Gunter's lyric 'You may have religion' with 'You may drive a pink Cadillac'.*

✱ Original by Arthur Gunter (Excello 2047) 1954.
◆ *Elvis' source:* Arthur Gunter (Excello 2047) 1954.
◉ Elvis recorded this title at Sun Studio, Memphis on 3 February 1955 (Sun 217, 1955) [see **4.15** for details].

North Junior High School Auditorium, Roswell, New Mexico
Monday, 14 February 1955 (9.30 pm)
Elvis Presley   Vocal and acoustic guitar (original Martin D-28)
Scotty Moore   Lead guitar (Gibson ES-295)
Bill Black   Double bass

This was the second of two shows that evening. The first show was at 7.30 pm.

Notable song(s) performed:

UNCLE PEN *(Monroe)*
Song written by Bill Monroe after his uncle, Pendleton Vandiver.

✱ Original by Bill Monroe – Voc. Bill Monroe & Jimmy Martin (Decca 46283) 1951.
◆ *Elvis' source:* Bill Monroe – Voc. Bill Monroe & Jimmy Martin (Decca 46283) 1951.
◉ Elvis recorded this title at Sun Studio, Memphis on 8 December 1954 (unissued) [see **4.12** for details].

5.38

West Monroe High School Auditorium, Monroe, Louisiana
Friday, 18 February 1955 (7.30 pm)
Elvis Presley   Vocal and acoustic guitar (original Martin D-28)
Scotty Moore   Lead guitar (Gibson ES-295)
Bill Black   Double bass

This was first of two shows that evening. The second show was at 9.30 pm.

Notable song(s) performed:

BREAKIN' THE RULES *(Blasingame/Gray/Thompson)*
C&W hit in 1954 for Hank Thompson (Capitol 2758).

✱ Original by Hank Thompson (Capitol 2758) 1954.
◆ Elvis' source: Hank Thompson (Capitol 2758) 1954.
○ Elvis recorded this title at Sun Studio, Memphis on 15 March 1955 (unissued) [see **4.17** for details].

5.39

City Auditorium, Camden, Arkansas
Monday, 21 February 1955 (8.00 pm)
Elvis Presley   Vocal and acoustic guitar (original Martin D-28)
Scotty Moore   Lead guitar (Gibson ES-295)
Bill Black   Double bass

Notable song(s) performed:

JUANITA *(Norton)*
Composition by Caroline Norton. Not to be confused with Big Joe Williams' 1951 recording of the same name (Trumpet 170), which was based on Sleepy John Estes' **VERNITA BLUES** *(Decca 7342) from 1937; or Chuck Willis' 1956 waxing (Atlantic 1112), later covered by Charlie Rich on his 1960 album, 'Lonely Weekends' (Phillips International PLP-1970).*

✱ Original by Rufus Thomas (Chess 1517) 1952.
◆ *Elvis' source:* Rufus Thomas (Chess 1517) 1952.
○ Elvis recorded this title at Sun Studio, Memphis on 8 December 1954 (unissued) [see **4.12** for details].

South Side Elementary School, Bastrop, Louisiana
Thursday, 24 February 1955 (7.30 pm)

Elvis Presley	Vocal and acoustic guitar (original Martin D-28)
Scotty Moore	Lead guitar (Gibson ES-295)
Bill Black	Double bass

This was first of two shows that evening. The second show was at 9.30 pm.

Notable song(s) performed:

GONNA PAINT THE TOWN RED *(Scott)*

★ Original by Ramblin' Tommy Scott (King 1054) 1952.
◆ *Elvis' source:* Ramblin' Tommy Scott (King 1054) 1952.

Porky's Rooftop Club, Newport, Arkansas
Wednesday, 2 March 1955 (Two sets at 10.00 pm and 10.45 pm)

Elvis Presley	Vocal and acoustic guitar (original Martin D-28)
Scotty Moore	Lead guitar (Gibson ES-295)
Bill Black	Double bass
Unknown	Pedal steel guitar

Prior to his appearances at Porky's, Elvis played a show at the US Armory, Newport at 8.00 pm.

Notable song(s) performed:

WABASH CANNONBALL *(Kindt)*
Song composed in 1905 by William Kindt, based on **THE GREAT ROCK ISLAND ROUTE** *by J.A. Rolfe, 1882. A hit in 1939 for Roy Acuff (Vocalion 04466).*

★ Original by Hugh Cross (Columbia 15439) 1929.
◆ *Elvis' sources:*   Carter Family (Victor 23731) 1933.
                         Roy Acuff (Vocalion 04466) 1938.
                         Roy Acuff (Conqueror 9121) 1938.
                         Bill Carlisle's Kentucky Boys (Decca 5713) 1939.
                         Carter Family (Bluebird 8350) 1939.
                         Roy Acuff (Columbia 37008) 1946.
                         Roy Acuff (Columbia 20034) 1947.
                         Roy Acuff (Columbia 20197) 1948.

5.42

Armory, Poplar Bluff, Missouri
Wednesday, 9 March 1955 (8.00 pm)

Elvis Presley	Vocal and acoustic guitar (original Martin D-28)
Scotty Moore	Lead guitar (Gibson ES-295)
Bill Black	Double bass
Jimmy Day	Pedal steel guitar

Notable song(s) performed:

ALWAYS LATE (WITH YOUR KISSES) *(Frizzell/Crawford)*
C&W hit in 1951 for Lefty Frizzell (Columbia 20837).

★ Original by Lefty Frizzell (Columbia 20837) 1951.
◆ *Elvis' source:* Lefty Frizzell (Columbia 20837) 1951.

5.43

Magnolia Garden, Houston, Texas
Sunday, 20 March 1955 (exact time unknown)

Elvis Presley	Vocal and acoustic guitar (original Martin D-28)
Scotty Moore	Lead guitar (Gibson ES-295)
Bill Black	Double bass

Notable song(s) performed:

MY BABY'S GONE *(Kesler/Taylor)*
Early arrangement of the Stan Kesler-Bill Taylor composition, **YOU'RE RIGHT, I'M LEFT, SHE'S GONE***, popularly known as the 'slow' or 'blues' version.*

★ Original by Elvis, **MY BABY'S GONE**, recorded at Sun Studio, Memphis on 15 November 1954 [see **4.11** for details].
◒ Elvis subsequently re-recorded the song at a faster (rockabilly) tempo on 6 March 1955 (**I'M LEFT, YOU'RE RIGHT, SHE'S GONE**, Sun 217) 1955 [see **4.16** for details].

Big Creek High School Gymnasium, Big Creek, Mississippi
Monday, 28 March 1955 (evening, exact time unknown)
Elvis Presley   Vocal and acoustic guitar (original Martin D-28)
Scotty Moore   Lead guitar (Gibson ES-295)
Bill Black   Double bass

Notable song(s) performed:

TENNESSEE PARTNER *(Traditional)*
Another mystery song, annotated in Marion Keisker's files simply as 'Country Trad.'. However, it seems strange that apparently no-one else — not even the Carter Family — has recorded it. Perhaps it was an adaptation of Jimmy Work's **TENNESSEE BORDER** *(Alben 501, released late 1948), a massive C&W hit in 1949 for Bob Atcher, Red Foley, Tennessee Ernie Ford and Jimmie Skinner, or* **TENNESSEE BORDER #2**, *a C&W hit that same year for Homer & Jethro and Ernest Tubb & Red Foley. We shall probably never know.*

★ Original by ?
O Elvis recorded this title at Sun Studio, Memphis on 15 March 1955 (unissued) [see **4.17** for details].

El Dorado High School Auditorium, El Dorado, Arkansas
Wednesday, 30 March 1955 (8.00 pm)
Elvis Presley   Vocal and acoustic guitar (original Martin D-28)
Scotty Moore   Lead guitar (Gibson ES-295)
Bill Black   Double bass

Notable song(s) performed:

THE LOVEBUG ITCH *(Carson/Botkin)*
C&W hit in 1950 for Eddy Arnold (RCA-Victor 0382).

★ Original by Eddy Arnold (RCA-Victor 2128) 1947.
◆ *Elvis' sources:* Eddy Arnold (RCA-Victor 2128) 1947.
                        Eddy Arnold (RCA-Victor 0382) 1950.
                        Red Foley, Ernest Tubb & Minnie Pearl (Decca 46278) 1950.

Reo Palm Isle, Longview, Texas
Thursday, 31 March 1955 (9.00 pm)
Elvis Presley   Vocal and acoustic guitar (original Martin D-28)
Scotty Moore   Lead guitar (Gibson ES-295)
Bill Black   Double bass

Notable song(s) performed:

HOW DO YOU THINK I FEEL *(Walker/Pierce)*

★ Original by Red Sovine (Decca 29068) early 1954.
◆ *Elvis' source:* Jimmie Rodgers Snow (RCA-Victor 5900) 1954.
◉ Elvis recorded this title at Sun Studio, Memphis on 6 March 1955 (unissued) [see **4.16** for details]. He re-recorded it at Radio Recorders, Hollywood on 1 September 1956 (released in 1956 on LP *Elvis*, RCA-Victor LPM-1382).

Court House, Corinth, Mississippi
Thursday, 7 April 1955 (8.00 pm)
Elvis Presley   Vocal and acoustic guitar (original Martin D-28)
Scotty Moore   Lead guitar (Gibson ES-295)
Bill Black   Double bass

This was second of two shows that day. The first show was at 2.30 pm.

Notable song(s) performed:

ROCKIN' LITTLE SALLY *(Gordon)*
Song written for Elvis by Rosco Gordon.

★ Original by Elvis, recorded at Sun Studio, Memphis on 15 March 1955 (unissued) [see **4.17** for details].

5.48

B&B Club, Gobler, Missouri
Friday, 8 April 1955 (Two sets at 8.00 pm and 10.00 pm)
Elvis Presley   Vocal and acoustic guitar (original Martin D-28)
Scotty Moore   Lead guitar (Gibson ES-295)
Bill Black   Double bass
Unknown   Drums

Notable song(s) performed:

ROCK THE JOINT *(Crafton/Keane/Bagby)*
R&B hit in 1949 for Jimmy Preston (Gotham 188). If any disc can lay claim to being the first rock'n'roll record, then it must surely be Preston's recording and not Jackie Brenston's **ROCKET 88** *(Chess 1458). Unutterably wild, with a great boogie-woogie piano and sax intro, honking saxes, handclaps and screams, it's infinitely more powerful than* **ROCKET 88** *— a comparatively straight R&B number — and years ahead of its time.*

★ Original by Jimmy Preston (Gotham 188) 1949.
◆ *Elvis' sources:* Jimmy Preston (Gotham 188) 1949.
                Bill Haley (Essex 303) 1952. *[Note: Haley changed some lyrics on his version.]*

5.49

American Legion Hut, Grenada, Mississippi
Wednesday, 20 April 1955 (8.00 pm)
Elvis Presley   Vocal and acoustic guitar (original Martin D-28)
Scotty Moore   Lead guitar (Gibson ES-295)
Bill Black   Double bass

Notable song(s) performed:

I'M LEFT, YOU'RE RIGHT, SHE'S GONE *(Kesler/Taylor)*
Later (rockabilly) arrangement of the Stan Kesler-Bill Taylor composition, **YOU'RE RIGHT, I'M LEFT, SHE'S GONE**.

★ Original by Elvis, **MY BABY'S GONE**, recorded at Sun Studio, Memphis on 15 November 1954 [see **4.11** for details].
◉ Elvis subsequently re-recorded the song at a faster (rockabilly) tempo on 6 March 1955 (**I'M LEFT, YOU'RE RIGHT, SHE'S GONE**, Sun 217) 1955 [see **4.16** for details].

5.50

Magnolia Gardens, Houston, Texas
Sunday, 24 April 1955 (3.00 pm)

Elvis Presley   Vocal and acoustic guitar (original Martin D-28)
Scotty Moore   Lead guitar (Gibson ES-295)
Bill Black   Double bass

Elvis also played a evening show at Cook's Hoedown Club, Houston on this date.

Notable song(s) performed:

NIGHTMARE *(Leiber/Stoller/Otis)*
Flip of **HOUND DOG**, *a R&B hit in 1953 for Big Mama Thornton (Peacock 1612).*

★ Original by Willie Mae 'Big Mama' Thornton (Peacock 1612) 1953.
◆ *Elvis' source:* Willie Mae 'Big Mama' Thornton (Peacock 1612) 1953.
○ Elvis recorded this title at Sun Studio, Memphis in March 1955 (rehearsal take, erased) [see **4.18** for details].

5.51

M-B Corral, Wichita Falls, Texas
Monday, 25 April 1955 (11.00 pm)

Elvis Presley   Vocal and acoustic guitar (original Martin D-28)
Scotty Moore   Lead guitar (Gibson ES-295)
Bill Black   Double bass

Immediately after his performance, Elvis travelled to do a midnight show at the High School in Seymour, Texas.

Notable song(s) performed:

THUNDERBOLT BOOGIE *(Stephens)*

★ Original by Todd Rhodes – Voc. LaVern Baker (King 4601) 1953.
◆ *Elvis' source:* Todd Rhodes – Voc. LaVern Baker (King 4601) 1953.
○ Elvis recorded this title at Sun Studio, Memphis on 13 December 1954 (unissued) [see **4.13** for details].

City Auditorium, Big Spring, Texas
Tuesday, 26 April 1955 (8.00 pm)

Elvis Presley	Vocal and acoustic guitar (original Martin D-28)
Scotty Moore	Lead guitar (Gibson ES-295)
Bill Black	Double bass

Notable song(s) performed:

I PLAYED THE FOOL *(Alexis)*
R&B hit in 1953 for the Clovers (Atlantic 977).

★ Original by the Clovers (Atlantic 977) 1952.
◆ *Elvis' source:* Clovers (Atlantic 977) 1952.
❍ Elvis recorded this title at Sun Studio, Memphis in March 1955 (rehearsal take, erased) [see **4.18** for details].

5.53

High School Auditorium, Baton Rouge, Louisiana
Monday, 2 May 1955 (7.00 pm)

Elvis Presley	Vocal and acoustic guitar (original Martin D-28)
Scotty Moore	Lead guitar (Gibson ES-295)
Bill Black	Double bass

This was first of two shows that evening. The second show was at 9.00 pm.

Notable song(s) performed:

NIGHT TRAIN TO MEMPHIS *(Hughes/Bradley/Smith)*

★ Original by Roy Acuff (OKeh 6693) 1943.
◆ *Elvis' sources:* Roy Acuff (OKeh 6693) 1943.
Roy Acuff (Columbia 37029) 1946.
Roy Acuff (Columbia 20054) 1947.
❍ Elvis recorded this title at Sun Studio, Memphis on 15 November 1954 (unissued) [see **4.11** for details].

Fort Homer Hesterly Armory, Tampa, Florida
Sunday, 8 May 1955 (8.15 pm)
Elvis Presley   Vocal and acoustic guitar (original Martin D-28)
Scotty Moore   Lead guitar (Gibson ES-295)
Bill Black   Double bass

This was second of two shows that day. The first show was at 2.30 pm.

Notable song(s) performed:

COOL DISPOSITION *(Crudup)*

✱ Original by Arthur 'Big Boy' Crudup (Bluebird 34-0738) 1945.
◆ *Elvis' source:* Arthur 'Big Boy' Crudup (Bluebird 34-0738) 1945.
❍ Elvis recorded this title at Sun Studio, Memphis on 5 July 1954 (unissued) [see **4.6** for details].

Mosque Theater, Richmond, Virginia
Monday, 16 May 1955 (8.00 pm)
Elvis Presley   Vocal and acoustic guitar (model unknown)
Scotty Moore   Lead guitar (Gibson ES-295)
Bill Black   Double bass

Notable song(s) performed:

I'M MOVIN' ON *(Snow)*
Crossover (pop and C&W) hit in 1950 for Hank Snow (RCA-Victor 0328).

✱ Original by Hank Snow (RCA-Victor 0328) 1950.
◆ *Elvis' source:* Hank Snow (RCA-Victor 0328) 1950.
❍ Elvis later recorded this title at American Sound Studio, Memphis on 15 January 1969 (released in 1969 on LP *From Elvis In Memphis*, RCA-Victor LSP-4155).

5.56

Memorial Auditorium, Raleigh, North Carolina
Thursday, 19 May 1955 (8.00 pm)
Elvis Presley   Vocal and acoustic guitar (model unknown)
Scotty Moore   Lead guitar (Gibson ES-295)
Bill Black   Double bass

Notable song(s) performed:

I DON'T HURT ANYMORE *(Robertson/Rollins)*
C&W hit in 1954 for Hank Snow (RCA-Victor 5698).

✱ Original by Hank Snow (RCA-Victor 5698) 1954.
◆ *Elvis' source:* Hank Snow (RCA-Victor 5698) 1954.

5.57

American Legion Hall, Meridian, Mississippi
Wednesday, 25 May 1955 (9.00 pm)
Elvis Presley   Vocal and acoustic guitar (model unknown)
Scotty Moore   Lead guitar (Gibson ES-295)
Bill Black   Double bass

Notable song(s) performed:

COLD, COLD HEART *(Williams)*
Crossover (pop and C&W) hit in 1951 for Hank Williams (MGM 10904). Pop hit in 1951 for Tony Bennett (Columbia 39449), Tony Fontane (Mercury 5693), the Fontane Sisters (RCA-Victor 4274) and Eileen Wilson (Decca 27761). R&B hit in 1951 for Dinah Washington (Mercury 5728).

✱ Original by Hank Williams (MGM 10904) 1951.
◆ *Elvis' sources:* Tony Bennett (Columbia 39449) 1951.
                     Tony Fontane (Mercury 5693) 1951.
                     Fontane Sisters (RCA-Victor 4274) 1951.
                     Eddie Johnson (Chess 1488) 1951.
                     Dinah Washington (Mercury 5728) 1951.
                     Hank Williams (MGM 10904) 1951.
                     Eileen Wilson (Decca 27761) 1951.

MEAN MAMA BLUES *(Tubb)*
C&W hit in 1949 for Ernest Tubb (Decca 46162) *based on Jimmie Rodgers'* **JIMMIE'S MEAN MAMA BLUES** *(Victor 23503) 1931.*

✱ Original by Ernest Tubb (Decca 46162) 1949.
◆ *Elvis' source:* Ernest Tubb (Decca 46162) 1949.

THAT'S THE STUFF YOU GOTTA WATCH *(Johnson)*
Crossover (pop and R&B) hit in 1945 for Buddy Johnson (Decca 8671).

✱ Original by Buddy Johnson – Voc. Ella Johnson (Decca 8671) 1944.
◆ *Elvis' sources:*   Buddy Johnson – Voc. Ella Johnson (Decca 8671) 1944.
                                    Rubberlegs Williams (Savoy 564) 1945.

Big D Jamboree concert *[not broadcast]*
Sportatorium, corner of Industrial Boulevard and Cadix Boulevard, Dallas, Texas
Sunday, 29 May 1955 (8.00 pm)

Elvis Presley	Vocal and acoustic guitar (original Martin D-28)
Scotty Moore	Lead guitar (Gibson ES-295)
Bill Black	Double bass
Others?	

Earlier in the day, Elvis played a show at the North Side Coliseum, Fort Worth at 4.00 pm. At 9.00 pm, 16 year old Eddie Cochran went backstage and met Elvis for the first time.

THAT'S ALL RIGHT *(Crudup)*

✱ Original by Arthur 'Big Boy' Crudup (RCA-Victor 20-2205) 1947.
◆ *Elvis' sources:*   Arthur 'Big Boy' Crudup (RCA-Victor 2205) 1947.
                                    Arthur 'Big Boy' Crudup (RCA-Victor 50-0000) 1949.
○ Elvis recorded this title at Sun Studio, Memphis on 5 July 1954 (Sun 209, 1954) [see **4.6** for details].

SHAKE, RATTLE AND ROLL *(Calhoun)*
Crossover (pop and R&B) hit in 1954 for Joe Turner (Atlantic 1026). Pop hit in 1954 for Bill Haley (Decca 29124).

✱ Original by Joe Turner (Atlantic 1026) 1954.
◆ *Elvis' sources:*   Bill Haley (Decca 29124) 1954.
                                    Joe Turner (Atlantic 1026) 1954.
○ Elvis later recorded this title at CBS-TV studio, New York on 28 January 1956 for the Dorsey brothers' *Stage Show* in medley with **FLIP, FLOP AND FLY** (released in 1984 on 6-LP box set *Elvis: A Golden Celebration*, RCA-Victor CPM6-5172) and subsequently at RCA, New York on 3 February 1956 (released in 1956 on EP *Elvis Presley*, RCA-Victor EPA-830).

GOOD ROCKIN' TONIGHT *(Brown)*
R&B hit in 1948 and 1949 for Roy Brown (DeLuxe 1093), and in 1948 for Wynonie Harris (King 4210).

✱ Original by Roy Brown (DeLuxe 1093) 1947.
◆ *Elvis' sources:*   Roy Brown (DeLuxe 1093) 1947.
                                    Wynonie Harris (King 4210) 1948.
○ Elvis recorded this title at Sun Studio, Memphis on 15 September 1954 (Sun 210, 1954) [see **4.10** for details].

BREAKIN' THE RULES *(Blasingame/Gray/Thompson)*
C&W hit in 1954 for Hank Thompson (Capitol 2758).

★ Original by Hank Thompson (Capitol 2758) 1954.
◆ Elvis' source: Hank Thompson (Capitol 2758) 1954.
○ Elvis recorded this title at Sun Studio, Memphis on 15 March 1955 (unissued) [see **4.17** for details].

BABY LET'S PLAY HOUSE *(Gunter)*
1955 R&B hit for Arthur Gunter (Excello 2047) based on Eddy Arnold's **I WANNA PLAY HOUSE WITH YOU** *(RCA-Victor 0476) 1951. Elvis memorably replaced Gunter's lyric 'You may have religion' with 'You may drive a pink Cadillac'.*

★ Original by Arthur Gunter (Excello 2047) 1954.
◆ *Elvis' source:* Arthur Gunter (Excello 2047) 1954.
○ Elvis recorded this title at Sun Studio, Memphis on 3 February 1955 (Sun 217, 1955) [see **4.15** for details].

Fair Park Auditorium, Abilene, Texas
Monday, 30 May 1955 (evening, exact time unknown)

Elvis Presley	Vocal and acoustic guitar (original Martin D-28)
Scotty Moore	Lead guitar (Gibson ES-295)
Bill Black	Double bass

Notable song(s) performed:

GONE *(Rogers)*
Song composed by Smokey Rogers. Not to be confused with the Drifters' **GONE** *(Atlantic 1055) 1955.*

★ Original by Terry Preston *[Ferlin Husky]* (Capitol 2298) 1952.
◆ *Elvis' source:* Terry Preston (Capitol 2298) 1952.

5.60

High School Auditorium, Guymon, Oklahoma
Wednesday, 1 June 1955 (8.00 pm)
Elvis Presley   Vocal and acoustic guitar (original Martin D-28)
Scotty Moore   Lead guitar (Gibson ES-295)
Bill Black   Double bass

Notable song(s) performed:

COTTONFIELDS *(Traditional)*
Folk-song of black origin dating from the 1850s popularised by Leadbelly during the 1940s. A 16-inch acetate recorded by him for WNYC (New York) in November or December 1941 is currently in the Smithsonian-Folkways Archive. Elvis first heard it in Shakerag.

★ Original by ?
◆ *Elvis' source:* **THE COTTON SONG** by Leadbelly (10-inch LP *Rock Island Line: Huddie Ledbetter Memorial Album (Volume 2)*, Folkways 2014) 1951.
○ Jam during rehearsals at MGM Soundstage, Hollywood on 15 July 1970. Released in 1998 on bootleg CD *Get Down And Get With It* (Fort Baxter 2204). Officially released in 2000 on CD box set *Elvis – That's The Way It Is: Special Edition* (BMG/RCA 07863 67938-2).

5.61

Municipal Auditorium, Sweetwater, Texas
Wednesday, 8 June 1955 (8.00 pm)
Elvis Presley   Vocal and acoustic guitar (model unknown)
Scotty Moore   Lead guitar (Gibson ES-295)
Bill Black   Double bass

Notable song(s) performed:

CORRINE, CORRINA *(Vincson/Chatmon)*
Traditional African American theme with several variants. A hit in 1931 for Red Nichols (Brunswick 6058). Crossover hit (pop and R&B) in 1956 for Joe Turner (Atlantic 1088).

★ Original by Bo Chatman (Brunswick 7080) 1928.
◆ *Elvis' sources:*   Bo Chatman (Brunswick 7080) 1928.
                      Tampa Red & Georgia Tom (Vocalion 1450) 1929.
                      Red Nichols (Brunswick 6058) 1931.
                      Art Tatum – Voc. Joe Turner (Decca 8563) 1941.
                      Bob Wills (OKeh 06530) 1942.
                      Bob Wills (Columbia 37428) 1947.

Belden High School Gymnasium, Belden, Mississippi
Wednesday, 15 June 1955 (8.00 pm)
Elvis Presley   Vocal and acoustic guitar (model unknown)
Scotty Moore   Lead guitar (Gibson ES-295)
Bill Black   Double bass

Notable song(s) performed:

DOWN THE LINE *(Holly/Montgomery)*
Rockabilly number written by Buddy Holly and Bob Montgomery. Holly sang it to Elvis on Friday, 3 June 1955. Buddy & Bob recorded a demo of it at the Nesman Studio in Wichita Falls, Texas on Tuesday, 7 June 1955 along with **BABY LET'S PLAY HOUSE**.

○ Elvis subsequently recorded this title at Sun Studio, Memphis in July 1955 (rehearsal take, erased) [see **4.21** for details].

City Auditorium, Beaumont, Texas
Tuesday, 21 June 1955 (7.00 pm)
Elvis Presley   Vocal and acoustic guitar (model unknown)
Scotty Moore   Lead guitar (Gibson ES-295)
Bill Black   Double bass

This was first of two shows that evening. The second show was at 9.00 pm.

Notable song(s) performed:

MUSIC MAKIN' MAMA FROM MEMPHIS *(Snow)*
C&W hit in 1952 for Hank Snow (RCA-Victor 4346).

★ Original by Hank Snow (RCA-Victor 4346) 1951.
◆ *Elvis' source:* Hank Snow (RCA-Victor 4346) 1951.

5.64

Southern Club, Lawton, Oklahoma
Friday, 24 June 1955 (2.00 pm)

Elvis Presley   Vocal and acoustic guitar (model unknown)
Scotty Moore   Lead guitar (Gibson ES-295)
Bill Black   Double bass

Notable song(s) performed:

MEAN HEART BLUES *(Presley/Brown)*
Actually **CRYIN' HEART BLUES** *(1951 C&W hit for Johnnie & Jack, RCA-Victor 0478) with new lyrics by Elvis.*

* Original by Johnnie & Jack (RCA-Victor 0478) 1951.
◆ *Elvis' source:* Johnnie & Jack (RCA-Victor 0478) 1951.
O Elvis recorded **CRYIN' HEART BLUES** at Sun Studio, Memphis in August 1955 (rehearsal take, erased) [see **4.24** for details].

5.65

Slavonian Lodge, Biloxi, Mississippi
Sunday, 26 June 1955 (8.00 pm)

Elvis Presley   Vocal and acoustic guitar (model unknown)
Scotty Moore   Lead guitar (Gibson ES-295)
Bill Black   Double bass

Notable song(s) performed:

SHOUT SISTER SHOUT *(Crudup)*

* Original by Arthur 'Big Boy' Crudup (RCA-Victor 0029) 1949.
◆ *Elvis' source:* Arthur 'Big Boy' Crudup (RCA-Victor 0029) 1949.

5.66

Curtis Gordon's Radio Ranch Club, Mobile, Alabama
Thursday, 30 June 1955 (8.30 pm)

Elvis Presley	Vocal and acoustic guitar (model unknown)
Scotty Moore	Lead guitar (Gibson ES-295)
Bill Black	Double bass

Notable song(s) performed:

MEAN MAMA BOOGIE *(Bond)*

★ Original by Johnny Bond (Columbia 20704) 1950.
◆ *Elvis' source:* Johnny Bond (Columbia 20704) 1950.

SITTING ON TOP OF THE WORLD *(Vincson/Chatmon)*
Composition by Walter Vincson and Bo Chatmon/Chatman/Carter. Not to be confused with Frank Crumit's **I'M SITTING ON TOP OF THE WORLD (JUST ROLLING ALONG, JUST ROLLING ALONG)** *(Victor 19928) 1926.*

★ Original by the Mississippi Sheiks (OKeh 8784) 1930.
◆ *Elvis' sources:* Mississippi Sheiks (OKeh 8784) 1930.
　　　　　　　　　　 Bob Wills (Vocalion 03139) 1935.

Note　*Club owner and Mercury recording artist Curtis Gordon was inspired by Elvis to cut his own rockabilly version of the song in 1957 (Mercury 71097).*

5.67

Gospel Meeting At The Bill
Hodges Park, DeLeon, Texas
Monday, 4 July 1955 (3.00–3.25 pm)

Elvis Presley	Vocal and acoustic guitar (model unknown)
Scotty Moore	Lead guitar (Gibson ES-295)
Bill Black	Double bass

Other acts appearing on the W.B. Nowlin-promoted gospel show were the Statesmen Quartet, the Deep South Stamps, the Stamps Ozark Quartet, Minnie Pearl, the Faren Twins and the Blackwood Brothers. Elvis also played two later shows on this date at the Recreation Hall, Stephenville, Texas and the Memorial Hall, Brownwood, Texas.

Elvis sang the following five songs in between dialogues (not in order of performance):

HE'S GOT THE WHOLE WORLD IN HIS HANDS *(Traditional)*
Negro spiritual. Heard in black churches in the South from circa 1890; in white churches from ?

★ Original by Rev. F.W. McGee (Victor 38513) 1929.
　 A variation on this theme, **GOT THE GREAT BIG WORLD IN HIS HANDS**, was recorded by the Megginson Female Quartette (Victor 20581) in 1927.
◆ *Elvis' radio sources:* Boyer Brothers (Excello 2010) 1953.

HIS HAND IN MINE *(Lister)*
Hymn composed in 1953 by the Statesmen's own composer, Mosie Lister.

✱ Original by the Statesmen Quartet (Statesmen 1035/1036) 1953.
◆ *Elvis' radio source:* Statesmen Quartet (Statesmen 1035/1036) 1953.
        Blackwood Brothers (RCA-Victor 5709) 1954.
❍ Elvis later made a private recording of this title at his army house at 14 Goethestrasse, Bad Nauheim, West Germany in April 1959 (tape lost). He subsequently recorded it at RCA Studio B, Nashville on 30 October 1960 (released in 1960 on LP *His Hand In Mine*, RCA-Victor LPM/LSP-2328).

KNOWN ONLY TO HIM *(Hamblen)*
Hymn composed in 1952 by Stuart Hamblen.

✱ Original by Stuart Hamblen (Columbia 21012) 1952.
◆ *Elvis' radio sources:* Stuart Hamblen (Columbia 21012) 1952.
        Statesmen Quartet (Statesmen 1049/1050) 1953.
❍ Elvis later recorded this title at RCA Studio B, Nashville on 31 October 1960 (released in 1960 on LP *His Hand In Mine*, RCA-Victor LPM/LSP-2328).

TAKE MY HAND, PRECIOUS LORD *(Dorsey)*
Gospel song composed in 1932 by Rev. Thomas A. Dorsey.

✱ Original **PRECIOUS LORD, TAKE MY HAND**
        by the Heavenly Gospel Singers (Bluebird 6846) 1937.
◆ *Elvis' radio sources:* Golden Gate Jubilee Quartet (Bluebird 8190) 1939.
        Selah Jubilee Singers (Decca 7598) 1939.
        PRECIOUS LORD, HOLD MY HAND
            Rosetta Tharpe (Decca 8610) 1941.
        Five Soul Stirrers (Bronze 103) recorded 1939, released 1945.
        Selah Jubilee Singers (Decca 48003) 1946.
        Brother John Sellers (Miracle 106) 1947.
        Floyd Dixon (Modern 20-724) 1949.
        Harmonizing Four (MGM 10457) 1949.
        Prof. James Earle Hines (Modern 20-690) 1949.
        Richmond Harmonizers (MGM 10457) 1949.
        Jimmy Davis (Decca 14580) 1950.
        Brother Joe May (Specialty 815) 1950.
        Wally Fowler & The Oak Ridge Quartet (Bullet 131) 1951.
        Clara Ward (Gotham 690) 1951.
        Blackwood Brothers Quartet (RCA-Victor 4793) 1952.
        Eddy Arnold (RCA-Victor 4490) 1952.
        Myrtle Jackson (Brunswick 84013) 1953.
❍ Elvis recorded this title at Radio Recorders, Hollywood on 13 January 1957 (released in 1957 on EP *Peace In The Valley*, RCA-Victor EPA-4054). He later also made a private recording of it at his army house at 14 Goethestrasse, Bad Nauheim, West Germany in April 1959 (tape lost).

(THERE'LL BE) PEACE IN THE VALLEY (FOR ME) *(Dorsey)*
Gospel song composed in 1939 by Rev. Thomas A. Dorsey. Adaptation of the Negro spiritual **WE SHALL WALK THROUGH THE VALLEY IN PEACE.** *C&W hit in 1951 for Red Foley (Decca 14573, 27856 and 46319).*

✱ Original by the Flying Clouds Of Detroit (Haven 510) 1946.
◆ *Elvis' radio sources:* Paramount Singers (Trilon 1233) 1949.
        Southern Sons Quartette (Trumpet 119) 1950.
        Speer Family (Bullet 120) 1950.

> Robert A. Bracey (Sittin' In With 620) 1951.
> Red Foley (Decca 14573, 27856 and 46319) 1951.
> Harmoneers Quartet (RCA-Victor 0480) 1951.
> Paramount Singers (Coral 65066) 1951.
> Soul Stirrers (Specialty 802) 1951.
> Stamps Quartet (Columbia 20836) 1951.
> Statesmen Quartet (Capitol 1489) 1951.
> Sister Rosetta Tharpe (Decca 48279) 1952.
> Blackwood Brothers Quartet (RCA-Victor 4795) 1952.

O Elvis later recorded this title at the *Million Dollar Quartet* session at Sun Studio, Memphis on 4 December 1956 (released in 1990 on 2-LP/CD *The Million Dollar Quartet*, BMG/RCA 2023-1-R / 2023-2-R). He subsequently re-cut it at Radio Recorders, Hollywood on 13 January 1957 (released in 1957 on EP *Peace In The Valley*, RCA-Victor EPA-4054).

5.68

Cape Arena Building, Cape Girardeau, Missouri
Wednesday, 20 July 1955 (8.30 pm)

Elvis Presley	Vocal and acoustic guitar (new Martin D-28)
Scotty Moore	Lead guitar (Gibson L5)
Bill Black	Double bass

Scotty now switched to playing the Gibson L5, having reportedly traded in his ES-295 on 7 July. However, he did revert to playing an ES-295 on some occasions in September and October 1955.

Notable song(s) performed:

MYSTERY TRAIN *(Parker/Phillips)*
Elvis' recording is a combination of two Little Junior Parker tunes — the lyrics of **MYSTERY TRAIN** *and the* **LOVE MY BABY** *guitar riff — which were issued back-to-back on Sun 192. Parker's* **MYSTERY TRAIN** *itself was based on the Carter Family's* **WORRIED MAN BLUES** *(Bluebird 6020) 1930.*

★ Original by Little Junior's Blue Flames (Sun 192) 1953.
◆ *Elvis' source:* Little Junior's Blue Flames (Sun 192) 1953.
O Elvis recorded this title at Sun Studio, Memphis on 11 July 1955 (Sun 223, 1955) [see **4.20** for details].

124

5.69

Municipal Auditorium, Orlando, Florida
Tuesday, 26 July 1955 (8.15 pm)
Elvis Presley   Vocal and acoustic guitar (new Martin D-28)
Scotty Moore   Lead guitar (Gibson L5)
Bill Black   Double bass

Notable song(s) performed:

RAGS TO RICHES *(Adler/Ross)*
Pop hit in 1953 for Tony Bennett (Columbia 40048). R&B hit in 1953 for Billy Ward & His Dominoes (King 1280).

★ Original by Tony Bennett (Columbia 40048) 1953.
◆ *Elvis' sources:*   Tony Bennett (Columbia 40048) 1953.
                Billy Ward & His Dominoes (King 1280) 1953.
○ Elvis later recorded this title at RCA Studio B, Nashville on 22 September 1970 (released in 1971 as the flip side of single **WHERE DID THEY GO LORD**, RCA-Victor 9980).

5.70

New Baseball Stadium, Jacksonville, Florida
Friday, 29 July 1955 (8.15 pm)
Elvis Presley   Vocal and acoustic guitar (new Martin D-28)
Scotty Moore   Lead guitar (Gibson L5)
Bill Black   Double bass

Notable song(s) performed:

ROCK AROUND THE CLOCK *(DeKnight/Freeman)*
Pop hit in 1954 for Bill Haley (Decca 29124), which became a crossover hit (pop and R&B) when reissued in 1955.

★ Original by Sonny Dae (Arcade 123) 1953.
◆ *Elvis' source:* Bill Haley (Decca 29124) 1954.

5.71

Municipal Auditorium, Camden, Arkansas
Thursday, 4 August 1955 (9.30 pm)
Elvis Presley   Vocal and acoustic guitar (new Martin D-28)
Scotty Moore   Lead guitar (Gibson L5)
Bill Black   Double bass

This was second of two shows that evening. The first show was at 7.00 pm.

Notable song(s) performed:

I FORGOT TO REMEMBER TO FORGET *(Kesler/Feathers)*
Song written by Stan Kesler, who recorded a demo of it at the Sun studio on Saturday, 25 June 1955 between 3.00 and 3.30 pm, with himself on fiddle and Charlie Feathers on vocal and acoustic guitar. Feathers subsequently claimed that he had finished off the song and that he should be credited as co-composer. They also recorded a demo of **WE'RE GETTING CLOSER TO BEING APART** *at the same session. In 1973, Feathers cut a new version of* **I FORGOT TO REMEMBER TO FORGET** *for his 'Living Legend' LP (Redita 107, Netherlands).*

★ Original by Elvis, recorded at Sun Studio, Memphis on 11 July 1955 (Sun 223, 1955) [see **4.20** for details].

5.72

Large Auditorium, Mayfair Building, Tyler, Texas
Monday, 8 August 1955 (8.00 pm)
Elvis Presley   Vocal and acoustic guitar (new Martin D-28)
Scotty Moore   Lead guitar (Gibson L5)
Bill Black   Double bass
D.J. Fontana   Drums

D.J. Fontana became a permanent member of Elvis' group on this date.

Notable song(s) performed:

I FORGOT TO REMEMBER TO FORGET *(Kesler/Feathers)*
Song written by Stan Kesler, who recorded a demo of it at the Sun studio on Saturday, 25 June 1955 between 3.00 and 3.30 pm, with himself on fiddle and Charlie Feathers on vocal and acoustic guitar. Feathers subsequently claimed that he had finished off the song and that he should be credited as co-composer. They also recorded a demo of **WE'RE GETTING CLOSER TO BEING APART** *at the same session. In 1973, Feathers cut a new version of* **I FORGOT TO REMEMBER TO FORGET** *for his 'Living Legend' LP (Redita 107, Netherlands).*

★ Original by Elvis, recorded at Sun Studio, Memphis on 11 July 1955 (Sun 223, 1955) [see **4.20** for details].

MYSTERY TRAIN *(Parker/Phillips)*

Elvis' recording is a combination of two Little Junior Parker tunes — the lyrics of **MYSTERY TRAIN** *and the* **LOVE MY BABY** *guitar riff — which were issued back-to-back on Sun 192. Parker's* **MYSTERY TRAIN** *itself was based on the Carter Family's* **WORRIED MAN BLUES** *(Bluebird 6020) 1930.*

★ Original by Little Junior's Blue Flames (Sun 192) 1953.
◆ *Elvis' source:* Little Junior's Blue Flames (Sun 192) 1953.
○ Elvis recorded this title at Sun Studio, Memphis on 11 July 1955 (Sun 223) 1955 [see **4.20** for details].

Driller Park, Kilgore, Texas
Friday, 12 August 1955 (exact time unknown)

Elvis Presley	Vocal and acoustic guitar (new Martin D-28)
Scotty Moore	Lead guitar (Gibson L5)
Bill Black	Double bass
D.J. Fontana	Drums

Notable song(s) performed:

MAYBELLENE *(Berry)*

Crossover (pop and R&B) hit in 1955 for Chuck Berry (Chess 1604). R&B hit in 1955 for Jim Lowe (Dot 15407). C&W hit in 1955 for Marty Robbins (Columbia 21446).

★ Original by Chuck Berry (Chess 1604) 1955.
◆ *Elvis' source:* Chuck Berry (Chess 1604) 1955.
○ Elvis recorded this title at Sun Studio, Memphis in August 1955 (rehearsal take, erased) [see **4.22** for details].

Saddle Club, Bryan, Texas
Tuesday, 23 August 1955 (evening, exact time unknown)

Elvis Presley	Vocal and acoustic guitar (new Martin D-28)
Scotty Moore	Lead guitar (Gibson L5)
Bill Black	Double bass
D.J. Fontana	Drums

Notable song(s) performed:

TRYIN' TO GET TO YOU *(McCoy/Singleton)*

★ Original by the Eagles (Mercury 70391) 1954.
◆ *Elvis' source:* Eagles (Mercury 70391) 1954.
○ Elvis recorded this title at Sun Studio, Memphis on 3 February and 11 July 1955 [see **4.15** and **4.20** for details]. Earlier version unissued.

5.75

Baseball Park, Gonzales, Texas
Friday, 26 August 1955 (8.00 pm)

Elvis Presley	Vocal and acoustic guitar (new Martin D-28)
Scotty Moore	Lead guitar (Gibson L5)
Bill Black	Double bass
D.J. Fontana	Drums

Notable song(s) performed:

CRYIN' HEART BLUES *(Brown)*
C&W hit in 1951 for Johnnie & Jack (RCA-Victor 0478). This song was later retitled **MEAN HEART BLUES** *by Elvis* [see **5.63**].

★ Original by Johnnie & Jack (RCA-Victor 0478) 1951.
◆ *Elvis' source:* Johnnie & Jack (RCA-Victor 0478) 1951.
❍ Elvis recorded this title at Sun Studio, Memphis in August 1955 (rehearsal take, erased) [see **4.24** for details].

5.76

Lake Ponchartrain Beach, New Orleans, Louisiana
Thursday, 1 September 1955 (9.30 pm)

Elvis Presley	Vocal and acoustic guitar (new Martin D-28)
Scotty Moore	Lead guitar (Gibson L5)
Bill Black	Double bass
Joe Clay	Drums

D.J. Fontana had health problems during September 1955 and did not play with the group. His replacement on this occasion was Joe Clay, who went on to record rockabilly for the RCA subsidiary Vik in 1956.

UNKNOWN TITLES

5.77

Arkansas Municipal Auditorium, Texarkana, Arkansas
Friday, 2 September 1955 (7.00 pm)

Elvis Presley	Vocal and acoustic guitar (new Martin D-28)
Scotty Moore	Lead guitar (Gibson ES-295)
Bill Black	Double bass
D.J. Fontana?	Drums
Unknown	Piano

Notable song(s) performed:

TEXARKANA BABY *(Clarke/Rose)*
Crossover (pop and C&W) hit in 1948 for Eddy Arnold (RCA-Victor 2806), and also a C&W hit that same year for Bob Wills (Columbia 38179).

✱ Eddy Arnold (RCA-Victor 2806) 1948.
◆ *Elvis' source:* Eddy Arnold (RCA-Victor 2806) 1948.
      Eddie Hazelwood (Decca 46129) 1948.
      Bob Wills (Columbia 38179) 1948.

5.78

St. Francis County Fair & Livestock Show Jamboree
Smith Stadium, Forrest City, Arkansas
Monday, 5 September 1955 (8.00 pm)

Elvis Presley	Vocal and acoustic guitar (model unknown)
Scotty Moore	Lead guitar (Gibson ES-295)
Bill Black	Double bass

Notable song(s) performed:

TOO LATE TO CRY *(Stanley/Stanley)*

✱ Original by the Stanley Brothers (Columbia 20697) 1950.
◆ *Elvis' source:* Stanley Brothers (Columbia 20697) 1950.

5.79

National Guard Armory, Sikeston, Missouri
Wednesday, 7 September 1955 (8.00 pm)
Elvis Presley   Vocal and acoustic guitar (model unknown)
Scotty Moore   Lead guitar (Gibson ES-295)
Bill Black   Double bass

Notable song(s) performed:

THE COVERED WAGON ROLLED RIGHT ALONG *(Wood/Heath)*

✱ Original by Texas Jim Lewis (Decca 46063) 1947.
◆ *Elvis' source:* Texas Jim Lewis (Decca 46063) 1947.

5.80

McComb High School Auditorium, McComb, Mississippi
Friday, 9 September 1955 (8.00 pm)
Elvis Presley   Vocal and acoustic guitar (model unknown)
Scotty Moore   Lead guitar (Gibson ES-295)
Bill Black   Double bass

Notable song(s) performed:

LONG TALL MAMA *(Edwards)*
Song composed by Bernice Edwards in December 1927. R&B hit for Smokey Hogg in 1948 (Modern 574). Not to be confused with Big Bill Broonzy's eponymous 1932 recording (Banner 33085), or with Jimmie Rodgers' **LONG TALL MAMA BLUES** *(Victor 23766) from 1933, which are both completely different songs.*

✱ Original by Moanin' Bernice Edwards (Paramount 12633) 1928.
◆ *Elvis' source:* Smokey Hogg (Modern 574) 1948.

5.81

Memorial Auditorium, Raleigh, North Carolina
Wednesday, 21 September 1955 (8.00 pm)
Elvis Presley   Vocal and acoustic guitar (model unknown)
Scotty Moore   Lead guitar (Gibson ES-295)
Bill Black   Double bass

Notable song(s) performed:

ONLY YOU *(Ram/Rand)*
Crossover (pop and R&B) hit in 1955 for the Platters (Mercury 70633). Pop hit in 1955 for the Hilltoppers (Dot 15423).

★ Original by the Platters (Federal 12244) 1955.
◆ *Elvis' sources:* Billy Eckstine (MGM 11984) 1955.
                      Platters (Mercury 70633) 1955.
                      Hilltoppers (Dot 15423) 1955.

5.82

B&B Club, Gobler, Missouri
Wednesday, 28 September 1955 (evening, exact time unknown)
Elvis Presley   Vocal and acoustic guitar (new Martin D-28)
Scotty Moore   Lead guitar (Gibson ES-295)
Bill Black   Double bass

Notable song(s) performed:

MY BABE *(Dixon)*
R&B hit in 1955 for Little Walter (Checker 811).

★ Original by Little Walter (Checker 811) 1955.
◆ *Elvis' source:* Little Walter (Checker 811) 1955.
◉ Elvis later recorded this title at the International Hotel, Las Vegas on 25 August 1969 (released in 1969 on 2-LP *Elvis In Person (From Memphis To Vegas/From Vegas To Memphis)*, RCA-Victor LSP-6020).

5.83

Southwest Texas State University, San Marcos, Texas
Thursday, 6 October 1955 (3.00 pm)

Elvis Presley	Vocal and acoustic guitar (new Martin D-28)
Scotty Moore	Lead guitar (Gibson ES-295)
Bill Black	Double bass

Elvis also played an evening show at the Skyline Club, Austin, Texas on the same date.

Notable song(s) performed:

WHEN IT RAINS IT REALLY POURS *(Emerson)*

✱ Original by Billy 'The Kid' Emerson (Sun 214) 1954.
◆ *Elvis' source:* Billy 'The Kid' Emerson (Sun 214) 1954.
O Elvis recorded this title at Sun Studio, Memphis on 3 November 1955 (unissued) [see **4.26** for details].

5.84

Memorial Hall, Brownwood, Texas
Monday, 10 October 1955 (8.00 pm)

Elvis Presley	Vocal and acoustic guitar (new Martin D-28)
Scotty Moore	Lead guitar (Gibson ES-295)
Bill Black	Double bass
D.J. Fontana	Drums

D.J. Fontana returned to the group having been absent throughout September due to ill health.

Notable song(s) performed:

MOVE IT ON OVER *(Williams)* / ROCK AROUND THE CLOCK *(DeKnight/Freeman)*
MOVE IT ON OVER *was a C&W hit in 1947 for Hank Williams (MGM 10033).* **ROCK AROUND THE CLOCK** *was a pop hit in 1954 for Bill Haley (Decca 29124) and became a crossover hit (pop and R&B) when reissued in 1955.*

✱ Original of **MOVE IT ON OVER** by Hank Williams (MGM 10033) 1947.
◆ *Elvis' source:* Hank Williams (MGM 10033) 1947.

✱ Original of **ROCK AROUND THE CLOCK** by Sonny Dae (Arcade 123) 1953.
◆ *Elvis' source:* Bill Haley (Decca 29124) 1954.

5.85

Missouri Theater, St. Louis, Missouri
Saturday, 22 October 1955 (9.30 pm)
Elvis Presley   Vocal and acoustic guitar (new Martin D-28)
Scotty Moore   Lead guitar (Gibson L5)
Bill Black   Double bass
D.J. Fontana   Drums

This was second of two shows that evening. The first show was at 7.00 pm. Elvis played two further shows at the same venue the following day.

Notable song(s) performed:

ONLY YOU *(Ram/Rand)*
Crossover (pop and R&B) hit in 1955 for the Platters (Mercury 70633). Pop hit in 1955 for the Hilltoppers (Dot 15423).

✱ Original by the Platters (Federal 12244) 1955.
◆ *Elvis' sources:* Billy Eckstine (MGM 11984) 1955.
                        Platters (Mercury 70633) 1955.
                        Hilltoppers (Dot 15423) 1955.

5.86

Biloxi Community House, Biloxi, Mississippi
Sunday, 6 November 1955 (8.00 pm)
Elvis Presley   Vocal and acoustic guitar (new Martin D-28)
Scotty Moore   Lead guitar (Gibson L5)
Bill Black   Double bass
D.J. Fontana?   Drums?

Notable song(s) performed:

MY BABY LEFT ME *(Crudup)*

✱ Original by Arthur 'Big Boy' Crudup (RCA-Victor 0109) 1951.
◆ *Elvis' source:* Arthur 'Big Boy' Crudup (RCA-Victor 0109) 1951.
O Elvis later recorded this title at RCA, New York on 30 January 1956 (released in 1956 as flip side of single **I WANT YOU, I NEED YOU, I LOVE YOU**, RCA-Victor 6540).

5.87

Sports Arena, Atlanta, Georgia
Friday, 2 December 1955 (exact time unknown)
Elvis Presley   Vocal and acoustic guitar (new Martin D-28)
Scotty Moore   Lead guitar (Gibson L5)
Bill Black   Double bass
D.J. Fontana   Drums

Notable song(s) performed:

SIXTEEN TONS *(Travis)*
Crossover hit (pop and C&W) in 1955 for Tennessee Ernie Ford (Capitol 3262), and also a pop hit that same year for Johnny Desmond (Coral 61529).

✱ Original by Merle Travis (78 rpm 4-disc album *Folk Songs Of The Hills*, Capitol AD-50) 1947.
◆ *Elvis' sources:*   Johnny Desmond (Coral 61529) 1955.
                   Tennessee Ernie Ford (Capitol 3262) 1955.
                   B.B. King (RPM 451) 1955.

5.88

State Coliseum, Montgomery, Alabama
Saturday, 3 December 1955 (exact time unknown)
Elvis Presley   Vocal and acoustic guitar (new Martin D-28)
Scotty Moore   Lead guitar (Gibson L5)
Bill Black   Double bass
D.J. Fontana?   Drums?

Notable song(s) performed:

FLIP, FLOP AND FLY *(Calhoun/Turner)*
R&B hit in 1955 for Joe Turner (Atlantic 1053).

✱ Original by Joe Turner (Atlantic 1053) 1955.
◆ *Elvis' source:*   Joe Turner (Atlantic 1053) 1955.
● Elvis later recorded this title at CBS-TV studio, New York on 28 January 1956 for the Dorsey brothers' *Stage Show* in medley with **SHAKE, RATTLE AND ROLL** (released in 1984 on 6-LP box set *Elvis: A Golden Celebration*, RCA-Victor CPM6-5172). Another version was recorded in Memphis on 20 March 1974 in medley with other rock'n'roll songs (released in 1974 on LP *Elvis – Recorded Live On Stage In Memphis*, RCA-Victor CPL1-0606).

5.89

Lyric Theater, Indianapolis, Indiana
Monday, 5 December 1955 (exact time unknown)

Elvis Presley	Vocal and acoustic guitar (new Martin D-28)
Scotty Moore	Lead guitar (Gibson L5)
Bill Black	Double bass
D.J. Fontana	Drums

This was the second of four shows at the Lyric Theater, on 4, 5, 6 and 7 December.

Notable song(s) performed:

TUTTI FRUTTI *(LaBostrie/Penniman)*
Crossover (pop and R&B) hit in 1955-56 for Little Richard (Specialty 561).

★ Original by Little Richard (Specialty 561) 1955.
◆ *Elvis' source:* Little Richard (Specialty 561) 1955.
○ Elvis later recorded this title at RCA, New York on 31 January 1956 (released in 1956 on LP *Elvis Presley* (RCA-Victor LPM-1254) and subsequently at CBS-TV studio, New York on both 4 and 18 February 1956 for the Dorsey brothers' *Stage Show* (released in 1984 on 6-LP box set *Elvis: A Golden Celebration*, RCA-Victor CPM6-5172).

5.90

Lyric Theater, Indianapolis, Indiana
Wednesday, 7 December 1955 (evening, exact time unknown)

Elvis Presley	Vocal and acoustic guitar (new Martin D-28)
Scotty Moore	Lead guitar (Gibson L5)
Bill Black	Double bass
D.J. Fontana	Drums

This was the last of four shows at the Lyric Theater, on 4, 5, 6 and 7 December.

Notable song(s) performed:

ROCK AROUND THE CLOCK *(DeKnight/Freeman)*
Pop hit in 1954 for Bill Haley (Decca 29124), which became a crossover hit (pop and R&B) when reissued in 1955.

★ Original by Sonny Dae (Arcade 123) 1953.
◆ *Elvis' source:* Bill Haley (Decca 29124) 1954.

5.91

Philip Morris Employees' Night
Rialto Theater, Louisville, Kentucky
Thursday, 8 December 1955 (evening, exact time unknown)
Elvis Presley   Vocal and acoustic guitar (new Martin D-28)
Scotty Moore   Lead guitar (Gibson L5)
Bill Black   Double bass
D.J. Fontana   Drums

Notable song(s) performed:

LAWDY MISS CLAWDY *(Price)*
R&B hit in 1952 for Lloyd Price (Specialty 428).

★ Original by Lloyd Price (Specialty 428) 1952.
◆ *Elvis' source:* Lloyd Price (Specialty 428) 1952.
○ Elvis later recorded this title at RCA, New York on 3 February 1956 (released in 1956 on EP *Elvis Presley*, RCA-Victor EPA-830). Also at NBC-TV studio, Burbank, California on 27 June 1968 (released in 1968 on LP *Elvis TV Special*, RCA-Victor LPM-4088) and at Mid-South Coliseum, Memphis on 20 March 1974 (released in 1974 on LP *Elvis – Recorded Live On Stage In Memphis*, RCA-Victor CPL1-0606).

5.92

B&I Club, Swifton, Arkansas
Friday, 9 December 1955 (11.00 pm)
Elvis Presley   Vocal and acoustic guitar (new Martin D-28)
Scotty Moore   Lead guitar (Gibson L5)
Bill Black   Double bass
D.J. Fontana   Drums

Earlier that evening, Elvis played a show at Swifton High School.

Notable song(s) performed:

HEARTBREAK HOTEL *(Axton/Durden)*

★ Original by Elvis (RCA-Victor 6420), released Friday, 27 January 1956.

◆ SECTION 6 ◆

Informal Jams 1954-55

The songs that Elvis performed in public and recorded represented only a tiny fraction of his musical knowledge and repertoire. The informal jams listed below provide an illuminating insight into other songs that he knew, liked, and was inspired or influenced by at the time his career was starting to take off.

6.1

Scotty Moore's House, 983 Belz Avenue, Memphis, Tennessee
Sunday, 27 June and Sunday, 4 July 1954 (exact times unknown)
Elvis Presley   Vocal and acoustic guitar (old Martin D-18)
Scotty Moore   Lead guitar (Gibson ES-295)
Bill Black   Double bass

*At Sam Phillips' behest, Scotty Moore auditioned Elvis at his home. Scotty, who was with the Starlite Wranglers at the time, asked the band's bassist, Bill Black, to join them. They ran through the following songs as well as other unknown titles over a couple of weekends. (It is not known which songs were played on which day, or in what order.) Scotty and Bill were not overly impressed with the aspiring singer's talent, although Scotty did suggest to Sam that it might be worthwhile giving him another chance in the studio. He did so the following day: Monday, 5 July 1954 [see **4.6**].*

I APOLOGIZE *(Hoffman/Goodhart/Nelson)*
A hit in 1931 for Bing Crosby (Brunswick 6179) and Nat Shilkret (Victor 22781). Crossover (pop and R&B) hit in 1951 for Billy Eckstine (MGM 10903), and a pop hit for Champ Butler (Columbia 39189) and Tony Martin (RCA-Victor 4056).

✱ Original by Bing Crosby (Brunswick 6179) 1931.
◆ *Elvis' sources:*   Champ Butler (Columbia 39189) 1951.
                    Billy Eckstine (MGM 10903) 1951.
                    Tony Martin (RCA-Victor 4056) 1951.
                    Dinah Washington (Mercury 8209) 1951.

I DON'T HURT ANYMORE *(Robertson/Rollins)*
C&W hit in 1954 for Hank Snow (RCA-Victor 5698).

✱ Original by Hank Snow (RCA-Victor 5698) 1954.
◆ *Elvis' source:* Hank Snow (RCA-Victor 5698) 1954.

IF I DIDN'T CARE *(Lawrence)*
Pop hit in 1939 for the Ink Spots (Decca 2286) and in 1954 for the Hilltoppers (Dot 15220).

✱ Original by the Ink Spots (Decca 2286) 1939.
◆ *Elvis' sources:* Ink Spots (Decca 2286) 1939.
　　　　　　　　　　Hilltoppers (Dot 15220) 1954.

I'LL GO ON ALONE *(Robbins)*
C&W hit in 1952 for Webb Pierce (Decca 28534) and Marty Robbins (Columbia 21022).

✱ Original by Marty Robbins (Columbia 21022) 1952.
◆ *Elvis' sources:* Webb Pierce (Decca 28534) 1952.
　　　　　　　　　　Marty Robbins (Columbia 21022) 1952.

I LOVE YOU BECAUSE *(Payne)*
C&W hit in 1950 for Leon Payne (Capitol 40238), Clyde Moody (King 837) and Ernest Tubb (Decca 46213).

✱ Original by Leon Payne (Capitol 40238) 1949.
◆ *Elvis' sources:* Leon Payne (Capitol 40238) 1949.
　　　　　　　　　　Gene Autry (Columbia 20709) 1950.
　　　　　　　　　　Clyde Moody (King 837) 1950.
　　　　　　　　　　Ernest Tubb (Decca 46213) 1950.
◒ Elvis recorded this title at Sun Studio, Memphis on 5 July 1954 [see **4.6** for details].

I REALLY DON'T WANT TO KNOW *(Barnes/Robertson)*
C&W hit in 1954 for Eddy Arnold (RCA-Victor 5525). Pop hit in 1954 for Les Paul & Mary Ford (Capitol 2735).

✱ Original by Eddy Arnold (RCA-Victor 5525) 1953.
◆ *Elvis' sources:* Eddy Arnold (RCA-Victor 5525) 1953.
　　　　　　　　　　Dominoes (King 1368) 1954.
　　　　　　　　　　Les Paul & Mary Ford (Capitol 2735) 1954.

LOVE ME OR LEAVE ME ALONE *(Robbins)*

✱ Original by Marty Robbins (Columbia 20925) 1952.
◆ *Elvis' source:* Marty Robbins (Columbia 20925) 1952.

MY ISLE OF GOLDEN DREAMS *(Blaufuss/Kahn)*
A hit in 1920 for Ben Selvin (Paramount 20002), and in 1939 for Bing Crosby (Decca 2775) and Glenn Miller (Bluebird 10399).

✱ Original by Ben Selvin (Paramount 20002) 1920.
◆ *Elvis' sources:* Bing Crosby (Decca 2775) 1939.
　　　　　　　　　　Marty Robbins (Columbia 21213) 1954.

ONE KISS TOO MANY *(Arnold/Nelson/Nelson)*
Crossover (pop and C&W) hit in 1949 for Eddy Arnold (RCA-Victor 0083).

✱ Original by Eddy Arnold (RCA-Victor 0083) 1949.
◆ *Elvis' source:* Eddy Arnold (RCA-Victor 0083) 1949.

TOMORROW NIGHT *(Coslow/Grosz)*
A hit in 1939 for Horace Heidt (Columbia 35203). Crossover (pop and R&B) hit in 1948 for Lonnie Johnson (King 4201). Not to be confused with Louis Armstrong's 1933 recording 'Tomorrow Night (After Tonight)' (RCA-Victor 68-0774) or Junior Wells' 'Tomorrow Night' (States 143) 1954.

* ✱ Original by Horace Heidt (Columbia 35203) 1939.
* ◆ *Elvis' sources:* Horace Heidt (Columbia 35203) 1939.
    Lonnie Johnson (King 4201) 1948.
    Lonnie Johnson (Paradise 11) 1948.
* ○ Elvis recorded this title at Sun Studio, Memphis on 19 August and 8 December 1954 [see **4.8** and **4.12** for details]. Second version unissued/lost.

YOU BELONG TO ME *(King/Stewart/Price)*
Pop hit in 1952 for Dean Martin (Capitol 2165), Patti Page (Mercury 5899) and Jo Stafford (Columbia 39811).

* ✱ Original by Joni James (MGM 11295) 1952.
* ◆ *Elvis' sources:* Tamara Hayes (RCA-Victor 4943) 1952.
    Joni James (MGM 11295) 1952.
    Annie Laurie (OKeh 6915) 1952.
    Buddy Lucas (Jubilee 5094) 1952.
    Dean Martin (Capitol 2165) 1952.
    Orioles (Jubilee 5102) 1952.
    Patti Page (Mercury 5899) 1952.
    Tab Smith (United 131) 1952.
    Jo Stafford (Columbia 39811) 1952.

Songs sung by Elvis backstage and at informal jam sessions at the Eagle's Nest, Bon Air, Bel Air and Handy Club.
Memphis, 1954 (exact dates unknown)

On some occasions, Elvis sang unaccompanied; on others, he also played guitar or piano, or was accompanied by Scotty and Bill and/or other local musicians like Carl Perkins, Marcus Van Story, Malcolm Yelvington, Rosco Gordon, etc. Naturally, this list makes no pretence at being complete.

Popular recordings by white artists

FRANKIE AND JOHNNY (FRANKIE AND ALBERT) *(Traditional)*
There are several theories as to the origin of this song, which was first published by Hughie Cannon in 1904 under the title **HE DONE ME WRONG** *but appears to date back to the 1800s. One is that it originated in New Orleans around 1812, when it was known as* **FRANÇOISE ET JEAN**. *Another attributes it to an actual incident in St. Louis in 1888. It was a hit in 1927 for both Frank Crumit (Victor 20715) and Ted Lewis (Columbia 1017). Also a pop hit in 1942 for Guy Lombardo (Decca 4177).*

* ✱ Original recording on cylinder by the Standard Quartette (*no details*) 1891.
    Original recording on 78 rpm by the Fate Marable Society Syncopators (OKeh 40113) 1924.
* ◆ *Elvis' sources:* Gene Autry (Diva 6037, Velvet-Tone 7063) 1929.
    FRANKIE AND ALBERT by Charley Patton (Paramount 13110) 1929.
    Jimmie Rodgers (Victor 22143) 1929.

Gene Autry (Clarion 5026) 1931.
Clayton McMichen's Georgia Wildcats (Decca 5418) 1937.
FRANKIE AND ALBERT by Leadbelly (Musicraft 223) 1939.
Guy Lombardo (Decca 4177) 1942.
T. Texas Tyler (4 Star 1150) 1947.
Lena Horne (Black & White 500) 1948.
Choker Campbell (Fortune 808) 1952.

O Elvis later recorded this title at Radio Recorders, Hollywood on 15 May 1965 (released in 1966 on LP *Frankie And Johnny*, RCA-Victor LPM/LSP-3553).

M-I-S-S-I-S-S-I-P-P-I *(Simmons/Williams)*
Pop hit in 1950 for Bill Darnel (Coral 60220), Red Foley (Decca 46324), Art Mooney (MGM 10721) and Kay Starr (Capitol 1072).

★ Original by Kay Starr (Capitol 1072) 1950.
◆ *Elvis' sources:* Bill Darnel (Coral 60220) 1950.
Red Foley (Decca 46324) 1950.
Art Mooney – Voc. Allan Brooks (MGM 10721) 1950.
Kay Starr (Capitol 1072) 1950.

THE OLD CHISHOLM TRAIL *(Traditional)*
Traditional cowboy song.

★ Original by Mac McClintock (Victor 2421) 1928.
◆ *Elvis' sources:* Bob Atcher (Columbia 20621) 1948.
Tex Ritter (Capitol 40179) 1949.

RELEASE ME *(Miller/Williams/Yount)*
Jam with Malcolm Yelvington at the Eagle's Nest, October 1954.
C&W hit in 1954 for Jimmy Heap with Perk Williams (Capitol 2518), Ray Price (Columbia 21214) and Kitty Wells (Decca 29023).

★ Original by Eddie Miller (4 Star 1407) 1950.
◆ *Elvis' sources:* Eddie Miller (4 Star 1407) 1950.
Jimmy Heap with Perk Williams (Capitol 2518) 1953.
Four Aces (Big Town 112) 1954.
Ray Price (Columbia 21214) 1954.
Kitty Wells (Decca 29023) 1954.

O Elvis later recorded this title at a midnight show at the International Hotel, Las Vegas on 18 February 1970 (released in 1970 on LP *On Stage*, RCA-Victor LSP-4362). A stage rehearsal, also from 18 February 1970 was released in 1997 on 4-CD *Platinum – A Life In Music*, BMG/RCA 67489-2). Another version, from a concert in Greensboro, North Carolina on 14 April 1972 (an outtake from the MGM film, *Elvis On Tour*) was included in the 1992 video, *The Lost Performances*.

RIDERS IN THE SKY [GHOST RIDERS IN THE SKY] *(Jones)*
Composed by Stan Jones. From the 1949 film, 'Riders In The Sky'. Crossover (pop and C&W) hit in 1949 for Burl Ives (Columbia 38445) and Vaughn Monroe (RCA-Victor 2902). Pop hit in 1949 for Bing Crosby (Decca 24618) and Peggy Lee (Capitol 608).

★ Original by the Sons Of The Pioneers (RCA-Victor 0060) 1949.
◆ *Elvis' sources:* Bing Crosby (Decca 24618) 1949.
Burl Ives (Columbia 38445) 1949.
Peggy Lee (Capitol 608) 1949.
Vaughn Monroe (RCA-Victor 2902) 1949.
Sons Of The Pioneers (RCA-Victor 0060) 1949.

Popular recordings by black artists

BLUE SHADOWS *(Glenn)*
Jam with Rosco Gordon at the Handy Club.
R&B hit in 1950 for Lowell Fulson (Swing-Time 226).

✱ Original by Lowell Fulson (Swing-Time 226) 1950.
◆ *Elvis' source:* Lowell Fulson (Swing-Time 226) 1950.

DRIFTING BLUES *(Brown/Moore/Williams)*
R&B hit in 1946 for Johnny Moore's Three Blazers (Philo 112).

✱ Original by Johnny Moore's Three Blazers (Philo 112) 1946.
◆ *Elvis' sources:*   Johnny Moore's Three Blazers (Philo 112) 1946.
                    Amos Milburn (Aladdin 3038) 1949.

GOLDEN TEARDROPS *(Carter)*

✱ Original by the Flamingos (Chance 1145) 1953.
◆ *Elvis' source:* Flamingos (Chance 1145) 1953.

I HELD MY BABY LAST NIGHT *(James)*
Jam with Rosco Gordon at the Handy Club.
Flip of I BELIEVE, *a R&B hit in 1953 for Elmore James (Meteor 5000).*

✱ Original by Elmore James (Meteor 5000) 1953.
◆ *Elvis' source:* Elmore James (Meteor 5000) 1953.

ROCKET 88 *(Brenston)*
Jam with Rosco Gordon at the Handy Club.
R&B hit in 1951 for Jackie Brenston (Chess 1458).

✱ Original by Jackie Brenston (Chess 1458) 1951.
◆ *Elvis' source:* Jackie Brenston (Chess 1458) 1951.

Gospel songs and spirituals

EZEKIEL SAW DE WHEEL *(Traditional)*
Negro spiritual. Heard in black churches in the South from circa 1890; in white churches from ?

✱ Original by the Biddle University Quintet (Pathe 22400) 1920.
◆ *Elvis' radio sources:* Southernaires (Decca 2858) 1939.
                    EZEKIEL SAW THE WHEEL A-ROLLIN'
                        Jubalaires (Decca 48085) 1944.
                    Dixie Hummingbirds (Apollo 155) 1947.

141

IN THE UPPER ROOM *(Campbell)*
Gospel song composed by Lucie Eddie Campbell in 1947.

✱ Original by Famous Blue Jay Singers Of Birmingham, Alabama (Harlem 1027) 1947.
◆ *Elvis' radio sources:* Famous Blue Jay Singers Of Birmingham, Alabama (Harlem 1027) 1947.
IN THAT UPPER ROOM by Swan's Silvertone Singers (King 4193) 1948.
Gospel Harmonettes (RCA-Victor 0081) 1949.
Fairfield Four (Dot 1015) 1950.
Wings Over Dixie (Tennessee 104) 1951.
Mahalia Jackson (Apollo 262) 1952.

Backstage at Leachville High School Gymnasium, Leachville, Arkansas
Thursday, 20 January 1955 (exact time unknown)
Elvis Presley   Vocal, possibly with guitar or piano

A SONG IN MY SOUL *(Ackley/Smith)*
Gospel song composed by Alfred H. Ackley and Oswald J. Smith.

✱ Original by the Stamps Quartet (Mercury 6080) 1948.
◆ *Elvis' source:* Stamps Quartet (Mercury 6080) 1948.

UNKNOWN TITLES

Backstage at Jimmie Thompson's Arena, Alexandria, Louisiana
Friday, 11 March 1955 (exact time unknown)
Elvis Presley   Vocal, possibly with guitar or piano

WITH A BROKEN HEART *(Pierce)*

✱ Original by the Five Keys (Aladdin 3085) 1951.
◆ *Elvis' source:* Five Keys (Aladdin 3085) 1951.

UNKNOWN TITLES

6.5

Backstage at the Municipal Auditorium, New Orleans, Louisiana
Sunday, 1 May 1955 (evening, exact time unknown)
Elvis Presley   Vocal
Onie Wheeler   Vocal

LITTLE MAMA *(Crowe/Strange)*
Not to be confused with the Clovers song of the same title (Atlantic 1022) 1954.

✱ Original by Onie Wheeler (OKeh 18049) 1954.
◆ *Elvis' source:* Onie Wheeler (OKeh 18049) 1954.

UNKNOWN TITLES

6.6

Backstage at the Casino Club, Plaquemine, Louisiana
Friday, 1 July 1955 (evening, exact time unknown)
Elvis Presley   Vocal, possibly with guitar or piano

BLUES JAM

DON'T THINK 'CAUSE YOU'RE PRETTY *(Hopkins)*

✱ Original by Lightnin' Hopkins (Herald 425) 1954.
◆ *Elvis' source:* Lightnin' Hopkins (Herald 425) 1954.

UNKNOWN TITLES

Backstage at the Memorial Hall, Brownwood, Texas
Monday, 4 July 1955 (evening, exact time unknown)
Elvis Presley   Vocal, possibly with guitar or piano

SWING LOW, SWEET CHARIOT [SWING DOWN, SWEET CHARIOT] *(Traditional)*
Negro spiritual. Heard in black churches in the South from circa 1872; in white churches from circa 1874. Many variants, most notably **SWING DOWN CHARIOT, LET ME RIDE**. *A hit in 1910 for the Fisk University Jubilee Quartet (Victor 16453).*

✱ Original recording on cylinder by the Standard Quartette (Columbia, no number) 1894.
   Original recording on 78 rpm by the Fisk University Jubilee Quartet (Victor 16453) 1910.
◆ *Elvis' radio sources:* Wings Over Jordan Choir (Queen 4154) 1946.
                              Harmonaires (Varsity 5008) 1947.
                              SWING DOWN, CHARIOT by the Golden Gate Quartet (Columbia 37834) 1948.
                              Luvenia Nash Singers (Excelsior 155) 1949.
                              Sister Rosetta Tharpe (Decca 48160) 1950.
                              Bill Monroe (Decca 46325) 1951.

UNKNOWN TITLES

Backstage at the Robinson Auditorium, Little Rock, Arkansas
Wednesday, 3 August 1955 (evening, exact time unknown)
Elvis Presley   Vocal
Charlie Feathers   Vocal and acoustic guitar
Marcus Van Story   Double bass

WILL THE CIRCLE BE UNBROKEN *(Traditional)*
Negro spiritual. Heard circa 1795 in the USA's first black church — St. Thomas' in Philadelphia, founded in 1794 by Absalom Jones; heard in white churches in the East after 1795. The theme was reworked by the Carter Family as **CAN THE CIRCLE BE UNBROKEN** *(Banner 33465) — a hit in 1935 — and was heard thereafter in white churches across the South.*

✱ Original recording on cylinder by an unidentified female group (private collection) 1896.
   First commercial recording on 78 rpm: Rev. J.C. Burnett (Columbia 14385) 1928.
◆ *Elvis' radio sources:* Monroe Brothers (Bluebird 6820) 1936.
                              Roy Acuff (Vocalion 05587) 1940.
                              Roy Acuff (Conqueror 9671) 1941.
                              Swan's Silvertone Singers (Queen 4143) 1946.
                              Eddy Arnold (RCA-Victor 2491) 1947.
                              CAN THE CIRCLE BE UNBROKEN
                              by the Carter Family (Columbia 37669) 1948.
                              Dixieaires (Exclusive 66X) 1948.
                              Eddy Arnold (RCA-Victor 3311) 1949.
                              Paramount Singers (Trilon 235) 1949.

I FORGOT TO REMEMBER TO FORGET *(Kesler/Feathers)*

Song written by Stan Kesler, who recorded a demo of it at the Sun studio on Saturday, 25 June 1955 between 3.00 and 3.30 pm, with himself on fiddle and Charlie Feathers on vocal and acoustic guitar. Feathers subsequently claimed that he had finished off the song and that he should be credited as co-composer. They also recorded a demo of WE'RE GETTING CLOSER TO BEING APART *at the same session. In 1973, Feathers cut a new version of* I FORGOT TO REMEMBER TO FORGET *for his 'Living Legend' LP (Redita 107, Netherlands).*

✱ Original by Elvis, recorded at Sun Studio, Memphis on 11 July 1955 (Sun 223, 1955) [see **4.20** for details].

Backstage at the Community House, Biloxi, Mississippi
Sunday, 6 November 1955 (afternoon, exact time unknown)
Elvis Presley   Vocal, possibly with guitar or piano

UNCHAINED MELODY *(North/Zareth)*

Song from the 1955 film, 'Unchained'. Crossover (pop and R&B) hit in 1955 for Roy Hamilton (Epic 5-9102) and Al Hibbler (Decca 29441). Pop hit in 1955 for Les Baxter (Capitol 3055) and June Valli (RCA-Victor 6078).

✱ Original by Al Hibbler (Decca 29441) 1955.
◆ *Elvis' sources:*   Les Baxter (Capitol 3055) 1955.
                    Don Cornell (Coral 61407) 1955.
                    Crew-Cuts (Mercury 70598) 1955.
                    Roy Hamilton (Epic 5-9102) 1955.
                    Al Hibbler (Decca 29441) 1955.
                    June Valli (RCA-Victor 6078) 1955.
⭕ Elvis later recorded this title at Ann Arbor, Michigan on 24 April 1977 (released in 1977 on LP *Moody Blue*, RCA-Victor AFL1-2428).

Backstage at the Ellis Auditorium, 225 North Main Street, Memphis, Tennessee
Sunday, 13 November 1955 (between 11.00 pm and midnight, exact time unknown)
Elvis Presley   Vocal, possibly with guitar or piano
Carl Perkins   Vocal, possibly guitar

GONE, GONE, GONE *(Perkins)*

✱ Original by Carl Perkins (Sun 224) 1955.
◆ *Elvis' source:* Carl Perkins (Sun 224) 1955.

6.11

**Backstage at the Ellis Auditorium, 225 North Main Street, Memphis, Tennessee
Sunday, 13 November 1955 (between 11.00 pm and midnight, exact time unknown)**
Elvis Presley   Vocal, possibly with guitar or piano
Charline Arthur   Vocal

Elvis sang a jokey version of:

KISS THE BABY GOODNIGHT *(Welch)*

✱ Original by Charline Arthur (RCA-Victor 6204) 1955.
◆ *Elvis' source:* Charline Arthur (RCA-Victor 6204) 1955.

6.12

**On stage at the Ellis Auditorium, 225 North Main Street, Memphis, Tennessee
1955 (exact date and time unknown)**
Elvis Presley (vocal) with the Statesmen Quartet.

*The booklet accompanying the 1994 2-CD 'Amazing Grace' (BMG/RCA 07863-66421-2) contains
a photo of this event, but mistakenly identifies the group as the Blackwood Brothers.*

FARTHER ALONE *(Composer unknown)*
*Hymn composed in 1880 by an unknown Missourian preacher. Heard in white churches in the
South from circa 1880; in black churches from circa 1883. See also* **FARTHER ALONG** [1.1]*.*

✱ Original by Beauty Morris (University of Texas field recording, Austin, Texas) 1941.
  Original commercial release by ?
◆ *Elvis' radio source:* Royal Kings Quartette (Lance 1020) 1950.

JORDAN RIVER
*Negro spiritual. Heard in black churches in the East from circa 1806. Heard in white churches in
the South from circa 1807; in black churches from circa 1865.*

✱ Original by the Elks Quartette
               (Library Of Congress field recording, Phoebus, Virginia, ca.1937-40).
  First commercial recording by ?

JUST A CLOSER WALK WITH THEE *(Composer unknown)*
*Hymn by unknown composer based on the melody of a traditional folk-song. Heard in white and
black churches in the South from circa 1910. C&W hit in 1950 for Red Foley (Decca 14505).*

✱ Original by the Selah Jubilee Singers (Decca 7872) 1941.
◆ *Elvis' radio sources:* Selah Jubilee Singers (Decca 7872) 1941.
                     Sister Rosetta Tharpe (Decca 8594) 1942.
                     Elder Charles Beck (Eagle 104) 1946.

Sister Marie Knight with the Sunset Four (Haven 516) 1946.
Dixie Hummingbirds (Apollo 155) 1947.
Dixieaires (Exclusive 37X) 1948.
Selah Jubilee Singers (Continental 6063) 1948.
Wings Over Jordan Choir (RCA-Victor 0006) 1948.
Red Foley (Decca 'Faith Series' 14505) 1950.
Stamps Quartet (Columbia 20683) 1950.
Wings Over Dixie (Tennessee 103) 1951.
Statesmen Quartet (Statesmen 1023/1024) 1953.
Southern Tones (Duke 207) 1954.

KNOWN ONLY TO HIM *(Hamblen)*
Hymn composed in 1952 by Stuart Hamblen.

✱ Original by Stuart Hamblen (Columbia 21012) 1952.
◆ *Elvis' radio sources:* Stuart Hamblen (Columbia 21012) 1952.
　　　　　　　　　　　　　Statesmen Quartet (Statesmen 1049/1050) 1953.

NEAR THE CROSS *(Traditional)*
Negro spiritual. Heard in the South in black churches from circa 1870; in white churches from ?

✱ Original by Rev. R.A. Harris (Library of Congress field recording, Navasota, TX) 1941.
　First commercial recording by ?
◆ *Elvis' radio sources:* Silveraires (Gotham 637) 1950.
　　　　　　　　　　　　Argo Gospel Singers (Trumpet 163) 1951.

THE OLD WOODEN CHURCH *(Composer unknown)*
Untraced. Perhaps this is an alternative title for **LITTLE WOODEN CHURCH** *or* **OLD COUNTRY CHURCH**.

PRECIOUS MEMORIES *(Composer unknown)*
Hymn. R&B hit in 1948 for Sister Rosetta Tharpe & Marie Knight (Decca 48070).

✱ Original by the Turkey Mountain Singers *[Georgia Yellow Hammers]* (Bluebird 5542) 1928.
◆ *Elvis' radio sources:* Claude Sharpe (Columbia 20014) 1946.
　　　　　　　　　　　　Dixieaires (Lenox 506) 1947.
　　　　　　　　　　　　Roberta Martin Singers (Fidelity 2000) 1947.
　　　　　　　　　　　　Sister Rosetta Tharpe & Marie Knight (Decca 48070) 1948.
　　　　　　　　　　　　Sunshine Boys Quartet (Decca 46228) 1950.
　　　　　　　　　　　　Floyd Tillman (Columbia 20673) 1950.
　　　　　　　　　　　　Johnson Family (Columbia 20838) 1951.
　　　　　　　　　　　　Five Blind Boys Of Mississippi (Peacock 1701) 1952.

6.13

Songs sung informally by Elvis at Sun Studio during 1955 (Marion Keisker's recollections)

COLD, COLD HEART *(Williams)*
Crossover (pop and C&W) hit in 1951 for Hank Williams (MGM 10904). Pop hit in 1951 for Tony Bennett (Columbia 39449), Tony Fontane (Mercury 5693), the Fontane Sisters (RCA-Victor 4274) and Eileen Wilson (Decca 27761). R&B hit in 1951 for Dinah Washington (Mercury 5728).

✱ Original by Hank Williams (MGM 10904) 1951.
◆ *Elvis' sources:*   Tony Bennett (Columbia 39449) 1951.
                      Tony Fontane (Mercury 5693) 1951.
                      Fontane Sisters (RCA-Victor 4274) 1951.
                      Eddie Johnson (Chess 1488) 1951.
                      Dinah Washington (Mercury 5728) 1951.
                      Hank Williams (MGM 10904) 1951.
                      Eileen Wilson (Decca 27761) 1951.

DON'T MENTION MY NAME *(Cooper/White)*

✱ Original by the Ravens (Mercury 70060) 1952.
◆ *Elvis' source:* Ravens (Mercury 70060) 1952.

HEY, MISS FANNIE *(Nugetre)*
Composed by Atlantic's Ahmet Ertegun ('Nugetre' is 'Ertegun' backwards). R&B hit in 1952 for the Clovers (Atlantic 977).

✱ Original by the Clovers (Atlantic 977) 1952.
◆ *Elvis' source:* Clovers (Atlantic 977) 1952.

IF I DIDN'T CARE *(Lawrence)*
Pop hit in 1939 for the Ink Spots (Decca 2286) and in 1954 for the Hilltoppers (Dot 15220).

✱ Original by the Ink Spots (Decca 2286) 1939.
◆ *Elvis' sources:*   Ink Spots (Decca 2286) 1939.
                      Hilltoppers (Dot 15220) 1954.

PLEDGING MY LOVE *(Washington/Robey)*
Crossover (pop and R&B) hit in 1955 for Johnny Ace (Duke 136). Pop hit in 1955 for Teresa Brewer (Coral 61362).

✱ Original by Johnny Ace (Duke 136) 1955.
◆ *Elvis' sources:*   Johnny Ace (Duke 136) 1955.
                      Cowboy Copas (King 1456) 1955.
                      Teresa Brewer (Coral 61362) 1955.
                      Four Lads (Columbia 40436) 1955.
O Elvis later recorded this title at Graceland, Memphis on 30 October 1976 (released in 1977 on LP *Moody Blue*, RCA-Victor AFL1-2428).

RECONSIDER BABY *(Fulson)*
R&B hit in 1954 for Lowell Fulson (Checker 804).

★ Original by Lowell Fulson (Checker 804) 1954.
◆ *Elvis' source:* Lowell Fulson (Checker 804) 1954.
❍ Elvis later recorded this title at the *Million Dollar Quartet* session at Sun Studio, Memphis on 4 December 1956 (released in 1992 on 5-CD box set *The King Of Rock'n'Roll: The Complete 50s Masters*, BMG/RCA 07863 66050-2) and subsequently at RCA Studio B, Nashville on 4 April 1960 (released in 1960 on LP *Elvis Is Back!*, RCA-Victor LPM/LSP-2231). Also live versions at the Bloch Arena, Pearl Harbor in 1961, Las Vegas in 1969 and Madison Square Garden, New York in 1972.

YOU ARE MY SUNSHINE *(Davis/Mitchell)*
A hit in 1941 for Gene Autry (OKeh 06274), Bing Crosby (Decca 3952) and Wayne King (Victor 26767).

★ Original by the Pine Ridge Boys (Bluebird 8263) 1939.
◆ *Elvis' sources:*   Jimmie Davis (Decca 5813) 1940.
　　　　　　　　　　Gene Autry (OKeh 06274) 1941.
　　　　　　　　　　Bing Crosby (Decca 3952) 1941.
　　　　　　　　　　Wayne King (Victor 26767) 1941.
　　　　　　　　　　Gene Autry (Columbia 20047) 1947.

YOU TURN(ED) THE TABLES ON ME *(Alter/Corbell/Smith)*
Song from the 1936 film, 'Sing, Baby, Sing'. A hit in 1936 for Benny Goodman (Victor 25391).

★ Original **YOU TURNED THE TABLES ON ME** by Benny Goodman (Victor 25391) 1936.
◆ *Elvis' sources:*   **YOU TURN THE TABLES ON ME** by Patti Page (Mercury 5098) 1948.
　　　　　　　　　　YOU TURNED THE TABLES ON ME by Lou Welch (Capitol 15044) 1948.

6.14

Songs sung by Elvis backstage and at informal jam sessions in clubs (Handy Club, Flamingo, etc) and other locations in Memphis during 1955 (exact dates unknown)

On some occasions, Elvis sang unaccompanied; on others, he also played guitar or piano, or was accompanied by Scotty and Bill and/or other local musicians like Carl Perkins, Marcus Van Story, Charline Arthur, Charlie Feathers, Rosco Gordon, etc. Naturally, this list makes no pretence at being complete.

Popular recordings by white artists

GOOD DEAL, LUCILLE *(Terry/Miller/Theriot)*

Backstage at Ellis Auditorium.
C&W hit in 1954 for Al Terry (Hickory 1003).

★ Original by Al Terry (Hickory 1003) 1954.
◆ *Elvis' sources:*   Al Terry (Hickory 1003) 1954.
　　　　　　　　　　Werly Fairburn (Capitol 2770) 1954.

HIGH NOON (DO NOT FORSAKE ME) *(Washingon/Tiomkin)*
Backstage at Ellis Auditorium.

Title song from the 1952 film, 'High Noon'. Pop hit in 1952 for Frankie Laine (Columbia 39770) and Tex Ritter (Capitol 2120).

* ✹ Original by Tex Ritter (Capitol 1698) 1951.
* ◆ *Elvis' sources:*   Tex Ritter (Capitol 1698) 1951.
  Frankie Laine (Columbia 39770) 1952.
  Tex Ritter (Capitol 2120) 1952.
* O Elvis sang the opening line in between takes of **GUITAR MAN** at RCA Studio B, Nashville on 10 September 1967 (released in 1997 on 4-CD *Platinum – A Life In Music*, BMG/RCA 67489-2).

I COULDN'T KEEP FROM CRYING *(Robbins)*
Backstage at Ellis Auditorium.

C&W hit in 1953 for Marty Robbins (Columbia 21075).

* ✹ Original by Marty Robbins (Columbia 21075) 1953.
* ◆ *Elvis' source:* Marty Robbins (Columbia 21075) 1953.

INDIAN LOVE CALL *(Friml)*
At home at 1414 Getwell Road.

Song from the Broadway musical, 'Rose Marie', made into a film in 1936. A hit in 1925 for Leo Reisman (Columbia 242) and Paul Whiteman (Victor 19517), in 1937 for Jeanette MacDonald & Nelson Eddy (Victor 4323), in 1938 for Artie Shaw (Bluebird 7746). Crossover (pop and C&W) hit in 1952 for Slim Whitman (Imperial 8156).

* ✹ Original by Leo Reisman (Columbia 242) 1925.
* ◆ *Elvis' sources:*   Jeanette MacDonald & Nelson Eddy (Victor 4323) 1936.
  Artie Shaw – Voc. Tom Pastor (Bluebird 7746) 1938.
  Slim Whitman (Imperial 8156) 1952.

JUKE BOX BLUES *(Copas)*
Backstage at Ellis Auditorium.

* ✹ Original by Cowboy Copas (King 566) 1947.
* ◆ *Elvis' source:* Cowboy Copas (King 566) 1947.

MAKING BELIEVE *(Work)*
Backstage at Ellis Auditorium.

C&W hit in 1955 for Kitty Wells (Decca 29419) and Jimmy Work (Dot 1221).

* ✹ Original by Jimmy Work (Dot 1221) 1954.
* ◆ *Elvis' sources:*   Kitty Wells (Decca 29419) 1954.
  Jimmy Work (Dot 1221) 1954.

THE OLD COUNTRY CHURCH *(Vaughan)*
Backstage at Ellis Auditorium.

Hymn composed by James D. Vaughan, 'the father of Southern gospel'.

* ✹ Original by ?
* ◆ *Elvis' sources:*   Byron Parker (DeLuxe 5022) 1947.
  T. Texas Tyler (4 Star 1403) 1950.
  Cope Brothers (Federal 10028) 1951.

THINKING OF YOU *(Kalmar/Ruby)*

Backstage at Ellis Auditorium.

From the Broadway musical, 'The Five O'Clock Girl'. A hit in 1928 for Harry Archer (Brunswick 3704), Ben Selvin (Columbia 1164) and Nat Shilkret (Victor 20996), and in 1936 for Carlos Molina (Columbia 3122). Featured in the 1950 film, 'Three Little Words'. Pop hit in 1950 for Don Cherry (Decca 27128), Eddie Fisher (RCA-Victor 3901) and Sarah Vaughan (Columbia 38925).

* Original by Nat Shilkret (Victor 20996) 1928.
◆ *Elvis' sources:* Don Cherry (Decca 27128) 1950.
　　　　　　　　　Eddie Fisher (RCA-Victor 3901) 1950.
　　　　　　　　　Sarah Vaughan (Columbia 38925) 1950.

Popular recordings by black artists

ABERDEEN, MISSISSIPPI BLUES *(White)*

Elvis first heard this song as a boy in Shakerag, performed by Bukka White outside Eulysses Mayhorn's grocery store.

* Original by Bukka White (OKeh 05743) 1940.
◆ *Elvis' source:* Bukka White (OKeh 05743) 1940.

ALL NIGHT LONG *(Morganfield)*

Muddy Waters composition based on Arthur 'Big Boy' Crudup's **ROCK ME MAMMA** *(Bluebird 34-0725) 1945.*

* Original by Muddy Waters (Chess 1509) 1952.
◆ *Elvis' source:* Muddy Waters (Chess 1509) 1952.

BAD LUCK BLUES *(Austin)*

Elvis first heard this song as a boy in Shakerag.

* Original by Ma Rainey (Paramount 12081) 1924.
◆ *Elvis' source:* Ma Rainey (Paramount 12081) 1924.

BEALE STREET ON A SATURDAY NIGHT *(Crothers/Moffet)*

* Original by Calvin Boze (Aladdin 3079) 1951.
◆ *Elvis' source:* Calvin Boze (Aladdin 3079) 1951.

BEFORE LONG *(DeBerry)*

* Original by Jimmy & Walter *[Jimmy DeBerry and Walter Horton]* (Sun 180) 1953.
◆ *Elvis' source:* Jimmy & Walter (Sun 180) 1953.

BLUES BEFORE SUNRISE *(Carr/Blackwell)*

* Original by Leroy Carr (Vocalion 02657) 1934.
◆ *Elvis' source:* Leroy Carr (Vocalion 02657) 1934.

THE BLUES COME FALLING DOWN *(Traditional)*
Although purportedly 'traditional', this is in fact a version of Leroy Carr's **PRISON BOUND BLUES** *(Vocalion 1241) 1929.*

✱ Original by Al Hibbler (Atlantic 925) 1951.
◆ *Elvis' source:* Al Hibbler (Atlantic 925) 1951.

BLUES ON CENTRAL AVENUE *(Turner)*

✱ Original by Joe Turner (Decca 7889) 1941.
◆ *Elvis' source:* Joe Turner (Decca 7889) 1941.

BLUE VALENTINE *(Cain/Wilcox/Royal)*

✱ Original by the Solitaires (Old Town 1000) 1954.
◆ *Elvis' source:* Solitaires (Old Town 1000) 1954.

CALL IT STORMY MONDAY [STORMY MONDAY BLUES] *(Walker)*
R&B hit in 1948 for T-Bone Walker (Black & White 122, Capitol 70014), not to be confused with **STORMY MONDAY BLUES** *by Earl Hines – Voc. Billy Eckstine (Bluebird 11567), a crossover (pop and R&B) hit in 1943.*

✱ Original by T-Bone Walker (Black & White 122) 1947.
◆ *Elvis' source:* T-Bone Walker (Black & White 122, Capitol 70014) 1947.

COME BACK BABY *(Ross)*

✱ Original by Doctor Ross (Sun 193) 1953.
◆ *Elvis' source:* Doctor Ross (Sun 193) 1953.

COOL DOWN MAMA *(Lyndell/Woodson)*

✱ Original by Lost John Hunter (4 Star 1492) 1950.
◆ *Elvis' source:* Lost John Hunter (4 Star 1492) 1950.

CRYING ALL NIGHT LONG *(Taub)*

✱ Original by Robert Bland *[Bobby Bland]* (Modern 848) 1951.
◆ *Elvis' source:* Robert Bland (Modern 848) 1951.

DROP DOWN MAMA *(Estes)*
Elvis first heard this song as a boy in Shakerag.

✱ Original by Sleepy John Estes (Champion 50048) 1935.
◆ *Elvis' source:* Sleepy John Estes (Champion 50048) 1935.

FEELIN' GOOD *(Parker)*
R&B hit in 1953 for Little Junior's Blue Flames (Sun 187).

✱ Original by Little Junior's Blue Flames (Sun 187) 1953.
◆ *Elvis' source:* Little Junior's Blue Flames (Sun 187) 1953.

FIVE LONG YEARS *(Boyd)*
R&B hit in 1952 for Eddie Boyd (JOB 1007).

✱ Original by Eddie Boyd (JOB 1007) 1952.
◆ *Elvis' source:* Eddie Boyd (JOB 1007) 1952.

GOODNIGHT, SWEETHEART, GOODNIGHT *(Carter/Hudson)*
Crossover (pop and R&B) hit in 1954 for the Spaniels (Vee-Jay 107). Pop hit in 1954 for Sunny Gale (RCA-Victor 5746) and the McGuire Sisters (Coral 61187). C&W hit in 1954 for Johnnie & Jack (RCA-Victor 5775).

✱ Original by the Spaniels (Vee-Jay 107) 1954.
◆ *Elvis' sources:*   Sunny Gale (RCA-Victor 5746) 1954.
                   Johnnie & Jack (RCA-Victor 5775).
                   McGuire Sisters (Coral 61187) 1954.
                   Ella Mae Morse (Capitol 2800) 1954.
                   Spaniels (Vee-Jay 107) 1954.

GUITAR IN MY HAND *(Brown)*

✱ Original by Clarence 'Gatemouth' Brown (Aladdin 199) 1948.
◆ *Elvis' source:* Clarence 'Gatemouth' Brown (Aladdin 199) 1948.

HEAVENLY FATHER *(McGriff)*
Composed by sixteen year old vocalist/pianist Edna McGriff, who scored a No.4 R&B hit with it in 1952.

✱ Original by Edna McGriff (Jubilee 5073) 1952.
◆ *Elvis' radio sources:*   Edna McGriff (Jubilee 5073) 1952.
                         Castelles (Grand 122) 1954.

HIGHWAY 51 *(Jones)*
Elvis first heard this song as a boy in Shakerag.

✱ Original by Curtis Jones (Vocalion 03990) 1938.
◆ *Elvis' source:* Curtis Jones (Vocalion 03990) 1938.

HOME LAST NIGHT *(Dirty Red)*

✱ Original by Dirty Red (Aladdin 194) 1948.
◆ *Elvis' source:* Dirty Red (Aladdin 194) 1948.

I FEEL SO BAD [FEEL SO BAD] *(Willis)*
R&B hit in 1954 for Chuck Willis (OKeh 7029).

✱ Original by Chuck Willis (OKeh 7029) 1954.
◆ *Elvis' source:* Chuck Willis (OKeh 7029) 1954.
❍ Elvis later recorded this title at RCA Studio B, Nashville on 12 March 1961 (released in 1961 on single RCA-Victor 7880).

I LOVE THE SUNSHINE OF YOUR SMILE *(Hoffman/McDonald)*
Pop hit in 1951 for the Four Knights (Capitol 1587).

✱ Original by the Four Knights (Capitol 1587) 1951.
◆ *Elvis' source:* Four Knights (Capitol 1587) 1951.

I'M SO GLAD *(James)*
Not to be confused with Ida Cox's **I'M SO GLAD** *(Paramount 12965) 1929.*

✱ Original by Skip James (Paramount 13098) 1931.
◆ *Elvis' source:* Skip James (Paramount 13098) 1931.

IT'S RAINING *(Farr)*
Flip of **SO LONG**, *a R&B hit in 1949 for Ruth Brown (Atlantic 879).*

✱ Original by Ruth Brown (Atlantic 879) 1949.
◆ *Elvis' source:* Ruth Brown (Atlantic 879) 1949.

I WANT YOUR PICTURE *(Burnett)*

✱ Original by Howlin' Wolf (RPM 347) 1952.
◆ *Elvis' source:* Howlin' Wolf (RPM 347) 1952.

LEND ME YOUR LOVE *(Chatman)*
Elvis first heard this song as a boy in Shakerag.

✱ Original by Peter Chatman *[Memphis Slim]* (Bluebird 9028) 1942.
◆ *Elvis' source:* Peter Chatman (Bluebird 9028) 1942.

MAMA TALK TO YOUR DAUGHTER *(Lenoir)*
R&B hit in 1955 for J.B. Lenoir (Parrot 809).

✱ Original by J.B. Lenoir (Parrot 809) 1954.
◆ *Elvis' source:* J.B. Lenoir (Parrot 809) 1954.

MERRY CHRISTMAS BABY *(Baxter/Moore)*
R&B hit in 1947, 1948 and 1949 for Johnny Moore's Three Blazers (Exclusive 254).

✱ Original by Johnny Moore's Three Blazers (Exclusive 254) 1947.
◆ *Elvis' sources:*   Johnny Moore's Three Blazers (Exclusive 254) 1947.
                        Johnny Moore's Three Blazers (Exclusive 63X) 1947.
                        Charles Brown (Hollywood 1021) 1954.
○ Elvis later recorded this title at RCA Studio B, Nashville on 16 May 1971 (released in 1971 on LP *Elvis Sings The Wonderful World Of Christmas*, RCA-Victor LSP-4579).

MIDNIGHT SPECIAL *(Traditional)*
Prisoner song thought to have originated at the Texas State Prison Farm at Sugar Land. Popularised by Leadbelly, who recorded his first version of it for the folklorist Alan Lomax at the Louisiana State Penitentiary, Angola, in July 1934. R&B instrumental hit in 1948 for Tiny Grimes (Atlantic 865). Elvis first heard this song as a boy in Shakerag.

✱ Original by Sodarisa Miller (Paramount 12306) 1925.
◆ *Elvis' sources:*   Delmore Brothers (King 514) 1946.
                        Leadbelly (Disc 6043) 1946.

MOVE BABY MOVE *(Emerson)*

✱ Original by Billy 'The Kid' Emerson (Sun 214) 1954.
◆ *Elvis' source:* Billy 'The Kid' Emerson (Sun 214) 1954.

MY GAL IS GONE *(Whittaker)*
Elvis first heard this song as a boy in Shakerag.

✱ Original by Tampa Red (Bluebird 7010) 1937.
◆ *Elvis' source:* Tampa Red (Bluebird 7010) 1937.

MY REVERIE *(Clinton)*
Composition by Larry Clinton based on Debussy's 'Reverie'. A hit in 1938 for Clinton (Victor 26006), Mildred Bailey (Vocalion 04408), Bing Crosby (Decca 2123), Eddy Duchin (Brunswick 8224) and Glenn Miller (Bluebird 7853).

✱ Original by Larry Clinton (Victor 26006) 1938.
◆ *Elvis' sources:*   Larks (Apollo 1184) 1951.
                        Buddy Johnson – Voc. Arthur Prysock (Decca 27567) 1951.
                        Sarah Vaughan (Columbia 39446) 1951.

OLD MAID BOOGIE *(Vinson)*
R&B hit in 1948 for Eddie 'Cleanhead' Vinson (Mercury 8028).

✱ Original by Eddie 'Cleanhead' Vinson (Mercury 8028) 1947.
◆ *Elvis' source:* Eddie 'Cleanhead' Vinson (Mercury 8028) 1947.

PLEASE SEND ME SOMEONE TO LOVE *(Mayfield)*
Crossover (pop and R&B) hit in 1950 for Percy Mayfield (Specialty 375).

✱ Original by Percy Mayfield (Specialty 375) 1950.
◆ *Elvis' sources:*   Percy Mayfield (Specialty 375) 1950.
                        Dinah Washington (Mercury 8231) 1951.

POOR, POOR ME *(Domino)*
R&B hit in 1952 for Fats Domino (Imperial 5197).

✱ Original by Fats Domino (Imperial 5197) 1952.
◆ *Elvis' source:* Fats Domino (Imperial 5197) 1952.

RAINY DAY BLUES *(Lofton)*
Elvis first heard this song as a boy in Shakerag.

✱ Original by Poor Boy Lofton (Decca 7049) 1935.
◆ *Elvis' source:* Poor Boy Lofton (Decca 7049) 1935.

SHOULDN'T I KNOW *(Brothers/Azrael)*
R&B hit in 1951 for the Cardinals (Atlantic 938).

✱ Original by the Cardinals (Atlantic 938) 1951.
◆ *Elvis' source:* Cardinals (Atlantic 938) 1951.

STAGGER LEE [STAGOLEE, STACK O'LEE (BLUES)] *(Traditional)*
Folk-song of black origin first published 1910. Instrumental hit in 1924 for Fred Waring's Pennsylvanians (Victor 19189). Elvis first heard this song as a boy in Shakerag.

✱ Original **STACK O'LEE BLUES** by Fred Waring's Pennsylvanians (Victor 19189) 1923.
◆ *Elvis' sources:*   **STACK O'LEE BLUES** by Ma Rainey (Paramount 12357) 1926.
                        BILLY LYONS AND STACK O'LEE by Furry Lewis (Vocalion 1132) 1927.
                        STACK O'LEE BLUES by Mississippi John Hurt (OKeh 8654) 1929.
◯ Jam recorded during rehearsals at MGM Soundstage, Hollywood on 15 July 1970. Released on bootleg CDs *A Dinner Date With Elvis* (Presto CD-1021) and *Get Down And Get With It* (Fort Baxter 2204).

TAKE A LITTLE CHANCE *(DeBerry/Burns)*

✱ Original by Jimmy DeBerry (Sun 185) 1953.
◆ *Elvis' source:* Jimmy DeBerry (Sun 185) 1953.

TEARDROPS ON MY PILLOW *(Chester/Wolfe)*
Pop hit in 1953 for Sunny Gale (RCA-Victor 5103).

✱ Original by the Orioles (Jubilee 5108) 1953.
◆ *Elvis' sources:*   Sunny Gale (RCA-Victor 5103) 1953.
                        Orioles (Jubilee 5108) 1953.

156

THREE O'CLOCK BLUES [THREE O'CLOCK IN THE MORNING] *(Fulson)*
R&B hit in 1948 for Lowell Fulson (Down Town 2002) and in 1952 for B.B. King (RPM 339).

* ✷ Original by Lowell Fulson (Down Town 2002) 1948.
* ◆ *Elvis' sources:* Lowell Fulson (Down Town 2002) 1948.
                    B.B. King (RPM 339) 1951.

TROUBLE IN MIND *(Jones)*
Elvis first heard this song as a boy in Shakerag.

* ✷ Original by Thelma La Vizzo (Paramount 12206) 1924.
* ◆ *Elvis' sources:* Richard Jones (Bluebird 6563) 1936.
      Georgia White (Decca 7192) 1936.
      Lucky Millinder – Voc. Rosetta Thorpe (Decca 4041) 1942.
      Bertha 'Chippie' Hill (Circle 1003) 1946.
      Bob Wills (Columbia 37306) 1947.
      Duke Henderson (Modern 20-632) 1948.
      Dinah Washington (Mercury 8269) 1952.

YOU DON'T HAVE TO GO *(Reed)*
R&B hit in 1955 for Jimmy Reed (Vee-Jay 119).

* ✷ Original by Jimmy Reed (Vee-Jay 119) 1954.
* ◆ *Elvis' source:* Jimmy Reed (Vee-Jay 119) 1954.

Gospel songs and spirituals

ALL THE WAY *(Traditional)*
Negro spiritual. Heard in black churches in the South from circa 1900; in white churches from ?

* ✷ Original by the Pace Jubilee Singers (Victor 20947) 1927.

AMAZING GRACE *(Newton/Carrell/Clayton)*
English hymn composed in 1779 by reformed slave trader Rev. John Newton; music by James P. Carrell and David S. Clayton added in 1831. Popularised in the USA by the Baptist song leader, Singin' Billy Walker (1809-75). Initially heard in white churches in the East from 1780 onwards. By 1835, it had spread to all churches in the South.

* ✷ Original by the Wisdom Sisters (Columbia 15093) 1926.
* ◆ *Elvis' radio sources:* Dixie Hummingbirds (Apollo 108) 1946.
                    Fairfield Four (Bullet 292) 1948.
                    Mahalia Jackson (Apollo 194) 1948.
* ◉ Elvis later recorded this title at RCA Studio B, Nashville on 15 March 1971 (released in 1972 on LP *He Touched Me*, RCA-Victor LSP-4690).

GO WHERE I SEND THEE *(Traditional)*
Negro spiritual. Heard in black churches in the South from circa 1890; in white churches from ?

* ✷ Original by the Golden Gate Jubilee Quartet (Bluebird 7340) 1937.

HE'S MY ROCK *(Farley/Crain)*
Gospel song composed by Jesse Farley and Senior Roy Crain of the Five Soul Stirrers. Heard in white and black churches in the South from 1939 onwards.

✱ Original by the Five Soul Stirrers (Bronze 102) recorded 1939, released 1945.
◆ *Elvis' radio sources:* Five Soul Stirrers (Bronze 102) 1945.
                       Heavenly Gospel Singers (Manor 1033) 1945.
                       Flying Clouds Of Detroit (Haven 509) 1946.

IN THE MORNING *(Traditional)*
Negro spiritual. Heard in black churches in the South from circa 1880; in white churches from ?

✱ Original by the Fisk University Jubilee Quartet (Victor 16840) 1911.

JUST OVER THE HILL *(Brewster)*
Gospel song composed in 1949 by Rev. W. Herbert Brewster.

✱ Original by Clara Ward (Savoy 4012) 1949.
◆ *Elvis' radio source:* Clara Ward (Savoy 4012) 1949.

LEAD ME ON AND ON *(Traditional)*
Negro spiritual. Not to be confused with the better known **LEAD ME ON***, first recorded in 1932 by the Famous Blue Jay Singers Of Birmingham (Paramount 13135).*

✱ Original by the Golden Gate Jubilee Quartet (Bluebird 7617) 1938.

MILKY WHITE WAY *(Traditional)*
Negro spiritual. R&B hit in 1948 for the Trumpeteers (Score 5001).

✱ Original by ?
◆ *Elvis' sources:* Trumpeteers (Score 5001) 1948.
                 Sister Elizabeth Detharge with the Fisher Brothers (Mercury 8097) 1948.
                 Floyd Dixon (Modern 20-724) 1949.
                 Red Foley (Decca 14553) 1950.
                 Sister Rosetta Tharpe (Decca 48227) 1951.
                 Angelic Gospel Singers (Gotham 717) 1952.
⊙ Elvis later recorded this title at RCA Studio B, Nashville on 30 October 1960 (released in 1960 on LP *His Hand In Mine*, RCA-Victor LPM/LSP-2328).

MY ETERNAL HOME *(Traditional arr. Martin)*
Traditional hymn arranged by Roberta Martin.

✱ Original by the Pilgrim Travelers (Specialty 340) 1949.
◆ *Elvis' source:* Pilgrim Travelers (Specialty 340) 1949.
                 Roberta Martin Singers (Apollo 227) 1950.

MY LORD, WHAT A MORNING *(Traditional)*
Negro spiritual. Heard in black churches in the South from circa 1890; in white churches from ?

✱ Original by Marian Anderson (Victor 19560) 1924.
◆ *Elvis' radio source:* Golden Wing Quartet (Capitol 70020) 1949.

NEAR THE CROSS *(Traditional)*
Negro spiritual. Heard in the South in black churches from circa 1870; in white churches from ?

✱ Original by Rev. R.A. Harris (Library of Congress field recording, Navasota, Texas) 1941.
First commercial recording by ?
◆ *Elvis' radio sources:* Silveraires (Gotham 637) 1950.
Argo Gospel Singers (Trumpet 163) 1951.

NOAH *(Traditional)*
Negro spiritual. Heard in black churches in the South from circa 1868; in white churches from ?

✱ Original by Rev. Hammond
(Library of Congress field recording, Petersburg, Virginia, May 1937).
First commercial recording by the Golden Gate Jubilee Quartet (Bluebird 7962) 1938.
◆ *Elvis' radio sources:* Golden Gate Jubilee Quartet (Bluebird 7962) 1938.
Golden Gate Jubilee Quartet (Bluebird 8160) 1939.
Golden Gate Quartet (Victor 27323) 1941.
Selah Jubilee Quartet (Continental 6029) 1945.
Harmoneers (Queen 4139) 1946.
Coleman Brothers (Manor 1065) 1947.
Fairfield Four (Bullet 318) 1949.
Trumpeteers (Score 5019) 1949.

NOBODY KNOWS THE TROUBLE I'VE SEEN *(Traditional)*
Negro spiritual. Heard in black churches in the South from circa 1865; in white churches from ?
A hit in 1925 for the famed black American contralto, Marian Anderson (Victor 19560).

✱ Original **NOBODY KNOWS THE TROUBLE I SEE** by the Excelsior Quartet (OKeh 4636) 1922.
◆ *Elvis' radio sources:* Dixie Hummingbirds (Apollo 183) 1948.
Mahalia Jackson (Apollo 298) 1954.

ROCK OF AGES *(Toplady/Hastings)*
English hymn. Words written in 1776 by Rev. Augustus M. Toplady; music added in 1830 by Thomas Hastings. Popular in Southern white churches 1832-1940s. Heard in white and black churches in the East from circa 1832. Heard in white churches in the South from circa 1832; in black churches from circa 1865. A hit for Alma Gluck & Louise Homer in 1914 (Victor 87198).

✱ Original by Alma Gluck & Louise Homer (Victor 87198) 1914.
◆ *Elvis' radio sources:* Bing Crosby (Decca 'Faith Series' 14517) 1949.
Sister Jessie Mae Renfro (Peacock 1571) 1951.
Sister Rosetta Tharpe (Decca 14576) 1951.
Brother Rodney (OKeh 6923) 1952.
Joe Warren (Dot 1141) 1952.

STEAL AWAY *(Traditional)*
*Negro spiritual. Many variants (**STEAL AWAY HOME, STEAL AWAY TO JESUS**, etc). Heard in black churches in the East from 1798, after which it spread to white churches in the South. Heard in black churches in the South from circa 1865. A hit for Paul Robeson in 1925 (Victor 19742). C&W hit in 1950 for Red Foley (Decca 'Faith Series' 14505).*

✱ Original recording on cylinder by an unidentified black male quartet (private collection) 1896.
  Original recording on 78 rpm by the Dinwiddie Colored Quartet
                    (Victor 1716 [7-inch], Monarch 1716 [10-inch]) 1902.
◆ *Elvis' radio sources:* Luvenia Nash Singers (Excelsior 147) 1945.
                   Soul Stirrers (Aladdin 2001) 1946.
                   Fairfield Four (Bullet 318) 1949.
                   Red Foley (Decca 'Faith Series' 14505) 1950.

SWEET HOUR OF PRAYER *(Walford/Bradbury)*
Hymn composed in 1845 by the blind English preacher, William W. Walford; music by William B. Bradbury added in 1861. Heard in white and black churches in the South from circa 1898.

✱ Originally recording on cylinder by an unidentified black male quartet (private collection) 1896.
  First commercial recording on 78 rpm by the Trinity Choir (Victor 17013) 1911.
◆ *Elvis' radio sources:* Southernaires (Decca 3919) 1941.
                   Rev. Charles Glover (Gotham 695) 1951.
                   Spirit Of Memphis (Peacock 1734) 1954.

WADE IN THE WATER *(Traditional)*
Negro spiritual. Heard in black churches in the South from circa 1892; in white churches from ?

✱ Original by the Sunset Four (Paramount 12273) 1925.
◆ *Elvis' radio sources:* Golden Gate Quartet (Columbia 37833) 1947.
                   Dixieaires (Sunrise 2117) 1950.
                   Gospel Harmonettes (Specialty 869) 1953.
                   Spiritual Consolers (DeLuxe 6026) 1953.

WALK AROUND *(Harris)*
*Gospel song composed by R.H. Harris, based on **I WANT JESUS TO WALK AROUND MY BEDSIDE** by Lillian M. Bowles.*

✱ Original by the Five Soul Stirrers (Bronze 102) recorded 1939, released 1945.
◆ *Elvis' radio sources:* Wright Brothers Gospel Singers (OKeh 05642) 1940.
                   Five Soul Stirrers (Bronze 102) 1945.

WHEN THE SAINTS GO MARCHING IN *(Traditional)*
Very popular Negro spiritual with many variations. Popularised in the 1940s by Louis Armstrong and Pete Daily. A pop hit in 1939 for Louis Armstrong (Decca 2230), and in 1951 for Percy Faith (Columbia 39528) and the Weavers (Decca 27670).

✱ Original recording on cylinder by an unidentified black male sextet (private collection) 1896.
  Earliest commercial recordings on 78 rpm:
  WHEN ALL THE SAINTS COME MARCHING IN
                   by the Paramount Jubilee Singers (Paramount 12073) 1923.
  WHEN THE SAINTS GO MARCHING IN
                   by the Elkins–Payne Jubilee Singers (OKeh 8170) 1924.
  WHEN THE SAINTS COME MARCHING HOME
                   by Bo Weevil Jackson (Paramount 12390) 1926.

◆ *Elvis' radio sources:* Fiddlin' John Carson & Moonshine Kate (Bluebird 5560) 1934.
Monroe Brothers (Bluebird 6820) 1936.
Golden Gate Jubilee Quartet (Bluebird 7897) 1938.
Louis Armstrong (Decca 2230) 1939.
Delta Boys (Bluebird 8891) 1942.
Coleman Brothers (Manor 1055) 1947.
Golden Gate Quartet (RCA-Victor 2797) 1948.
Chuck Wagon Gang (Columbia 20630) 1949.
Pete Daily (Capitol 15434) 1949.
Five Trumpets (RCA-Victor 0080) 1949.
Golden Echoes (Specialty 331) 1949.
Stars Of Harmony (Swing-Time 288) 1949.
Progressive Four (Mercury 5469) 1950.
Bill Monroe (Decca 46325) 1951.
WHEN THE SAINTS GO MARCHING IN BOOGIE
Dave Bartholomew (Imperial 5273) 1954.

⦿ Elvis recorded this title at the *Million Dollar Quartet* session at Sun Studio, Memphis on 4 December 1956 (released in 1990 on 2-LP/CD *The Million Dollar Quartet*, BMG/RCA 2023-1-R / 2023-2-R). He also made a home recording of it at Audubon Drive, Memphis that same month (released in 1999 on CD *The Home Recordings*, BMG/RCA 07863 67676-2). He also included it in a medley with **DOWN BY THE RIVERSIDE** cut at Radio Recorders, Hollywood on 12-13 May 1965 (released in 1966 on LP *Frankie And Johnny*, RCA-Victor LPM/LSP-3553).

◆ SECTION 7 ◆

Radio, TV & Film 1954-55

This section contains a chronological listing of Elvis' key radio, television and film appearances and recordings during 1954 and 1955. As with other listings in this book, it does not claim to be exhaustive.

At the time they conducted their research (1968-75), Sam Barnes and Graham Metson were unable to access radio station archives for either the *Louisiana Hayride* or *Big D Jamboree*. It is known, however, that these are largely incomplete. Nevertheless, thanks to the efforts of various collectors and researchers, a considerable amount of information has emerged over the years to help complete the picture.

Elvis' first major radio appearance was on WSM's *Grand Ole Opry* on 2 October 1954. He did not go down particularly well with the traditionalist audience and never appeared on the flagship country music show again.

He fared much better with KWKH's *Louisiana Hayride*, appearing no fewer than forty-one times (or possibly forty-two — see **7.27**) between 16 October 1954 and 31 December 1955. The show was broadcast every Saturday evening between 8.00 and 11.30 pm, usually from the Municipal Auditorium in Shreveport, Louisiana, but occasionally from remote locations.

Three of Elvis' *Hayride* performances (5 March 1955, 24 September 1955 and 12 November 1955) were filmed in Kinescope 16 mm for broadcast on KWKH-TV; other shows may also have been filmed. Sadly, all these films are now lost.

Elvis also appeared on KRLD's *Big D Jamboree* five times between 16 April 1955 and 3 September 1955. The show was broadcast every Saturday evening from 8.30 pm until midnight from the Sportatorium in Dallas, Texas. It is not known whether any of his *Big D Jamboree* performances were filmed for television, but a ten-minute 8 mm amateur film exists of his 18 June 1955 show (see *Appendix E*).

Graham Metson's copyright research in Odessa and Midland, Texas disclosed details of Elvis' earliest TV appearances — on two Charline Arthur shows and two Roy Orbison shows. Graham also came across a note suggesting that Elvis may also have appeared on another TV show in Odessa on 16 February 1955. However, it was impossible to draw a firm conclusion as no other details were given, and this appearance has therefore not been listed.

In addition to live broadcasts, Elvis also recorded promotional material for various radio stations in advance of his shows. These sessions were usually informal and unrehearsed, and the choice of titles was spontaneous too. Some were recorded on tape, but the majority were cut 'direct to disc' onto 10-inch acetates running at either 33⅓ or 78 rpm. Others were field recordings cut on mobile recording equipment. All of these recordings are now either lost or secretly held in private collections.

The Poor Richard Show **(KWEM)**
West Memphis, Arkansas
Sunday, 1 August 1954 (exact time unknown)

Elvis Presley	Vocal and acoustic guitar (new Martin D-18)
Scotty Moore	Lead guitar (Gibson ES-295)
Bill Black	Double bass
Presenter	Dick Stuart ('Poor Richard'/'Uncle Richard')

This was Elvis, Scotty and Bill's first professional radio appearance.

BLUE MOON OF KENTUCKY *(Monroe)*
This number started life as a slow country ballad, but developed into something quite different when Elvis, Scotty and Bill decided to speed it up.

✱ Original by Bill Monroe (Columbia 37888) 1947.
◆ *Elvis' source:* Bill Monroe (Columbia 37888) 1947.
○ Elvis recorded this title at Sun Studio, Memphis on 6 July 1954 (Sun 209, 1954) [see **4.7** for details].

THAT'S ALL RIGHT *(Crudup)*

✱ Original by Arthur 'Big Boy' Crudup (RCA-Victor 20-2205) 1947.
◆ *Elvis' sources:* Arthur 'Big Boy' Crudup (RCA-Victor 2205) 1947.
                    Arthur 'Big Boy' Crudup (RCA-Victor 50-0000) 1949.
○ Elvis recorded this title at Sun Studio, Memphis on 5 July 1954 (Sun 209, 1954) [see **4.6** for details].

Grand Ole Opry **(WSM)**
Ryman Auditorium, 116 Fifth Avenue North, Nashville, Tennessee
Saturday, 2 October 1954 (10.15 pm)

Elvis Presley	Vocal and acoustic guitar (new Martin D-18)
Scotty Moore	Lead guitar (Gibson ES-295)
Bill Black	Double bass

This was Elvis' one and only appearance on the famous country music radio show.

BLUE MOON OF KENTUCKY *(Monroe)*
This number started life as a slow country ballad, but developed into something quite different when Elvis, Scotty and Bill decided to speed it up.

✱ Original by Bill Monroe (Columbia 37888) 1947.
◆ *Elvis' source:* Bill Monroe (Columbia 37888) 1947.
○ Elvis recorded this title at Sun Studio, Memphis on 6 July 1954 (Sun 209, 1954) [see **4.7** for details].

Louisiana Hayride (KWKH)
Municipal Auditorium, 705 Grand Avenue, Shreveport, Louisiana
Saturday, 16 October 1954

Elvis Presley	Vocal and acoustic guitar (new Martin D-18)
Scotty Moore	Lead guitar (Gibson ES-295)
Bill Black	Double bass

This was Elvis' first appearance on the 'Louisiana Hayride', and he is also reputed to have met his future drummer D.J. Fontana on this occasion (although some sources state November). He performed **THAT'S ALL RIGHT** *and* **BLUE MOON OF KENTUCKY** *twice during the course of the evening, and Scotty also played a brief instrumental.*

THAT'S ALL RIGHT *(Crudup)*

✱ Original by Arthur 'Big Boy' Crudup (RCA-Victor 20-2205) 1947.
◆ *Elvis' sources:*   Arthur 'Big Boy' Crudup (RCA-Victor 2205) 1947.
        Arthur 'Big Boy' Crudup (RCA-Victor 50-0000) 1949.
O Elvis recorded this title at Sun Studio, Memphis on 5 July 1954 (Sun 209, 1954) [see **4.6** for details].

Issued in 2002 on bootleg CD *The Elvis Broadcasts On Air* (Stardust, no number).

BLUE MOON OF KENTUCKY *(Monroe)*
This number started life as a slow country ballad, but developed into something quite different when Elvis, Scotty and Bill decided to speed it up.

✱ Original by Bill Monroe (Columbia 37888) 1947.
◆ *Elvis' source:* Bill Monroe (Columbia 37888) 1947.
O Elvis recorded this title at Sun Studio, Memphis on 6 July 1954 (Sun 209, 1954) [see **4.7** for details].

Issued in 2002 on bootleg CD *The Elvis Broadcasts On Air* (Stardust, no number).

SITTING ON TOP OF THE WORLD *(Vincson/Chatmon)*
Composition by Walter Vincson and Bo Chatmon/Chatman/Carter. Not to be confused with Frank Crumit's **I'M SITTING ON TOP OF THE WORLD (JUST ROLLING ALONG, JUST ROLLING ALONG)** *(Victor 19928) 1926.*

✱ Original by the Mississippi Sheiks (OKeh 8784) 1930.
◆ *Elvis' sources:*   Mississippi Sheiks (OKeh 8784) 1930.
        Bob Wills (Vocalion 03139) 1935.

Note   *Ernst Jorgensen says he has found no evidence that Elvis performed* **SITTING ON TOP OF THE WORLD** *on this occasion. Perhaps this was the 'brief instrumental' played by Scotty?*

KWKH studio, 509 Texas Street, Shreveport, Louisiana
25-28 October 1954 (radio session, exact date and times unknown)
Elvis Presley   Vocal and acoustic guitar (model unknown)
Scotty Moore   Lead guitar (Gibson ES-295)
Bill Black   Double bass
Bob Sullivan?   Producer and sound engineer

It is not known whether these recordings were made on acetate or tape.

ALWAYS LATE (WITH YOUR KISSES) *(Frizzell/Crawford)*
C&W hit in 1951 for Lefty Frizzell (Columbia 20837).

★ Original by Lefty Frizzell (Columbia 20837) 1951.
◆ *Elvis' source:* Lefty Frizzell (Columbia 20837) 1951.

BLUE GUITAR *(Wooley)*

★ Original by Sheb Wooley (MGM 11717) 1954.
◆ *Elvis' source:* Sheb Wooley (MGM 11717) 1954.

GIVE ME MORE, MORE, MORE (OF YOUR KISSES) *(Price/Frizzell/Beck)*
C&W hit in 1952 for Lefty Frizzell (Columbia 20885).

★ Original by Lefty Frizzell (Columbia 20885) 1951.
◆ *Elvis' source:* Lefty Frizzell (Columbia 20885) 1951.

THAT'S THE STUFF YOU GOTTA WATCH *(Johnson)*
Crossover (pop and R&B) hit in 1945 for Buddy Johnson (Decca 8671).

★ Original by Buddy Johnson – Voc. Ella Johnson (Decca 8671) 1944.
◆ *Elvis' sources:* Buddy Johnson – Voc. Ella Johnson (Decca 8671) 1944.
                    Rubberlegs Williams (Savoy 564) 1945.

Louisiana Hayride (KWKH)
Municipal Auditorium, 705 Grand Avenue, Shreveport, Louisiana
Saturday, 6 November 1954 (9.00–9.30 pm)

Elvis Presley	Vocal and acoustic guitar (new Martin D-18 or a Martin D-28 rented for the occasion)
Scotty Moore	Lead guitar (Gibson ES-295)
Bill Black	Double bass

This was Elvis' second appearance on the 'Louisiana Hayride'.

I'M GONNA SIT RIGHT DOWN AND CRY (OVER YOU) *(Thomas/Biggs)*
Flip of **YOU'LL NEVER WALK ALONE,** *a crossover (pop and R&B) hit in 1954 for Roy Hamilton (Epic 5-9015). Composed by Joe Thomas and Howard Biggs. (NB. This Joe Thomas is not the saxophonist/vocalist Joe Thomas who gained fame with Lunceford's band and went on to record for King, but the brother of Walter 'Foots' Thomas, former musician-turned-agent. He and Biggs, ex-pianist/arranger with Luis Russell and the Ravens, held A&R positions with Victor in the early 1950s, then OKeh, then Decca/Coral. Their other big song was* **GOT YOU ON MY MIND** *(RCA-Victor 4348), a R&B hit in 1951 for Big John Greer, former vocalist/tenor saxophonist with Lucky Millinder.)*

* Original by Roy Hamilton (Epic 5-9015) 1954.
* *Elvis' source:* Roy Hamilton (Epic 5-9015) 1954.
* Elvis later recorded this title at RCA, New York on 31 January 1956 (released in 1956 on LP *Elvis Presley*, RCA-Victor LPM-1254).

FOOL, FOOL, FOOL *(Nugetre)*
Composed by Atlantic's Ahmet Ertegun ('Nugetre' is 'Ertegun' backwards). R&B hit in 1951 for the Clovers (Atlantic 944). Pop hit in 1952 for Kay Starr (Capitol 2151).

* Original by the Clovers (Atlantic 944) 1951.
* *Elvis' sources:* Clovers (Atlantic 944) 1951.
     Kay Starr (Capitol 2151) 1952.

BLUE MOON OF KENTUCKY *(Monroe)*
This number started life as a slow country ballad, but developed into something quite different when Elvis, Scotty and Bill decided to speed it up.

* Original by Bill Monroe (Columbia 37888) 1947.
* *Elvis' source:* Bill Monroe (Columbia 37888) 1947.
* Elvis recorded this title at Sun Studio, Memphis on 6 July 1954 (Sun 209, 1954) [see **4.7** for details].

SITTING ON TOP OF THE WORLD *(Vincson/Chatmon)*
Composition by Walter Vincson and Bo Chatmon/Chatman/Carter. Not to be confused with Frank Crumit's **I'M SITTING ON TOP OF THE WORLD (JUST ROLLING ALONG, JUST ROLLING ALONG)** *(Victor 19928) 1926.*

* Original by the Mississippi Sheiks (OKeh 8784) 1930.
* *Elvis' sources:* Mississippi Sheiks (OKeh 8784) 1930.
     Bob Wills (Vocalion 03139) 1935.

7.6

Louisiana Hayride **(KWKH)**
Municipal Auditorium, 705 Grand Avenue, Shreveport, Louisiana
Saturday, 13 November 1954

Elvis Presley	Vocal and acoustic guitar (model unknown)
Scotty Moore	Lead guitar (Gibson ES-295)
Bill Black	Double bass

This was Elvis' third appearance on the 'Louisiana Hayride'.

UNKNOWN TITLES

7.7

Louisiana Hayride **(KWKH)**
Municipal Auditorium, 705 Grand Avenue, Shreveport, Louisiana
Saturday, 20 November 1954 (8.30–9.00 pm)

Elvis Presley	Vocal and acoustic guitar (model unknown)
Scotty Moore	Lead guitar (Gibson ES-295)
Bill Black	Double bass

This was Elvis' fourth appearance on the 'Louisiana Hayride'.

FOOL, FOOL, FOOL *(Nugetre)*
Composed by Atlantic's Ahmet Ertegun ('Nugetre' is 'Ertegun' backwards). R&B hit in 1951 for the Clovers (Atlantic 944). Pop hit in 1952 for Kay Starr (Capitol 2151).

✱ Original by the Clovers (Atlantic 944) 1951.
◆ *Elvis' sources:* Clovers (Atlantic 944) 1951.
                 Kay Starr (Capitol 2151) 1952.

JUST BECAUSE *(Shelton/Shelton/Robin)*
Crossover (pop and C&W) hit in 1948 for Frankie Yankovic (Columbia 12359), and a pop hit for Eddy Howard (Majestic 1231).

✱ Original by the Lone Star Cowboys *[Shelton Brothers – Bob and Joe]* (Bluebird 6052) 1933.
◆ *Elvis' sources:* Dick Stabile (Decca 716) 1937.
                 Shelton Brothers *[Bob and Joe]* (Decca 5872) 1942.
                 Eddy Howard (Majestic 1231) 1948.
                 Frankie Yankovic (Columbia 12359) 1948.
◯ Elvis recorded this title at Sun Studio, Memphis on 15 September 1954 [see **4.10** for details].

BLUE MOON OF KENTUCKY *(Monroe)*
This number started life as a slow country ballad, but developed into something quite different when Elvis, Scotty and Bill decided to speed it up.

★ Original by Bill Monroe (Columbia 37888) 1947.
◆ *Elvis' source:* Bill Monroe (Columbia 37888) 1947.
О Elvis recorded this title at Sun Studio, Memphis on 6 July 1954 (Sun 209, 1954) [see **4.7** for details].

THAT'S ALL RIGHT *(Crudup)*

★ Original by Arthur 'Big Boy' Crudup (RCA-Victor 20-2205) 1947.
◆ *Elvis' sources:* Arthur 'Big Boy' Crudup (RCA-Victor 2205) 1947.
                             Arthur 'Big Boy' Crudup (RCA-Victor 50-0000) 1949.
О Elvis recorded this title at Sun Studio, Memphis on 5 July 1954 (Sun 209, 1954) [see **4.6** for details].

KSIJ studio, Gladewater, Texas
November 1954 (radio session, exact date and times unknown)

Elvis Presley	Vocal and acoustic guitar (model unknown)
Scotty Moore	Lead guitar (Gibson ES-295)
Bill Black	Double bass
Unknown	Producer/sound engineer

It is not known whether these recordings were made on acetate or tape.

UNKNOWN TITLES

KWKH studio, 509 Texas Street, Shreveport, Louisiana
November 1954 (radio session, exact date and times unknown)

Elvis Presley	Vocal and acoustic guitar (new Martin D-18)
Scotty Moore	Lead guitar (Gibson ES-295)
Bill Black	Double bass
Bob Sullivan?	Producer and sound engineer

This was the first of two sessions recorded at KWKH in November 1954. It is not known whether these recordings were made on acetate or tape.

UNKNOWN TITLES

KWKH studio, 509 Texas Street, Shreveport, Louisiana
November 1954 (radio session, exact date and times unknown)
Elvis Presley   Vocal and acoustic guitar (new Martin D-18)
Scotty Moore   Lead guitar (Gibson ES-295)
Bill Black   Double bass
Bob Sullivan?   Producer and sound engineer

This was the second of two sessions recorded at KWKH in November 1954. It is not known whether these recordings were made on acetate or tape.

UNKNOWN TITLES

Louisiana Hayride (KWKH)
Municipal Auditorium, 705 Grand Avenue, Shreveport, Louisiana
Saturday, 4 December 1954 (10.45 pm)
Elvis Presley   Vocal and acoustic guitar (model unknown)
Scotty Moore   Lead guitar (Gibson ES-295)
Bill Black   Double bass
D.J. Fontana?   Drums?
Others?

This was Elvis' fifth appearance on the 'Louisiana Hayride'.

UNKNOWN TITLES

7.12

Louisiana Hayride (KWKH)
Municipal Auditorium, 705 Grand Avenue, Shreveport, Louisiana
Saturday, 11 December 1954
Elvis Presley   Vocal and acoustic guitar (model unknown)
Scotty Moore   Lead guitar (Gibson ES-295)
Bill Black   Double bass
D.J. Fontana?   Drums?

This was Elvis' sixth appearance on the 'Louisiana Hayride'.

UNKNOWN TITLES

7.13

Louisiana Hayride (KWKH)
Municipal Auditorium, 705 Grand Avenue, Shreveport, Louisiana
Saturday, 18 December 1954

Elvis Presley	Vocal and acoustic guitar (model unknown)
Scotty Moore	Lead guitar (Gibson ES-295)
Bill Black	Double bass
D.J. Fontana?	Drums?

This was Elvis' seventh appearance on the 'Louisiana Hayride'.

BLUE MOON OF KENTUCKY *(Monroe)*
This number started life as a slow country ballad, but developed into something quite different when Elvis, Scotty and Bill decided to speed it up.

✱ Original by Bill Monroe (Columbia 37888) 1947.
◆ *Elvis' source:* Bill Monroe (Columbia 37888) 1947.
○ Elvis recorded this title at Sun Studio, Memphis on 6 July 1954 (Sun 209, 1954) [see **4.7** for details].

THAT'S ALL RIGHT *(Crudup)*

✱ Original by Arthur 'Big Boy' Crudup (RCA-Victor 20-2205) 1947.
◆ *Elvis' sources:*   Arthur 'Big Boy' Crudup (RCA-Victor 2205) 1947.
                 Arthur 'Big Boy' Crudup (RCA-Victor 50-0000) 1949.
○ Elvis recorded this title at Sun Studio, Memphis on 5 July 1954 (Sun 209, 1954) [see **4.6** for details].

HEARTS OF STONE *(Ray/Jackson)*
R&B hit in 1954 for Otis Williams & His Charms (DeLuxe 6062).

✱ Original by the Jewels (R&B 1301) 1954.
◆ *Elvis' sources:*   Fontane Sisters (Dot 15265) 1954.
                 Jewels (R&B 1301) 1954.
                 McGuire Sisters (Coral 61335) 1954.
                 Otis Williams & His Charms (DeLuxe 6062) 1954.

SHAKE, RATTLE AND ROLL *(Calhoun)*
Crossover (pop and R&B) hit in 1954 for Joe Turner (Atlantic 1026). Pop hit in 1954 for Bill Haley (Decca 29124).

✱ Original by Joe Turner (Atlantic 1026) 1954.
◆ *Elvis' sources:*   Bill Haley (Decca 29124) 1954.
                 Joe Turner (Atlantic 1026) 1954.
○ Elvis later recorded this title at CBS-TV studio, New York on 28 January 1956 for the Dorsey brothers' *Stage Show* in medley with **FLIP, FLOP AND FLY** (released in 1984 on 6-LP box set *Elvis: A Golden Celebration*, RCA-Victor CPM6-5172) and subsequently at RCA, New York on 3 February 1956 (released in 1956 on EP *Elvis Presley*, RCA-Victor EPA-830).

171

KWKH studio, 509 Texas Street, Shreveport, Louisiana
December 1954 (radio session, exact date and times unknown)
Elvis Presley   Vocal and acoustic guitar (new Martin D-18)
Scotty Moore   Lead guitar (Gibson ES-295)
Bill Black   Double bass
Bob Sullivan?   Producer and sound engineer

It is not known whether these recordings were made on acetate or tape.

UNKNOWN TITLES

KDAV studio, 6602 Quirt Avenue, Lubbock, Texas
Thursday, 6 January 1955 (radio session: 7.15–7.30 pm)
Elvis Presley   Vocal and acoustic guitar (model unknown)
Scotty Moore   Lead guitar (Gibson ES-295)
Bill Black   Double bass
Unknown   Producer and sound engineer

'Direct-to-disc' recordings onto a 10-inch 78 rpm Presto acetate.

FOOL, FOOL, FOOL *(Nugetre)* 1.52 ⊙
Composed by Atlantic's Ahmet Ertegun ('Nugetre' is 'Ertegun' backwards). R&B hit in 1951 for the Clovers (Atlantic 944). Pop hit in 1952 for Kay Starr (Capitol 2151).

✱ Original by the Clovers (Atlantic 944) 1951.
◆ *Elvis' sources:* Clovers (Atlantic 944) 1951.
                     Kay Starr (Capitol 2151) 1952.

Acetate was incorrectly labelled **WHAT A FOOL I WAS**.

RCA master WPA5-2533. First released in 1992 on 5-CD box set *The King Of Rock'n'Roll: The Complete 50s Masters* (BMG/RCA 07863 66050-2). Reissued in 1999 on 2-CD *Sunrise* (BMG/RCA 07863 67675-2).

SHAKE, RATTLE AND ROLL *(Calhoun)* 2.19 ⊙
Crossover (pop and R&B) hit in 1954 for Joe Turner (Atlantic 1026). Pop hit in 1954 for Bill Haley (Decca 29124).

✱ Original by Joe Turner (Atlantic 1026) 1954.
◆ *Elvis' sources:* Bill Haley (Decca 29124) 1954.
                     Joe Turner (Atlantic 1026) 1954.
❍ Elvis later recorded this title at CBS-TV studio, New York on 28 January 1956 for the Dorsey
  brothers' *Stage Show* in medley with **FLIP, FLOP AND FLY** (released in 1984 on 6-LP box set
  Elvis: A Golden Celebration, RCA-Victor CPM6-5172) and subsequently at RCA, New York on
  3 February 1956 (released in 1956 on EP *Elvis Presley*, RCA-Victor EPA-830).

172

RCA master WPA5-2534. First released in 1992 on 5-CD box set *The King Of Rock'n'Roll: The Complete 50s Masters* (BMG/RCA 07863 66050-2). Reissued in 1999 on 2-CD *Sunrise* (BMG/RCA 07863 67675-2).

Louisiana Hayride (KWKH)
Municipal Auditorium, 705 Grand Avenue, Shreveport, Louisiana
Saturday, 8 January 1955

Elvis Presley	Vocal and acoustic guitar (model unknown)
Scotty Moore	Lead guitar (Gibson ES-295)
Bill Black	Double bass
D.J. Fontana?	Drums?

This was Elvis' eighth appearance on the 'Louisiana Hayride'.

THAT'S ALL RIGHT *(Crudup)*

✱ Original by Arthur 'Big Boy' Crudup (RCA-Victor 20-2205) 1947.
◆ *Elvis' sources:* Arthur 'Big Boy' Crudup (RCA-Victor 2205) 1947.
                 Arthur 'Big Boy' Crudup (RCA-Victor 50-0000) 1949.
❍ Elvis recorded this title at Sun Studio, Memphis on 5 July 1954 (Sun 209, 1954) [see **4.6** for details].

HEARTS OF STONE *(Ray/Jackson)*
R&B hit in 1954 for Otis Williams & His Charms (DeLuxe 6062).

✱ Original by the Jewels (R&B 1301) 1954.
◆ *Elvis' sources:* Fontane Sisters (Dot 15265) 1954.
                 Jewels (R&B 1301) 1954.
                 McGuire Sisters (Coral 61335) 1954.
                 Otis Williams & His Charms (DeLuxe 6062) 1954.

BLUE MOON OF KENTUCKY *(Monroe)*
This number started life as a slow country ballad, but developed into something quite different when Elvis, Scotty and Bill decided to speed it up.

✱ Original by Bill Monroe (Columbia 37888) 1947.
◆ *Elvis' source:* Bill Monroe (Columbia 37888) 1947.
❍ Elvis recorded this title at Sun Studio, Memphis on 6 July 1954 (Sun 209, 1954) [see **4.7** for details].

FOOL, FOOL, FOOL *(Nugetre)*
Composed by Atlantic's Ahmet Ertegun ('Nugetre' is 'Ertegun' backwards). R&B hit in 1951 for the Clovers (Atlantic 944). Pop hit in 1952 for Kay Starr (Capitol 2151).

✱ Original by the Clovers (Atlantic 944) 1951.
◆ *Elvis' sources:* Clovers (Atlantic 944) 1951.
                 Kay Starr (Capitol 2151) 1952.

7.17

Louisiana Hayride **(KWKH)**
Municipal Auditorium, 705 Grand Avenue, Shreveport, Louisiana
Saturday, 15 January 1955

Elvis Presley	Vocal and acoustic guitar (model unknown)
Scotty Moore	Lead guitar (Gibson ES-295)
Bill Black	Double bass
Leon Post	Piano
Sonny Trammell	Pedal steel guitar
Others?	

This was Elvis' ninth appearance on the 'Louisiana Hayride'.

HEARTS OF STONE *(Ray/Jackson)*
R&B hit in 1954 for Otis Williams & His Charms (DeLuxe 6062).

✱ Original by the Jewels (R&B 1301) 1954.
◆ *Elvis' sources:* Fontane Sisters (Dot 15265) 1954.
Jewels (R&B 1301) 1954.
McGuire Sisters (Coral 61335) 1954.
Otis Williams & His Charms (DeLuxe 6062) 1954.

Issued in 2002 on bootleg CD *The Elvis Broadcasts On Air* (Stardust, no number).

THAT'S ALL RIGHT *(Crudup)*

✱ Original by Arthur 'Big Boy' Crudup (RCA-Victor 20-2205) 1947.
◆ *Elvis' sources:* Arthur 'Big Boy' Crudup (RCA-Victor 2205) 1947.
Arthur 'Big Boy' Crudup (RCA-Victor 50-0000) 1949.
⭘ Elvis recorded this title at Sun Studio, Memphis on 5 July 1954 (Sun 209, 1954) [see **4.6** for details].

Issued in 2002 on bootleg CD *The Elvis Broadcasts On Air* (Stardust, no number).

TWEEDLE DEE *(Scott)*
Crossover (pop and R&B) hit in 1954-55 for LaVern Baker (Atlantic 1047). Pop hit in 1955 for Georgia Gibbs (Mercury 70517).

✱ Original by LaVern Baker (Atlantic 1047) 1954.
◆ *Elvis' sources:* LaVern Baker (Atlantic 1047) 1954.
Georgia Gibbs (Mercury 70517) 1955.

First issued in 1999 on 2-CD *Sunrise* (BMG/RCA 07863 67675-2). Also issued in 2002 on bootleg CD *The Elvis Broadcasts On Air* (Stardust, no number) with incorrect date of 22 January 1955.

7.18

WCMA studio, Corinth, Mississippi
Tuesday, 18 January 1955 (radio session: 3.00–3.20 pm)

Elvis Presley	Vocal and acoustic guitar (model unknown)
Scotty Moore	Lead guitar (Gibson ES-295)
Bill Black	Double bass
Unknown	Producer/sound engineer

'Direct-to-disc' recordings onto a 10-inch 78 rpm Presto acetate.

NIGHT TRAIN TO MEMPHIS *(Hughes/Bradley/Smith)* 2.40

✱ Original by Roy Acuff (OKeh 6693) 1943.
◆ *Elvis' sources:*   Roy Acuff (OKeh 6693) 1943.
                          Roy Acuff (Columbia 37029) 1946.
                          Roy Acuff (Columbia 20054) 1947.
❍ Elvis recorded this title at Sun Studio, Memphis on 15 November 1954 (unissued) [see **4.11** for details].

MAMA DON'T ALLOW ME *(Presley/Brown)* 2.28
Popular theme with many variations. Elvis based his interpretation on Milton Brown's.

✱ Original **MAMA DON'T ALLOW NO EASY RIDERS** by Cow Cow Davenport (Vocalion 1434) 1929.
◆ *Elvis' sources:*   **MAMA DON'T ALLOW NO EASY RIDERS** by Cow Cow Davenport (Vocalion 1434) 1929
                          MAMA DON'T ALLOW NO EASY RIDERS HERE by Tampa Red (Vocalion 1429) 1929.
                          MAMA DON'T ALLOW No. 1 by Washboard Sam (Vocalion 03275) 1935.
                          MAMA DON'T ALLOW IT by Milton Brown (Decca 5281) 1936.
                          MAMA DON'T ALLOW IT by Julia Lee (Capitol 1589) 1951.

7.19

***Louisiana Hayride* (KWKH)**
Municipal Auditorium, 705 Grand Avenue, Shreveport, Louisiana
Saturday, 22 January 1955

Elvis Presley	Vocal and acoustic guitar (model unknown)
Scotty Moore	Lead guitar (Gibson ES-295)
Bill Black	Double bass
Leon Post	Piano
Sonny Trammell	Pedal steel guitar

This was Elvis' 10th appearance on the 'Louisiana Hayride'.

MONEY HONEY *(Stone)*
R&B hit in 1953 for the Drifters (Atlantic 1006).

✱ Original by the Drifters (Atlantic 1006) 1953.
◆ *Elvis' source:* Drifters (Atlantic 1006) 1953.
◉ Elvis later recorded this title at RCA, Nashville on 10 January 1956 (released in 1956 on EP *Elvis Presley*, RCA-Victor EPA-821).

Issued in 2002 on bootleg CD *The Elvis Broadcasts On Air* (Stardust, no number).

BLUE MOON OF KENTUCKY *(Monroe)*
This number started life as a slow country ballad, but developed into something quite different when Elvis, Scotty and Bill decided to speed it up.

✱ Original by Bill Monroe (Columbia 37888) 1947.
◆ *Elvis' source:* Bill Monroe (Columbia 37888) 1947.
◉ Elvis recorded this title at Sun Studio, Memphis on 6 July 1954 (Sun 209, 1954) [see **4.7** for details].

Issued in 2002 on bootleg CD *The Elvis Broadcasts On Air* (Stardust, no number).

I DON'T CARE IF THE SUN DON'T SHINE *(David)*
Pop hit in 1950 for Patti Page (Mercury 5396).

✱ Original by Patti Page (Mercury 5396) 1950.
◆ *Elvis' sources:*   Dean Martin (Capitol 981) 1950.
                       Patti Page (Mercury 5396) 1950.
◉ Elvis recorded this title at Sun Studio, Memphis on 15 September 1954 (Sun 210, 1954) [see **4.10** for details].

Issued in 2002 on bootleg CD *The Elvis Broadcasts On Air* (Stardust, no number).

THAT'S ALL RIGHT *(Crudup)*

✱ Original by Arthur 'Big Boy' Crudup (RCA-Victor 20-2205) 1947.
◆ *Elvis' sources:*   Arthur 'Big Boy' Crudup (RCA-Victor 2205) 1947.
                       Arthur 'Big Boy' Crudup (RCA-Victor 50-0000) 1949.
◉ Elvis recorded this title at Sun Studio, Memphis on 5 July 1954 (Sun 209, 1954) [see **4.6** for details].

Issued in 2002 on bootleg CD *The Elvis Broadcasts On Air* (Stardust, no number).

Field recording in Tyler, Texas for KSIJ, Gladewater, Texas
Tuesday, 25 January 1955 (morning, exact time unknown)
Elvis Presley Vocal and acoustic guitar (model unknown)
Scotty Moore Lead guitar (Gibson ES-295)
Bill Black   Double bass
Unknown   Producer/sound engineer

It is not known whether these recordings were made on acetate or tape.

UNKNOWN TITLES

***Louisiana Hayride* (KWKH)**
Municipal Auditorium, 705 Grand Avenue, Shreveport, Louisiana
Saturday, 29 January 1955
Elvis Presley Vocal and acoustic guitar (model unknown)
Scotty Moore Lead guitar (Gibson ES-295)
Bill Black   Double bass

This was Elvis' 11th appearance on the 'Louisiana Hayride'.

UNKNOWN TITLES

7.22

KWKH studio, 509 Texas Street, Shreveport, Louisiana
Saturday, 5 February 1955 (radio session, exact time unknown)
Elvis Presley Vocal and acoustic guitar (original Martin D-28)
Scotty Moore Lead guitar (Gibson ES-295)
Bill Black   Double bass
Bob Sullivan? Producer and sound engineer

It is not known whether these recordings were made on acetate or tape.

UNKNOWN TITLES

7.23

Louisiana Hayride (KWKH)
Municipal Auditorium, 705 Grand Avenue, Shreveport, Louisiana
Saturday, 5 February 1955 (8.30-9.00 pm)

Elvis Presley   Vocal and acoustic guitar (original Martin D-28)
Scotty Moore   Lead guitar (Gibson ES-295)
Bill Black   Double bass
D.J. Fontana?   Drums?

This was Elvis' 12th appearance on the 'Louisiana Hayride'.

TWEEDLE DEE *(Scott)*

Crossover (pop and R&B) hit in 1954-55 for LaVern Baker (Atlantic 1047). Pop hit in 1955 for Georgia Gibbs (Mercury 70517).

★ Original by LaVern Baker (Atlantic 1047) 1954.
◆ *Elvis' sources:* LaVern Baker (Atlantic 1047) 1954.
                     Georgia Gibbs (Mercury 70517) 1955.

THAT'S ALL RIGHT *(Crudup)*

★ Original by Arthur 'Big Boy' Crudup (RCA-Victor 20-2205) 1947.
◆ *Elvis' sources:* Arthur 'Big Boy' Crudup (RCA-Victor 2205) 1947.
                     Arthur 'Big Boy' Crudup (RCA-Victor 50-0000) 1949.
◉ Elvis recorded this title at Sun Studio, Memphis on 5 July 1954 (Sun 209, 1954) [see **4.6** for details].

BLUE MOON OF KENTUCKY *(Monroe)*

This number started life as a slow country ballad, but developed into something quite different when Elvis, Scotty and Bill decided to speed it up.

★ Original by Bill Monroe (Columbia 37888) 1947.
◆ *Elvis' source:* Bill Monroe (Columbia 37888) 1947.
◉ Elvis recorded this title at Sun Studio, Memphis on 6 July 1954 (Sun 209, 1954) [see **4.7** for details].

MONEY HONEY *(Stone)*

R&B hit in 1953 for the Drifters (Atlantic 1006).

★ Original by the Drifters (Atlantic 1006) 1953.
◆ *Elvis' source:* Drifters (Atlantic 1006) 1953.
◉ Elvis later recorded this title at RCA, Nashville on 10 January 1956 (released in 1956 on EP *Elvis Presley*, RCA-Victor EPA-821).

7.24

Louisiana Hayride (KWKH)
Municipal Auditorium, 705 Grand Avenue, Shreveport, Louisiana
Saturday, 19 February 1955

Elvis Presley	Vocal and acoustic guitar (model unknown)
Scotty Moore	Lead guitar (Gibson ES-295)
Bill Black	Double bass
D.J. Fontana?	Drums?

This was Elvis' 13th appearance on the 'Louisiana Hayride'.

UNKNOWN TITLES

7.25

Louisiana Hayride (KWKH)
Municipal Auditorium, 705 Grand Avenue, Shreveport, Louisiana
Saturday, 5 March 1955 (9.00-9.30 pm)

Elvis Presley	Vocal and acoustic guitar (model unknown)
Scotty Moore	Lead guitar (Gibson ES-295)
Bill Black	Double bass
D.J. Fontana?	Drums?

This was Elvis' 14th appearance on the 'Louisiana Hayride'. The show was also filmed for broadcast on KWKH-TV (film lost). Except for the unconfirmed Odessa, Texas show of 16 February 1955 referred to in the introduction to this section, this is Elvis' earliest known television appearance.

TWEEDLE DEE *(Scott)*
Crossover (pop and R&B) hit in 1954-55 for LaVern Baker (Atlantic 1047). Pop hit in 1955 for Georgia Gibbs (Mercury 70517).

✱ Original by LaVern Baker (Atlantic 1047) 1954.
◆ *Elvis' sources:* LaVern Baker (Atlantic 1047) 1954.
　　　　　　　　　Georgia Gibbs (Mercury 70517) 1955.

LITTLE MAMA *(Taylor/Carroll/Ertegun/Wexler)*
R&B hit in 1954 for the Clovers (Atlantic 1022). Not to be confused with the Onie Wheeler song of the same title (OKeh 18049) 1954.

✱ Original by the Clovers (Atlantic 1022) 1954.
◆ *Elvis' source:* Clovers (Atlantic 1022) 1954.

MONEY HONEY *(Stone)*
R&B hit in 1953 for the Drifters (Atlantic 1006).

✱ Original by the Drifters (Atlantic 1006) 1953.
◆ *Elvis' source:* Drifters (Atlantic 1006) 1953.
○ Elvis later recorded this title at RCA, Nashville on 10 January 1956 (released in 1956 on EP *Elvis Presley*, RCA-Victor EPA-821).

SHAKE, RATTLE AND ROLL *(Calhoun)*
Crossover (pop and R&B) hit in 1954 for Joe Turner (Atlantic 1026). Pop hit in 1954 for Bill Haley (Decca 29124).

✱ Original by Joe Turner (Atlantic 1026) 1954.
◆ *Elvis' sources:* Bill Haley (Decca 29124) 1954.
                Joe Turner (Atlantic 1026) 1954.
○ Elvis later recorded this title at CBS-TV studio, New York on 28 January 1956 for the Dorsey brothers' *Stage Show* in medley with **FLIP, FLOP AND FLY** (released in 1984 on 6-LP box set *Elvis: A Golden Celebration*, RCA-Victor CPM6-5172) and subsequently at RCA, New York on 3 February 1956 (released in 1956 on EP *Elvis Presley*, RCA-Victor EPA-830).

Some researchers have claimed that Elvis also performed the following song:

UNCLE PEN *(Monroe)*
Song written by Bill Monroe after his uncle, Pendleton Vandiver.

✱ Original by Bill Monroe – Voc. Bill Monroe & Jimmy Martin (Decca 46283) 1951.
◆ *Elvis' source:* Bill Monroe – Voc. Bill Monroe & Jimmy Martin (Decca 46283) 1951.
○ Elvis recorded this title at Sun Studio, Memphis on 8 December 1954 (unissued) [see **4.12** for details].

Louisiana Hayride **(KWKH)**
Municipal Auditorium, 705 Grand Avenue, Shreveport, Louisiana
Saturday, 12 March 1955

Elvis Presley   Vocal and acoustic guitar (model unknown)
Scotty Moore   Lead guitar (Gibson ES-295)
Bill Black   Double bass
D.J. Fontana?   Drums?

This was Elvis' 15th appearance on the 'Louisiana Hayride'.

UNKNOWN TITLES

7.27

Louisiana Hayride **(KWKH)**
G. Rolle White Coliseum, Texas A&M University, College Station, Texas
Saturday, 19 March 1955

Elvis Presley	Vocal and acoustic guitar (model unknown)
Scotty Moore	Lead guitar (Gibson ES-295)
Bill Black	Double bass
D.J. Fontana?	Drums?

This was Elvis' 16th appearance on the 'Louisiana Hayride' — possibly. Although a poster of this show apparently exists, Ernst Jorgensen is dubious as to its authenticity: it is not corroborated by newspaper ads, the artists listed (Lester Flatt & Earl Scruggs, Little Jimmie [sic] Dickens, Archie Campbell, Wilma Burgess and Debbie Day) did not normally appear on the 'Louisiana Hayride', plus there was a 'Hayride' show in Shreveport that evening as usual. On the other hand, Elvis was in Texas that day and later performed at the Eagles Hall in Houston (see below).

UNKNOWN TITLES

7.28

Grand Prize Saturday Night Jamboree **(KPRC-TV)**
Eagles Hall, Houston, Texas (11.00 pm)
Saturday, 19 March 1955

Elvis Presley	Vocal and acoustic guitar (model unknown)
Scotty Moore	Lead guitar (Gibson ES-295)
Bill Black	Double bass

This show was filmed for broadcast on KPRC-TV (film lost). Some sources state that it was also broadcast by KNUZ.

GOOD ROCKIN' TONIGHT *(Brown)*
R&B hit in 1948 and 1949 for Roy Brown (DeLuxe 1093), and in 1948 for Wynonie Harris (King 4210).

★ Original by Roy Brown (DeLuxe 1093) 1947.
◆ *Elvis' sources:* Roy Brown (DeLuxe 1093) 1947.
Wynonie Harris (King 4210) 1948.
○ Elvis recorded this title at Sun Studio, Memphis on 15 September 1954 (Sun 210, 1954) [see **4.10** for details].

Issued in 1997 on bootleg CD *Elvis Raw* (Out West DRC1-1739). A doctored version of this cut also appeared in 2002 on bootleg CD *The Elvis Broadcasts On Air* (Stardust, no number), incorrectly attributed to a *Louisiana Hayride* show of 19 April 1955 — a Tuesday!

BABY LET'S PLAY HOUSE *(Gunter)*
1955 R&B hit for Arthur Gunter (Excello 2047) based on Eddy Arnold's I WANNA PLAY HOUSE WITH YOU *(RCA-Victor 0476) 1951. Elvis memorably replaced Gunter's lyric 'You may have religion' with 'You may drive a pink Cadillac'.*

✱ Original by Arthur Gunter (Excello 2047) 1954.
◆ *Elvis' source:* Arthur Gunter (Excello 2047) 1954.
◉ Elvis recorded this title at Sun Studio, Memphis on 3 February 1955 (Sun 217, 1955) [see **4.15** for details].

Issued in 1997 on bootleg CD *Elvis Raw* (Out West DRC1-1739).

BLUE MOON OF KENTUCKY *(Monroe)*
This number started life as a slow country ballad, but developed into something quite different when Elvis, Scotty and Bill decided to speed it up.

✱ Original by Bill Monroe (Columbia 37888) 1947.
◆ *Elvis' source:* Bill Monroe (Columbia 37888) 1947.
◉ Elvis recorded this title at Sun Studio, Memphis on 6 July 1954 (Sun 209, 1954) [see **4.7** for details].

Issued in 1997 on bootleg CD *Elvis Raw* (Out West DRC1-1739).

I GOT A WOMAN *(Charles)*
R&B hit in 1955 for Ray Charles (Atlantic 1050).

✱ Original by Ray Charles (Atlantic 1050) 1955.
◆ *Elvis' source:* Ray Charles (Atlantic 1050) 1955.
◉ Elvis recorded this title at Sun Studio, Memphis on 3 February 1955 (unissued) [see **4.15** for details]. He re-recorded it at RCA, Nashville on 10 January 1956 (released in 1956 on LP *Elvis Presley*, RCA-Victor LPM-1254).

Issued in 1997 on bootleg CD *Elvis Raw* (Out West DRC1-1739). A doctored version of this cut also appeared in 2002 on bootleg CD *The Elvis Broadcasts On Air* (Stardust, no number), incorrectly attributed to a *Louisiana Hayride* show of 19 April 1955 — a Tuesday!

THAT'S ALL RIGHT *(Crudup)*

✱ Original by Arthur 'Big Boy' Crudup (RCA-Victor 20-2205) 1947.
◆ *Elvis' sources:*   Arthur 'Big Boy' Crudup (RCA-Victor 2205) 1947.
                       Arthur 'Big Boy' Crudup (RCA-Victor 50-0000) 1949.
◉ Elvis recorded this title at Sun Studio, Memphis on 5 July 1954 (Sun 209, 1954) [see **4.6** for details].

Issued in 1997 on bootleg CD *Elvis Raw* (Out West DRC1-1739).

Audition for *Arthur Godfrey's Talent Scouts* (CBS-TV)
501 Madison Avenue, New York City
Wednesday, 23 March 1955 (Arrival: 2.30 pm. Audition: 2.50–3.10 pm)
Elvis Presley   Vocal and acoustic guitar (model unknown)
Scotty Moore   Lead guitar (Gibson ES-295)
Bill Black   Double bass

It is not known how many songs Elvis performed, or whether the audition was filmed for a screen test. During the 1970s, it was rumoured that he performed **YOU'RE A HEARTBREAKER**, *although this remains unconfirmed.*

UNKNOWN TITLE(S)

***Louisiana Hayride* (KWKH)**
Municipal Auditorium, 705 Grand Avenue, Shreveport, Louisiana
Saturday, 26 March 1955
Elvis Presley   Vocal and acoustic guitar (model unknown)
Scotty Moore   Lead guitar (Gibson ES-295)
Bill Black   Double bass
D.J. Fontana?   Drums?

This was Elvis' 17th appearance on the 'Louisiana Hayride'.

UNKNOWN TITLES

7.31

The Charline Arthur Show (KMID-TV)
[Local TV show for Midland, Texas broadcast on Channel 2]
Aircraft hangar at Odessa–Midland Airport
Filmed Friday, 1 April 1955 (6.00–6.30 pm). Broadcast date unknown.

Elvis Presley	Vocal and acoustic guitar (model unknown)
Scotty Moore	Lead guitar (Gibson ES-295)
Bill Black	Double bass

Show sponsored by the Pioneer Furniture Company, filmed before an audience of approximately 50 in a disused aircraft hangar at Odessa-Midland Airport (film lost). The same hangar was also used by KOSA-TV (Odessa) at this time.

SCRIPT

Announcements and station ID.
Sponsors.
Opening credits.
Introduction by Charline.
Dialogue and jokes.
Song by Charline.
Dialogue.
Charline introduces Elvis & The Blue Moon Boys.
Elvis' first song: **THAT'S ALL RIGHT**.
Dialogue and jokes with Charline.
Sponsors and credit-title TV.
Dialogue.
Song by Charline.
Dialogue.
Elvis' second song: **BLUE MOON OF KENTUCKY**.
Dialogue.
Song by Charline.
Sponsors.
Announcements and closing credits.

THAT'S ALL RIGHT *(Crudup)*

✱ Original by Arthur 'Big Boy' Crudup (RCA-Victor 20-2205) 1947.
◆ *Elvis' sources:* Arthur 'Big Boy' Crudup (RCA-Victor 2205) 1947.
Arthur 'Big Boy' Crudup (RCA-Victor 50-0000) 1949.
◐ Elvis recorded this title at Sun Studio, Memphis on 5 July 1954 (Sun 209, 1954) [see **4.6** for details].

BLUE MOON OF KENTUCKY *(Monroe)*
This number started life as a slow country ballad, but developed into something quite different when Elvis, Scotty and Bill decided to speed it up.

✱ Original by Bill Monroe (Columbia 37888) 1947.
◆ *Elvis' source:* Bill Monroe (Columbia 37888) 1947.
◐ Elvis recorded this title at Sun Studio, Memphis on 6 July 1954 (Sun 209, 1954) [see **4.7** for details].

7.32

Louisiana Hayride **(KWKH)**
City Auditorium, Houston, Texas
Saturday, 2 April 1955 (9.00 pm)

Elvis Presley	Vocal and acoustic guitar (model unknown)
Scotty Moore	Lead guitar (Gibson ES-295)
Bill Black	Double bass
D.J. Fontana?	Drums?

This was Elvis' 18th appearance on the 'Louisiana Hayride'.

LITTLE MAMA *(Taylor/Carroll/Ertegun/Wexler)*
R&B hit in 1954 for the Clovers (Atlantic 1022). Not to be confused with the Onie Wheeler song of the same title (OKeh 18049) 1954.

✱ Original by the Clovers (Atlantic 1022) 1954.
◆ *Elvis' source:* Clovers (Atlantic 1022) 1954.

THAT'S ALL RIGHT *(Crudup)*

✱ Original by Arthur 'Big Boy' Crudup (RCA-Victor 20-2205) 1947.
◆ *Elvis' sources:* Arthur 'Big Boy' Crudup (RCA-Victor 2205) 1947.
  Arthur 'Big Boy' Crudup (RCA-Victor 50-0000) 1949.
○ Elvis recorded this title at Sun Studio, Memphis on 5 July 1954 (Sun 209, 1954) [see **4.6** for details].

YOU'RE A HEARTBREAKER *(Sallee)*
Composition by Jack Sallee. Flip of **WILD HORSES**, *a pop hit in 1953 for Ray Anthony (Capitol 2349). This is not the same song as Jimmy Heap's* **(YOU'RE A) HEARTBREAKER** *(Capitol 2294) 1952.*

✱ Original by Ray Anthony — Voc. Jo Ann Greer (Capitol 2349) 1953.
◆ *Elvis' source:* Ray Anthony — Voc. Jo Ann Greer (Capitol 2349) 1953.
○ Elvis recorded this title at Sun Studio, Memphis on 20 December 1954 (Sun 215, 1954) [see **4.14** for details]. He re-recorded it on 6 March 1955 (unissued) [see **4.16** for details].

SHAKE, RATTLE AND ROLL *(Calhoun)*
Crossover (pop and R&B) hit in 1954 for Joe Turner (Atlantic 1026). Pop hit in 1954 for Bill Haley (Decca 29124).

✱ Original by Joe Turner (Atlantic 1026) 1954.
◆ *Elvis' sources:* Bill Haley (Decca 29124) 1954.
  Joe Turner (Atlantic 1026) 1954.
○ Elvis later recorded this title at CBS-TV studio, New York on 28 January 1956 for the Dorsey brothers' *Stage Show* in medley with **FLIP, FLOP AND FLY** (released in 1984 on 6-LP box set *Elvis: A Golden Celebration*, RCA-Victor CPM6-5172) and subsequently at RCA, New York on 3 February 1956 (released in 1956 on EP *Elvis Presley*, RCA-Victor EPA-830).

7.33

Louisiana Hayride **(KWKH)**
Municipal Auditorium, 705 Grand Avenue, Shreveport, Louisiana
Saturday, 9 April 1955 (9.30 pm)

Elvis Presley	Vocal and acoustic guitar (model unknown)
Scotty Moore	Lead guitar (Gibson ES-295)
Bill Black	Double bass
D.J. Fontana?	Drums?

This was Elvis' 19th appearance on the 'Louisiana Hayride'.

THAT'S ALL RIGHT *(Crudup)*

✱ Original by Arthur 'Big Boy' Crudup (RCA-Victor 20-2205) 1947.
◆ *Elvis' sources:* Arthur 'Big Boy' Crudup (RCA-Victor 2205) 1947.
     Arthur 'Big Boy' Crudup (RCA-Victor 50-0000) 1949.
❍ Elvis recorded this title at Sun Studio, Memphis on 5 July 1954 (Sun 209, 1954) [see **4.6** for details].

I GOT A WOMAN *(Charles)*
R&B hit in 1955 for Ray Charles (Atlantic 1050).

✱ Original by Ray Charles (Atlantic 1050) 1955.
◆ *Elvis' source:* Ray Charles (Atlantic 1050) 1955.
❍ Elvis recorded this title at Sun Studio, Memphis on 3 February 1955 (unissued) [see **4.15** for details]. He re-recorded it at RCA, Nashville on 10 January 1956 (released in 1956 on LP *Elvis Presley*, RCA-Victor LPM-1254).

BLUE MOON OF KENTUCKY *(Monroe)*
This number started life as a slow country ballad, but developed into something quite different when Elvis, Scotty and Bill decided to speed it up.

✱ Original by Bill Monroe (Columbia 37888) 1947.
◆ *Elvis' source:* Bill Monroe (Columbia 37888) 1947.
❍ Elvis recorded this title at Sun Studio, Memphis on 6 July 1954 (Sun 209, 1954) [see **4.7** for details].

7.34

Big D Jamboree **(KRLD)**
Sportatorium, corner of Industrial and Cadix Boulevards, Dallas, Texas
Saturday, 16 April 1955 (8.00 pm)

Elvis Presley	Vocal and acoustic guitar (original Martin D-28)
Scotty Moore	Lead guitar (Gibson ES-295)
Bill Black	Double bass

This was Elvis' first appearance on the 'Big D Jamboree'.

UNKNOWN TITLES

7.35

Louisiana Hayride **(KWKH)**
Heart O'Texas Arena, Waco, Texas
Saturday, 23 April 1955

Elvis Presley	Vocal and acoustic guitar (model unknown)
Scotty Moore	Lead guitar (Gibson ES-295)
Bill Black	Double bass
D.J. Fontana?	Drums?

This was Elvis' 20th appearance on the 'Louisiana Hayride'.

UNKNOWN TITLES

7.36

Louisiana Hayride **(KWKH)**
Gladewater High School, Gladewater, Texas
Saturday, 30 April 1955

Elvis Presley	Vocal and acoustic guitar (model unknown)
Scotty Moore	Lead guitar (Gibson ES-295)
Bill Black	Double bass
Floyd Cramer	Piano
Jimmy Day	Pedal steel guitar

This was Elvis' 21st appearance on the 'Louisiana Hayride'. It is not known whether Floyd Cramer and Jimmy Day played on any titles other than **TWEEDLE DEE***.*

TWEEDLE DEE *(Scott)*
Crossover (pop and R&B) hit in 1954-55 for LaVern Baker (Atlantic 1047). Pop hit in 1955 for Georgia Gibbs (Mercury 70517).

★ Original by LaVern Baker (Atlantic 1047) 1954.
◆ *Elvis' sources:* LaVern Baker (Atlantic 1047) 1954.
　　　　　　　　　　Georgia Gibbs (Mercury 70517) 1955.

RCA master WPA5-2535. First issued in 1992 on 5-CD box set *The King Of Rock'n'Roll: The Complete 50s Masters* (BMG/RCA 07863 66050-2) with recording date incorrectly stated as 18 December 1954. Also issued in 2002 on bootleg CD *The Elvis Broadcasts On Air* (Stardust, no number).

UNKNOWN TITLES

7.37

KWKH studio, 509 Texas Street, Shreveport, Louisiana
April 1955 (radio session, exact date and times unknown)
Elvis Presley   Vocal and acoustic guitar (model unknown)
Scotty Moore   Lead guitar (Gibson ES-295)
Bill Black   Double bass
Bob Sullivan?   Producer and sound engineer

It is not known whether these recordings were made on acetate or tape.

UNKNOWN TITLES

7.38

KWKH studio, 509 Texas Street, Shreveport, Louisiana
April 1955 (radio session, exact date and times unknown)
Elvis Presley   Vocal and acoustic guitar (model unknown)
Scotty Moore   Lead guitar (Gibson ES-295)
Bill Black   Double bass
Bob Sullivan?   Producer and sound engineer

It is not known whether these recordings were made on acetate or tape.

UNKNOWN TITLES

7.39

WXOK studio, Baton Rouge, Louisiana
Monday, 2 May 1955 (radio session: 11.00–11.15 pm)
Elvis Presley   Vocal and acoustic guitar (model unknown)
Scotty Moore   Lead guitar (Gibson ES-295)
Bill Black   Double bass
Unknown   Producer/sound engineer

'Direct-to-disc' recording onto a Soundcraft 10-inch 33⅓ rpm single-sided acetate.

ROCKIN' ROLLIN' MAMA *(Jones)* 2.20

✱ Original by Buddy Jones (Decca 5731) 1939.
◆ *Elvis' source:* Buddy Jones (Decca 5731) 1939.

Two other songs were also recorded at the same session (no details):

UNKNOWN TITLES

7.40

Louisiana Hayride **(KWKH)**
Municipal Auditorium, 705 Grand Avenue, Shreveport, Louisiana
Saturday, 21 May 1955

Elvis Presley	Vocal and acoustic guitar (model unknown)
Scotty Moore	Lead guitar (Gibson ES-295)
Bill Black	Double bass
D.J. Fontana?	Drums?

This was Elvis' 22nd appearance on the 'Louisiana Hayride'.

UNKNOWN TITLES

7.41

Big D Jamboree **(KRLD)**
Sportatorium, corner of Industrial and Cadix Boulevards, Dallas, Texas
Saturday, 28 May 1955 (8.00 pm)

Elvis Presley	Vocal and acoustic guitar (original Martin D-28)
Scotty Moore	Lead guitar (Gibson ES-295)
Bill Black	Double bass

*This was Elvis' second appearance on the 'Big D Jamboree'. The following evening, Elvis performed at another 'Big D Jamboree' concert [see **5.58**]. This concert was not broadcast.*

UNKNOWN TITLES

7.42

The Charline Arthur Show **(KMID-TV)**
[Local TV show for Midland, Texas broadcast on Channel 2]
Aircraft hangar at Odessa–Midland Airport
Filmed Tuesday, 31 May 1955 (6.00–6.40 pm). Broadcast date unknown.

Elvis Presley	Vocal and acoustic guitar (original Martin D-28)
Scotty Moore	Lead guitar (Gibson ES-295)
Bill Black	Double bass

Show sponsored by the Pioneer Furniture Company, filmed before an audience of approximately 50 in a disused aircraft hangar at Odessa-Midland Airport (film lost). The same hangar was also used by KOSA-TV (Odessa) at this time.

SCRIPT

Announcements and station ID.
Sponsors.
Opening credits.
Introduction by Charline.
Dialogue.
Elvis' introduction.
Elvis' first song: **THAT'S ALL RIGHT**.
Sponsors + station ID.
Dialogue.
Song by Charline.
Dialogue + sponsors.
Dialogue.
Elvis' second song: **GOOD ROCKIN' TONIGHT**.
Dialogue.
Song by Charline.
Sponsors + station ID.
Dialogue.
Elvis' third song: **BABY LET'S PLAY HOUSE**.
Dialogue.
Song by Charline.
Sponsors.
Announcements + closing credits.

THAT'S ALL RIGHT *(Crudup)*

★ Original by Arthur 'Big Boy' Crudup (RCA-Victor 20-2205) 1947.
◆ *Elvis' sources:* Arthur 'Big Boy' Crudup (RCA-Victor 2205) 1947.
     Arthur 'Big Boy' Crudup (RCA-Victor 50-0000) 1949.
◉ Elvis recorded this title at Sun Studio, Memphis on 5 July 1954 (Sun 209, 1954) [see **4.6** for details].

GOOD ROCKIN' TONIGHT *(Brown)*
R&B hit in 1948 and 1949 for Roy Brown (DeLuxe 1093), and in 1948 for Wynonie Harris (King 4210).

* ✱ Original by Roy Brown (DeLuxe 1093) 1947.
* ◆ *Elvis' sources:* Roy Brown (DeLuxe 1093) 1947.
                 Wynonie Harris (King 4210) 1948.
* ● Elvis recorded this title at Sun Studio, Memphis on 15 September 1954 (Sun 210, 1954) [see **4.10** for details].

BABY LET'S PLAY HOUSE *(Gunter)*
*1955 R&B hit for Arthur Gunter (Excello 2047) based on Eddy Arnold's **I WANNA PLAY HOUSE WITH YOU** (RCA-Victor 0476) 1951. Elvis memorably replaced Gunter's lyric 'You may have religion' with 'You may drive a pink Cadillac'.*

* ✱ Original by Arthur Gunter (Excello 2047) 1954.
* ◆ *Elvis' source:* Arthur Gunter (Excello 2047) 1954.
* ● Elvis recorded this title at Sun Studio, Memphis on 3 February 1955 (Sun 217, 1955) [see **4.15** for details].

City Auditorium, Amarillo, Texas (KGNC-TV)
Thursday, 2 June 1955 (exact time unknown)

Elvis Presley	Vocal and acoustic guitar (model unknown)
Scotty Moore	Lead guitar (Gibson ES-295)
Bill Black	Double bass
Al Rogers	Announcer

Filmed partly or entirely at the City Auditorium for broadcast on KGNC-TV (film lost).

UNKNOWN TITLES

KDAV studio, Lubbock, Texas
Friday, 3 June 1955 (radio session: 11.30–11.50 pm)

Elvis Presley	Vocal and acoustic guitar (model unknown)
Scotty Moore	Lead guitar (Gibson ES-295)
Bill Black	Double bass
Unknown	Producer/sound engineer

'Direct to disc' recording onto a single-sided 10-inch 78 rpm Presto acetate.

DOWN THE LINE *(Holly/Montgomery)* 2.30
*Rockabilly number written by Buddy Holly and Bob Montgomery. Holly sang it to Elvis on Friday, 3 June 1955. Buddy & Bob recorded a demo of it at the Nesman Studio in Wichita Falls, Texas on Tuesday, 7 June 1955 along with **BABY LET'S PLAY HOUSE.***

* ● Elvis subsequently recorded this title at Sun Studio, Memphis in July 1955 (rehearsal take, erased) [see **4.21** for details].

7.45

Louisiana Hayride (KWKH)
Municipal Auditorium, 705 Grand Avenue, Shreveport, Louisiana
Saturday, 4 June 1955

Elvis Presley	Vocal and acoustic guitar (model unknown)
Scotty Moore	Lead guitar (Gibson ES-295)
Bill Black	Double bass
D.J. Fontana?	Drums?

This was Elvis' 23rd appearance on the 'Louisiana Hayride'.

UNKNOWN TITLES

7.46

KWKH studio, 509 Texas Street, Shreveport, Louisiana
Saturday, 11 June 1955 (radio session, exact time unknown)

Elvis Presley	Vocal and acoustic guitar (model unknown)
Scotty Moore	Lead guitar (Gibson ES-295)
Bill Black	Double bass
Bob Sullivan?	Producer and sound engineer

It is not known whether these recordings were made on acetate or tape.

UNKNOWN TITLES

7.47

Louisiana Hayride (KWKH)
Municipal Auditorium, 705 Grand Avenue, Shreveport, Louisiana
Saturday, 11 June 1955

Elvis Presley	Vocal and acoustic guitar (model unknown)
Scotty Moore	Lead guitar (Gibson ES-295)
Bill Black	Double bass
D.J. Fontana?	Drums?

This was Elvis' 24th appearance on the 'Louisiana Hayride'.

UNKNOWN TITLES

7.48

Big D Jamboree (KRLD)
Sportatorium, corner of Industrial and Cadix Boulevards, Dallas, Texas
Saturday, 18 June 1955 (9.00 pm)

Elvis Presley	Vocal and acoustic guitar (original Martin D-28)
Scotty Moore	Lead guitar (Gibson ES-295)
Bill Black	Double bass
Others?	

This was Elvis' third appearance on the 'Big D Jamboree'.

THAT'S ALL RIGHT *(Crudup)*

✶ Original by Arthur 'Big Boy' Crudup (RCA-Victor 20-2205) 1947.
◆ *Elvis' sources:* Arthur 'Big Boy' Crudup (RCA-Victor 2205) 1947.
　　　　　　　　　Arthur 'Big Boy' Crudup (RCA-Victor 50-0000) 1949.
○ Elvis recorded this title at Sun Studio, Memphis on 5 July 1954 (Sun 209, 1954) [see **4.6** for details].

BABY LET'S PLAY HOUSE *(Gunter)*
1955 R&B hit for Arthur Gunter (Excello 2047) based on Eddy Arnold's **I WANNA PLAY HOUSE WITH YOU** *(RCA-Victor 0476) 1951. Elvis memorably replaced Gunter's lyric 'You may have religion' with 'You may drive a pink Cadillac'.*

✶ Original by Arthur Gunter (Excello 2047) 1954.
◆ *Elvis' source:* Arthur Gunter (Excello 2047) 1954.
○ Elvis recorded this title at Sun Studio, Memphis on 3 February 1955 (Sun 217, 1955) [see **4.15** for details].

UNKNOWN TITLES

7.49

KLEE studio, Houston, Texas
Sunday, 19 June 1955 (radio session: 5.00–5.20 pm)

Elvis Presley	Vocal and acoustic guitar (model unknown)
Scotty Moore	Lead guitar (Gibson ES-295)
Bill Black	Double bass
Unknown	Producer/sound engineer

'Direct to disc' recordings onto a J&S 10-inch 78 rpm acetate.

ROCKIN' DADDY *(Fisher)* 2.26

✶ Original by Sonny Fisher (Starday 179) 1955.
◆ *Elvis' source:* Sonny Fisher (Starday 179) 1955.

TIGER MAN (KING OF THE JUNGLE) *(Louis/Burns)* 2.15
Song written by Joe Hill Louis and Sam Burns (the latter a pseudonym for Sam Phillips). Louis was also the first to cut it (in the spring of 1953), but it was not released at the time. It was subsequently recorded by Rufus Thomas. During one of his August 1970 shows in Las Vegas, Elvis performed **TIGER MAN**, *after which he explained to the audience: 'This is my second record, but not too many people got to heard it.' The flip side of the* **TIGER MAN** *single was to have been* **BLUE MOON**, *recorded on 19 August 1954* [see **4.8**].

✱ Original by Rufus Thomas (Sun 188) 1953.
◆ *Elvis' source:* Rufus Thomas (Sun 188) 1953.
◉ Elvis recorded this title at Sun Studio, Memphis on 5 July 1954 (unissued) [see **4.6** for details]. He re-recorded at NBC-TV studio, Burbank, CA on 27 June 1968 (released in 1968 on LP *Singer Presents Elvis Singing Flaming Star And Others*, PRS 279). Another version dates from a midnight show at the International Hotel, Las Vegas on 25 August 1969 (released in 1969 on 2-LP *Elvis In Person (From Memphis To Vegas/From Vegas To Memphis)*, RCA-Victor LSP-6020).

Louisiana Hayride (KWKH)
Municipal Auditorium, 705 Grand Avenue, Shreveport, Louisiana
Saturday, 25 June 1955

Elvis Presley	Vocal and acoustic guitar (model unknown)
Scotty Moore	Lead guitar (Gibson ES-295)
Bill Black	Double bass
D.J. Fontana?	Drums?

This was Elvis' 25th appearance on the 'Louisiana Hayride'.

BABY LET'S PLAY HOUSE *(Gunter)*
1955 R&B hit for Arthur Gunter (Excello 2047) based on Eddy Arnold's **I WANNA PLAY HOUSE WITH YOU** *(RCA-Victor 0476) 1951. Elvis memorably replaced Gunter's lyric 'You may have religion' with 'You may drive a pink Cadillac'.*

✱ Original by Arthur Gunter (Excello 2047) 1954.
◆ *Elvis' source:* Arthur Gunter (Excello 2047) 1954.
◉ Elvis recorded this title at Sun Studio, Memphis on 3 February 1955 (Sun 217, 1955) [see **4.15** for details].

GOOD ROCKIN' TONIGHT *(Brown)*
R&B hit in 1948 and 1949 for Roy Brown (DeLuxe 1093), and in 1948 for Wynonie Harris (King 4210).

✱ Original by Roy Brown (DeLuxe 1093) 1947.
◆ *Elvis' sources:* Roy Brown (DeLuxe 1093) 1947.
                     Wynonie Harris (King 4210) 1948.
◉ Elvis recorded this title at Sun Studio, Memphis on 15 September 1954 (Sun 210, 1954) [see **4.10** for details].

BLUE MOON OF KENTUCKY *(Monroe)*
This number started life as a slow country ballad, but developed into something quite different when Elvis, Scotty and Bill decided to speed it up.

★ Original by Bill Monroe (Columbia 37888) 1947.
◆ *Elvis' source:* Bill Monroe (Columbia 37888) 1947.
O Elvis recorded this title at Sun Studio, Memphis on 6 July 1954 (Sun 209, 1954) [see **4.7** for details].

WVMI studio, Biloxi, Mississippi
Sunday, 26 June 1955 (6.00–6.30 pm)
Elvis Presley   Vocal and acoustic guitar (model unknown)
Scotty Moore   Lead guitar (Gibson ES-295)
Bill Black   Double bass
Unknown   Producer/sound engineer

It is not known whether these recordings were made on acetate or tape.

UNKNOWN TITLES

Louisiana Hayride **(KWKH)**
Municipal Auditorium, 705 Grand Avenue, Shreveport, Louisiana
Saturday, 2 July 1955
Elvis Presley   Vocal and acoustic guitar (original or new Martin D-28)
Scotty Moore   Lead guitar (Gibson ES-295)
Bill Black   Double bass
D.J. Fontana?   Drums?

This was Elvis' 26th appearance on the 'Louisiana Hayride'.

UNKNOWN TITLES

7.53

KEYS studio, Corpus Christi, Texas
3 July 1955 *or* 16 April 1956 (radio session, exact date/time unknown)
Elvis Presley   Vocal and acoustic guitar (original or new Martin D-28)
Scotty Moore   Lead guitar (Gibson ES-295 if 1955, Gibson L5 if 1956)
Bill Black   Double bass
D.J. Fontana?   Drums?
Unknown   Producer/sound engineer

'Direct to disc' recordings onto a 78 rpm acetate (KEYS acetate #947).

UNKNOWN TITLES

7.54

Louisiana Hayride **(KWKH)**
Municipal Auditorium, 705 Grand Avenue, Shreveport, Louisiana
Saturday, 16 July 1955
Elvis Presley   Vocal and acoustic guitar (new Martin D-28)
Scotty Moore   Lead guitar (Gibson L5)
Bill Black   Double bass
D.J. Fontana?   Drums?

This was Elvis' 27th appearance on the 'Louisiana Hayride'.

I'M LEFT, YOU'RE RIGHT, SHE'S GONE *(Kesler/Taylor)*
Later arrangement of the Stan Kesler-Bill Taylor composition, **YOU'RE RIGHT, I'M LEFT, SHE'S GONE***, popularly known as the 'rockabilly' version.*

✸ Original by Elvis, **MY BABY'S GONE** recorded at Sun Studio, Memphis on 15 November 1954 [see **4.11** for details].
⦾ Elvis subsequently re-recorded the song at a faster tempo on 6 March 1955 (**I'M LEFT, YOU'RE RIGHT, SHE'S GONE**, Sun 217) 1955 [see **4.16** for details].

Issued in 2002 on bootleg CD *The Elvis Broadcasts On Air* (Stardust, no number) with the incorrect date of 15 July 1955.

UNKNOWN TITLES

7.55

Big D Jamboree (KRLD)
Sportatorium, corner of Industrial and Cadix Boulevards, Dallas, Texas
Saturday, 23 July 1955
Elvis Presley   Vocal and acoustic guitar (new Martin D-28)
Scotty Moore   Lead guitar (Gibson ES-295 or Gibson L5)
Bill Black   Double bass

This was Elvis' fourth appearance on the 'Big D Jamboree'.

MYSTERY TRAIN *(Parker/Phillips)*
Elvis' recording is a combination of two Little Junior Parker tunes — the lyrics of **MYSTERY TRAIN** *and the* **LOVE MY BABY** *guitar riff — which were issued back-to-back on Sun 192. Parker's* **MYSTERY TRAIN** *itself was based on the Carter Family's* **WORRIED MAN BLUES** *(Bluebird 6020) 1930.*

✱ Original by Little Junior's Blue Flames (Sun 192) 1953.
◆ *Elvis' source:* Little Junior's Blue Flames (Sun 192) 1953.
❍ Elvis recorded this title at Sun Studio, Memphis on 11 July 1955 (Sun 223, 1955) [see **4.20** for details].

UNKNOWN TITLES

7.56

KSIJ studio, Gladewater, Texas
Wednesday, 10 August 1955 (radio session: 11.00–11.25 am)
Elvis Presley   Vocal and acoustic guitar (new Martin D-28)
Scotty Moore   Lead guitar (Gibson L5)
Bill Black   Double bass
D.J. Fontana   Drums
Unknown   Producer/sound engineer

It is not known whether these recordings were made on acetate or tape.

UNKNOWN TITLES

7.57

Louisiana Hayride (KWKH)
Municipal Auditorium, 705 Grand Avenue, Shreveport, Louisiana
Saturday, 13 August 1955

Elvis Presley	Vocal and acoustic guitar (new Martin D-28)
Scotty Moore	Lead guitar (Gibson L5)
Bill Black	Double bass
D.J. Fontana?	Drums?

This was Elvis' 28th appearance on the 'Louisiana Hayride'.

UNKNOWN TITLES

7.58

Louisiana Hayride (KWKH)
Municipal Auditorium, 705 Grand Avenue, Shreveport, Louisiana
Saturday, 20 August 1955

Elvis Presley	Vocal and acoustic guitar (new Martin D-28)
Scotty Moore	Lead guitar (Gibson L5)
Bill Black	Double bass

This was Elvis' 29th appearance on the 'Louisiana Hayride'.

BABY LET'S PLAY HOUSE *(Gunter)*
1955 R&B hit for Arthur Gunter (Excello 2047) based on Eddy Arnold's **I WANNA PLAY HOUSE WITH YOU** *(RCA-Victor 0476) 1951. Elvis memorably replaced Gunter's lyric 'You may have religion' with 'You may drive a pink Cadillac'.*

✱ Original by Arthur Gunter (Excello 2047) 1954.
◆ *Elvis' source:* Arthur Gunter (Excello 2047) 1954.
❍ Elvis recorded this title at Sun Studio, Memphis on 3 February 1955 (Sun 217, 1955) [see **4.15** for details].

Issued in 2002 on bootleg CD *The Elvis Broadcasts On Air* (Stardust, no number).

MAYBELLENE *(Berry)*
Crossover (pop and R&B) hit in 1955 for Chuck Berry (Chess 1604). R&B hit in 1955 for Jim Lowe (Dot 15407). C&W hit in 1955 for Marty Robbins (Columbia 21446).

✱ Original by Chuck Berry (Chess 1604) 1955.
◆ *Elvis' source:* Chuck Berry (Chess 1604) 1955.

Issued in 2002 on bootleg CD *The Elvis Broadcasts On Air* (Stardust, no number). RCA master WPA5-2536.

THAT'S ALL RIGHT *(Crudup)*

★ Original by Arthur 'Big Boy' Crudup (RCA-Victor 20-2205) 1947.
◆ *Elvis' sources:* Arthur 'Big Boy' Crudup (RCA-Victor 2205) 1947.
                Arthur 'Big Boy' Crudup (RCA-Victor 50-0000) 1949.
⦿ Elvis recorded this title at Sun Studio, Memphis on 5 July 1954 (Sun 209, 1954) [see **4.6** for details].

Issued in 2002 on bootleg CD *The Elvis Broadcasts On Air* (Stardust, no number).

Louisiana Hayride (KWKH)
Municipal Auditorium, 705 Grand Avenue, Shreveport, Louisiana
Saturday, 27 August 1955

Elvis Presley	Vocal and acoustic guitar (new Martin D-28)
Scotty Moore	Lead guitar (Gibson L5)
Bill Black	Double bass
D.J. Fontana	Drums

This was Elvis' 30th appearance on the 'Louisiana Hayride'.

UNKNOWN TITLES

7.60

KWKH studio, 509 Texas Street, Shreveport, Louisiana
August 1955 (radio session, exact date and times unknown)

Elvis Presley	Vocal and acoustic guitar (new Martin D-28)
Scotty Moore	Lead guitar (Gibson ES-295)
Bill Black	Double bass
Bob Sullivan?	Producer and sound engineer

It is not known whether these recordings were made on acetate or tape.

UNKNOWN TITLES

7.61

Big D Jamboree (KRLD)
Sportatorium, corner of Industrial and Cadix Boulevards, Dallas, Texas
Saturday, 3 September 1955 (9.30 pm)

Elvis Presley   Vocal and acoustic guitar (new Martin D-28)
Scotty Moore   Lead guitar (Gibson ES-295)
Bill Black   Double bass

This was Elvis' fifth and last appearance on the 'Big D Jamboree'.

MYSTERY TRAIN *(Parker/Phillips)*

Elvis' recording is a combination of two Little Junior Parker tunes — the lyrics of **MYSTERY TRAIN** *and the* **LOVE MY BABY** *guitar riff — which were issued back-to-back on Sun 192. Parker's* **MYSTERY TRAIN** *itself was based on the Carter Family's* **WORRIED MAN BLUES** *(Bluebird 6020) 1930.*

★ Original by Little Junior's Blue Flames (Sun 192) 1953.
◆ *Elvis' source:* Little Junior's Blue Flames (Sun 192) 1953.
⦾ Elvis recorded this title at Sun Studio, Memphis on 11 July 1955 (Sun 223, 1955) [see **4.20** for details].

I FORGOT TO REMEMBER TO FORGET *(Kesler/Feathers)*

Song written by Stan Kesler, who recorded a demo of it at the Sun studio on Saturday, 25 June 1955 between 3.00 and 3.30 pm, with himself on fiddle and Charlie Feathers on vocal and acoustic guitar. Feathers subsequently claimed that he had finished off the song and that he should be credited as co-composer. They also recorded a demo of **WE'RE GETTING CLOSER TO BEING APART** *at the same session. In 1973, Feathers cut a new version of* **I FORGOT TO REMEMBER TO FORGET** *for his 'Living Legend' LP (Redita 107, Netherlands).*

★ Original by Elvis, recorded at Sun Studio, Memphis on 11 July 1955 (Sun 223, 1955) [see **4.20** for details].

THAT'S ALL RIGHT *(Crudup)*

★ Original by Arthur 'Big Boy' Crudup (RCA-Victor 20-2205) 1947.
◆ *Elvis' sources:*   Arthur 'Big Boy' Crudup (RCA-Victor 2205) 1947.
                     Arthur 'Big Boy' Crudup (RCA-Victor 50-0000) 1949.
⦾ Elvis recorded this title at Sun Studio, Memphis on 5 July 1954 (Sun 209, 1954) [see **4.6** for details].

UNKNOWN TITLES

7.62

Louisiana Hayride (KWKH)
Municipal Auditorium, 705 Grand Avenue, Shreveport, Louisiana
Saturday, 10 September 1955

Elvis Presley	Vocal and acoustic guitar (model unknown)
Scotty Moore	Lead guitar (Gibson ES-295 or L5)
Bill Black	Double bass

This was Elvis' 31st appearance on the 'Louisiana Hayride'.

UNKNOWN TITLES

7.63

Louisiana Hayride (KWKH)
Municipal Auditorium, 705 Grand Avenue, Shreveport, Louisiana
Saturday, 24 September 1955

Elvis Presley	Vocal and acoustic guitar (model unknown)
Scotty Moore	Lead guitar (Gibson ES-295 or L5)
Bill Black	Double bass

This was Elvis' 32nd appearance on the 'Louisiana Hayride'. The show was also filmed for broadcast on KWKH-TV (film lost).

UNKNOWN TITLES

7.64

Field recording in Gobler, Missouri for KBOA, Kennett, Missouri
Wednesday, 28 September 1955 (evening, exact time unknown)

Elvis Presley	Vocal and acoustic guitar (model unknown)
Scotty Moore	Lead guitar (Gibson ES-295)
Bill Black	Double bass
Unknown	Producer/sound engineer

It is not known whether these recordings were made on acetate or tape.

UNKNOWN TITLES

7.65

***Louisiana Hayride* (KWKH)**
Municipal Auditorium, 705 Grand Avenue, Shreveport, Louisiana
Saturday, 1 October 1955
Elvis Presley   Vocal and acoustic guitar (model unknown)
Scotty Moore   Lead guitar (Gibson ES-295 or L5)
Bill Black   Double bass

This was Elvis' 33rd appearance on the 'Louisiana Hayride'.

UNKNOWN TITLES

7.66

***Louisiana Hayride* (KWKH)**
City Auditorium, Houston, Texas
Saturday, 8 October 1955
Elvis Presley   Vocal and acoustic guitar (model unknown)
Scotty Moore   Lead guitar (Gibson ES-295 or L5)
Bill Black   Double bass

This was Elvis' 34th appearance on the 'Louisiana Hayride'.

UNKNOWN TITLES

7.67

Roy Orbison TV show, unknown title (KMID-TV)
[Local TV show for Midland, Texas broadcast on Channel 2]
Aircraft hangar at Odessa–Midland Airport
Filmed Wednesday, 12 October 1955 (4.30–5.00 pm). Broadcast date unknown.
Elvis Presley   Vocal and acoustic guitar (model unknown)
Scotty Moore   Lead guitar (Gibson ES-295)
Bill Black   Double bass

Show filmed in a disused aircraft hangar at Odessa-Midland Airport. The same hangar was also used by KOSA-TV (Odessa) at this time.

MYSTERY TRAIN *(Parker/Phillips)*
Elvis' recording is a combination of two Little Junior Parker tunes — the lyrics of **MYSTERY TRAIN** *and the* **LOVE MY BABY** *guitar riff — which were issued back-to-back on Sun 192. Parker's* **MYSTERY TRAIN** *itself was based on the Carter Family's* **WORRIED MAN BLUES** *(Bluebird 6020) 1930.*

✱ Original by Little Junior's Blue Flames (Sun 192) 1953.
◆ *Elvis' source:* Little Junior's Blue Flames (Sun 192) 1953.
O Elvis recorded this title at Sun Studio, Memphis on 11 July 1955 (Sun 223, 1955) [see **4.20** for details.]

7.68

The Roy Orbison Show (KOSA-TV)
[Local TV show for Odessa, Texas broadcast on Channel 7]
Aircraft hangar at Odessa–Midland Airport
Filmed Friday, 14 October 1955 (4.30–5.00 pm)
Broadcast Saturday, 15 October 1955

Elvis Presley	Vocal and acoustic guitar (model unknown)
Scotty Moore	Lead guitar (Gibson ES-295 or L5)
Bill Black	Double bass

Show sponsored by the Pioneer Furniture Company, Deram's Jewelry, the T.L. Miller Jewelry Store Co. and the local Pontiac dealership in Odessa, filmed before an audience of approximately 60 in a disused aircraft hangar at Odessa-Midland Airport (film lost). The same hangar was also used by KMID-TV (Midland) at this time.

Before the show, Elvis sang Arthur 'Big Boy' Crudup's **SHOUT SISTER SHOUT** *backstage. Johnny Cash, the other guest that day, suggested to Roy that he ought to try his luck at Sun Records, which he subsequently did in March 1956.*

SCRIPT

Announcements and station ID.
Sponsors.
Opening credits.
Introduction by Roy Orbison.
Dialogue.
Sponsors.
Roy talks to Johnny Cash.
Roy introduces Johnny Cash & The Tennessee Two.
Dialogue.
Sponsors.
Roy talks to Johnny Cash.
Johnny Cash's first song: **HEY! PORTER**.
Roy talks.
Sponsors.
Roy talks and introduces Johnny Cash & The
    Tennessee Two.
Johnny Cash's second song: **CRY, CRY, CRY**.
Roy talks.
Sponsors and station ID.
Roy talks and jokes.
Roy introduces Elvis.
Roy talks and jokes with Elvis.
Elvis' first song: **THAT'S ALL RIGHT**.
Roy talks.
Sponsors.
Roy talks to Elvis.
Elvis' second song: **MYSTERY TRAIN**.
Roy talks.
Sponsors.
Roy talks to Elvis & Johnny Cash.
Announcers + sponsors.
Closing credits.
Announcements + closing credits.

THAT'S ALL RIGHT (Crudup)

✱ Original by Arthur 'Big Boy' Crudup (RCA-Victor 20-2205) 1947.
◆ Elvis' sources: Arthur 'Big Boy' Crudup (RCA-Victor 2205) 1947.
                Arthur 'Big Boy' Crudup (RCA-Victor 50-0000) 1949.
◉ Elvis recorded this title at Sun Studio, Memphis on 5 July 1954 (Sun 209, 1954) [see **4.6** for details].

MYSTERY TRAIN (Parker/Phillips)

Elvis' recording is a combination of two Little Junior Parker tunes — the lyrics of **MYSTERY TRAIN** and the **LOVE MY BABY** guitar riff — which were issued back-to-back on Sun 192. Parker's **MYSTERY TRAIN** itself was based on the Carter Family's **WORRIED MAN BLUES** (Bluebird 6020) 1930.

✱ Original by Little Junior's Blue Flames (Sun 192) 1953.
◆ Elvis' source: Little Junior's Blue Flames (Sun 192) 1953.
◉ Elvis recorded this title at Sun Studio, Memphis on 11 July 1955 (Sun 223, 1955) [see **4.20** for details].

The Pied Piper Of Cleveland (A Day In The Life Of A Famous Disc Jockey)
Universal Studios [unreleased film]
Brooklyn High School Auditorium, Cleveland, Ohio
Thursday, 20 October 1955 (1.30–1.50 pm)
Elvis Presley   Vocal and acoustic guitar (new Martin D-28)
Scotty Moore   Lead guitar (Gibson L5)
Bill Black   Double bass

Unreleased 35 mm black-and-white film by Universal Studios. Thirty minutes of film was shot, but was edited down to fifteen minutes. The footage features deejay Bill Randle of WERE (Cleveland), Bill Haley, Pat Boone, the Four Lads and Elvis. A second show at St. Michael's Hall, Cleveland at 8.00 pm was also filmed that evening (no details). It is not known whether drummer D.J. Fontana was present at either.

THAT'S ALL RIGHT (Crudup)

✱ Original by Arthur 'Big Boy' Crudup (RCA-Victor 20-2205) 1947.
◆ Elvis' sources: Arthur 'Big Boy' Crudup (RCA-Victor 2205) 1947.
                Arthur 'Big Boy' Crudup (RCA-Victor 50-0000) 1949.
◉ Elvis recorded this title at Sun Studio, Memphis on 5 July 1954 (Sun 209, 1954) [see **4.6** for details].

BLUE MOON OF KENTUCKY (Monroe)

This number started life as a slow country ballad, but developed into something quite different when Elvis, Scotty and Bill decided to speed it up.

✱ Original by Bill Monroe (Columbia 37888) 1947.
◆ Elvis' source: Bill Monroe (Columbia 37888) 1947.
◉ Elvis recorded this title at Sun Studio, Memphis on 6 July 1954 (Sun 209, 1954) [see **4.7** for details].

GOOD ROCKIN' TONIGHT *(Brown)*
R&B hit in 1948 and 1949 for Roy Brown (DeLuxe 1093), and in 1948 for Wynonie Harris (King 4210).

* ★ Original by Roy Brown (DeLuxe 1093) 1947.
* ◆ *Elvis' sources:*   Roy Brown (DeLuxe 1093) 1947.
                       Wynonie Harris (King 4210) 1948.
* ⊙ Elvis recorded this title at Sun Studio, Memphis on 15 September 1954 (Sun 210, 1954) [see **4.10** for details].

I FORGOT TO REMEMBER TO FORGET *(Kesler/Feathers)*
Song written by Stan Kesler, who recorded a demo of it at the Sun studio on Saturday, 25 June 1955 between 3.00 and 3.30 pm, with himself on fiddle and Charlie Feathers on vocal and acoustic guitar. Feathers subsequently claimed that he had finished off the song and that he should be credited as co-composer. They also recorded a demo of **WE'RE GETTING CLOSER TO BEING APART** *at the same session. In 1973, Feathers cut a new version of* **I FORGOT TO REMEMBER TO FORGET** *for his 'Living Legend' LP (Redita 107, Netherlands).*

* ★ Original by Elvis, recorded at Sun Studio, Memphis on 11 July 1955 (Sun 223, 1955) [see **4.20** for details].

MYSTERY TRAIN *(Parker/Phillips)*
Elvis' recording is a combination of two Little Junior Parker tunes — the lyrics of **MYSTERY TRAIN** *and the* **LOVE MY BABY** *guitar riff — which were issued back-to-back on Sun 192. Parker's* **MYSTERY TRAIN** *itself was based on the Carter Family's* **WORRIED MAN BLUES** *(Bluebird 6020) 1930.*

* ★ Original by Little Junior's Blue Flames (Sun 192) 1953.
* ◆ *Elvis' source:* Little Junior's Blue Flames (Sun 192) 1953.
* ⊙ Elvis recorded this title at Sun Studio, Memphis on 11 July 1955 (Sun 223, 1955) [see **4.20** for details].

Louisiana Hayride **(KWKH)**
Municipal Auditorium, 705 Grand Avenue, Shreveport, Louisiana
Saturday, 29 October 1955

Elvis Presley   Vocal and acoustic guitar (new Martin D-28)
Scotty Moore   Lead guitar (Gibson ES-295)
Bill Black   Double bass
D.J. Fontana   Drums
Others?

This was Elvis' 35th appearance on the 'Louisiana Hayride'.

UNKNOWN TITLES

7.71

Louisiana Hayride **(KWKH)**
Municipal Auditorium, 705 Grand Avenue, Shreveport, Louisiana
Saturday, 5 November 1955

Elvis Presley	Vocal and acoustic guitar (new Martin D-28)
Scotty Moore	Lead guitar (Gibson L5)
Bill Black	Double bass
D.J. Fontana	Drums

This was Elvis' 36th appearance on the 'Louisiana Hayride'.

UNKNOWN TITLES

7.72

WVMI studio, Biloxi, Mississippi
Sunday, 6 November 1955 (radio session: 4.45–5.10 pm)

Elvis Presley	Vocal and acoustic guitar (new Martin D-28)
Scotty Moore	Lead guitar (Gibson L5)
Bill Black	Double bass
D.J. Fontana	Drums
Unknown	Producer/sound engineer

It is not known whether these recordings were made on acetate or tape.

UNKNOWN TITLES

7.73

Louisiana Hayride **(KWKH)**
Municipal Auditorium, 705 Grand Avenue, Shreveport, Louisiana
Saturday, 12 November 1955

Elvis Presley	Vocal and acoustic guitar (new Martin D-28)
Scotty Moore	Lead guitar (Gibson L5)
Bill Black	Double bass
D.J. Fontana	Drums

This was Elvis' 37th appearance on the 'Louisiana Hayride'. The show was also filmed for broadcast on KWKH-TV (film lost).

UNKNOWN TITLES

7.74

Louisiana Hayride **(KWKH)**
Gladewater High School, Gladewater, Texas
Saturday, 19 November 1955

Elvis Presley	Vocal and acoustic guitar (new Martin D-28)
Scotty Moore	Lead guitar (Gibson L5)
Bill Black	Double bass
D.J. Fontana	Drums

This was Elvis' 38th appearance on the 'Louisiana Hayride'.

BABY LET'S PLAY HOUSE *(Gunter)*
1955 R&B hit for Arthur Gunter (Excello 2047) based on Eddy Arnold's **I WANNA PLAY HOUSE WITH YOU** *(RCA-Victor 0476) 1951. Elvis memorably replaced Gunter's lyric 'You may have religion' with 'You may drive a pink Cadillac'.*

✱ Original by Arthur Gunter (Excello 2047) 1954.
◆ *Elvis' source:* Arthur Gunter (Excello 2047) 1954.
○ Elvis recorded this title at Sun Studio, Memphis on 3 February 1955 (Sun 217, 1955) [see **4.15** for details].

THAT'S ALL RIGHT *(Crudup)*

✱ Original by Arthur 'Big Boy' Crudup (RCA-Victor 20-2205) 1947.
◆ *Elvis' sources:* Arthur 'Big Boy' Crudup (RCA-Victor 2205) 1947.
　　　　　　　　　Arthur 'Big Boy' Crudup (RCA-Victor 50-0000) 1949.
○ Elvis recorded this title at Sun Studio, Memphis on 5 July 1954 (Sun 209, 1954) [see **4.6** for details].

ROCK AROUND THE CLOCK *(DeKnight/Freeman)*
Pop hit in 1954 for Bill Haley (Decca 29124), which became a crossover hit (pop and R&B) when reissued in 1955.

✱ Original by Sonny Dae (Arcade 123) 1953.
◆ *Elvis' source:* Bill Haley (Decca 29124) 1954.

7.75

Louisiana Hayride **(KWKH)**
Municipal Auditorium, 705 Grand Avenue, Shreveport, Louisiana
Saturday, 26 November 1955

Elvis Presley	Vocal and acoustic guitar (new Martin D-28)
Scotty Moore	Lead guitar (Gibson L5)
Bill Black	Double bass
D.J. Fontana	Drums

This was Elvis' 39th appearance on the 'Louisiana Hayride'.

UNKNOWN TITLES

7.76

KWKH studio, 509 Texas Street, Shreveport, Louisiana
November 1955 (radio session, exact date and times unknown)
Elvis Presley   Vocal and acoustic guitar (new Martin D-28)
Scotty Moore   Lead guitar (Gibson L5)
Bill Black   Double bass
D.J. Fontana   Drums
Bob Sullivan?   Producer and sound engineer

It is not known whether these recordings were made on acetate or tape.

UNKNOWN TITLES

7.77

Louisiana Hayride **(KWKH)**
Municipal Auditorium, 705 Grand Avenue, Shreveport, Louisiana
Saturday, 10 December 1955
Elvis Presley   Vocal and acoustic guitar (new Martin D-28)
Scotty Moore   Lead guitar (Gibson L5)
Bill Black   Double bass
D.J. Fontana   Drums

This was Elvis' 40th appearance on the 'Louisiana Hayride'.

UNKNOWN TITLES

7.78

KWKH studio, 509 Texas Street, Shreveport, Louisiana
17 December 1955 (radio session, exact time unknown)
Elvis Presley   Vocal and acoustic guitar (new Martin D-28)
Scotty Moore   Lead guitar (Gibson L5)
Bill Black   Double bass
D.J. Fontana   Drums
Bob Sullivan?   Producer and sound engineer

It is not known whether these recordings were made on acetate or tape.

UNKNOWN TITLES

7.79

Louisiana Hayride (KWKH)
Municipal Auditorium, 705 Grand Avenue, Shreveport, Louisiana
Saturday, 17 December 1955

Elvis Presley	Vocal and acoustic guitar (new Martin D-28)
Scotty Moore	Lead guitar (Gibson L5)
Bill Black	Double bass
D.J. Fontana	Drums

This was Elvis' 41st appearance on the 'Louisiana Hayride'.

BABY LET'S PLAY HOUSE *(Gunter)*
1955 R&B hit for Arthur Gunter (Excello 2047) based on Eddy Arnold's **I WANNA PLAY HOUSE WITH YOU** *(RCA-Victor 0476) 1951. Elvis memorably replaced Gunter's lyric 'You may have religion' with 'You may drive a pink Cadillac'.*

★ Original by Arthur Gunter (Excello 2047) 1954.
◆ *Elvis' source:* Arthur Gunter (Excello 2047) 1954.
○ Elvis recorded this title at Sun Studio, Memphis on 3 February 1955 (Sun 217, 1955) [see **4.15** for details].

SIXTEEN TONS *(Travis)*
Crossover hit (pop and C&W) in 1955 for Tennessee Ernie Ford (Capitol 3262), and also a pop hit that same year for Johnny Desmond (Coral 61529).

★ Original by Merle Travis (78 rpm 4-disc album *Folk Songs Of The Hills*, Capitol AD-50) 1947.
◆ *Elvis' sources:* Johnny Desmond (Coral 61529) 1955.
　　　　　　　　Tennessee Ernie Ford (Capitol 3262) 1955.
　　　　　　　　B.B. King (RPM 451) 1955.

ONLY YOU *(Ram/Rand)*
Crossover (pop and R&B) hit in 1955 for the Platters (Mercury 70633). Pop hit in 1955 for the Hilltoppers (Dot 15423).

★ Original by the Platters (Federal 12244) 1955.
◆ *Elvis' sources:* Billy Eckstine (MGM 11984) 1955.
　　　　　　　　Platters (Mercury 70633) 1955.
　　　　　　　　Hilltoppers (Dot 15423) 1955.

I GOT A WOMAN *(Charles)*
R&B hit in 1955 for Ray Charles (Atlantic 1050).

★ Original by Ray Charles (Atlantic 1050) 1955.
◆ *Elvis' source:* Ray Charles (Atlantic 1050) 1955.
○ Elvis recorded this title at Sun Studio, Memphis on 3 February 1955 (unissued) [see **4.15** for details]. He re-recorded it at RCA, Nashville on 10 January 1956 (released in 1956 on LP *Elvis Presley*, RCA-Victor LPM-1254).

TUTTI FRUTTI *(LaBostrie/Penniman)*
Crossover (pop and R&B) hit in 1955-56 for Little Richard (Specialty 561).

★ Original by Little Richard (Specialty 561) 1955.
◆ *Elvis' source:* Little Richard (Specialty 561) 1955.

THAT'S ALL RIGHT *(Crudup)*

★ Original by Arthur 'Big Boy' Crudup (RCA-Victor 20-2205) 1947.
◆ *Elvis' sources:*   Arthur 'Big Boy' Crudup (RCA-Victor 2205) 1947.
                    Arthur 'Big Boy' Crudup (RCA-Victor 50-0000) 1949.
❍ Elvis recorded this title at Sun Studio, Memphis on 5 July 1954 (Sun 209, 1954) [see **4.6** for details].

Louisiana Hayride **(KWKH)**
Municipal Auditorium, 705 Grand Avenue, Shreveport, Louisiana
Saturday, 31 December 1955

Elvis Presley	Vocal and acoustic guitar (new Martin D-28)
Scotty Moore	Lead guitar (Gibson L5)
Bill Black	Double bass
D.J. Fontana	Drums

This was Elvis' 42nd appearance on the 'Louisiana Hayride'. It was also the first time that he performed **BLUE SUEDE SHOES** *on stage. Carl Perkins had sung his new composition to him on Monday, 19 December (exact time unknown) and recorded it later that same day. Perkins' record (Sun 234) was released in Memphis on 28 or 29 December 1955.*

BLUE SUEDE SHOES *(Perkins)*

★ Original by Carl Perkins (Sun 234) 1955.
◆ *Elvis' source:* Carl Perkins (Sun 234) 1955.
❍ Elvis later recorded this title at RCA Studios, New York on 30 January 1956 (released in 1956 on LP *Elvis Presley*, RCA LPM-1254). He subsequently re-recorded it at RCA Studios, Hollywood on 28 April 1960 (released in 1960 on LP *G.I. Blues*, RCA-Victor LPM/LSP-2256).

UNKNOWN TITLES
Some researchers claim that Elvis also sang **HEARTBREAK HOTEL** *and* **PEACE IN THE VALLEY** *on this show.*

7.81

List of other titles Elvis is known to have performed on the *Louisiana Hayride* 1954–55 (exact dates unknown)

I FORGOT TO REMEMBER TO FORGET
Song written by Stan Kesler, who recorded a demo of it at the Sun studio on Saturday, 25 June 1955 between 3.00 and 3.30 pm, with himself on fiddle and Charlie Feathers on vocal and acoustic guitar. Feathers subsequently claimed that he had finished off the song and that he should be credited as co-composer. They also recorded a demo of **WE'RE GETTING CLOSER TO BEING APART** *at the same session. In 1973, Feathers cut a new version of* **I FORGOT TO REMEMBER TO FORGET** *for his 'Living Legend' LP (Redita 107, Netherlands).*

✱ Original by Elvis, recorded at Sun Studio, Memphis on 11 July 1955 (Sun 223, 1955) [see **4.20** for details].

MILKCOW BLUES BOOGIE *(Arnold)*
The **'BOOGIE'** *was probably added by Elvis or Sam Phillips.*

✱ Original **MILK COW BLUES** by Freddie Spruell (OKeh 8422) 1926. [Incidentally, this record was issued under the same catalogue number with two different 'B' sides.]
Sleepy John Estes recorded his variation on the theme (Victor 38614) in 1930.
Kokomo Arnold subsequently reworked the theme in five different versions:
MILK COW BLUES (Decca 7026) 1934.
MILK COW BLUES No. 2 (Decca 7059) 1935.
MILK COW BLUES No. 3 (Decca 7116) 1935.
MILK COW BLUES No. 4 (Decca 7163) 1936.
MILK COW BLUES No. 5 (Decca, unissued), recorded 1936.
◆ *Elvis' sources:* Kokomo Arnold (Decca 7026) 1934.
      Johnny Lee Wills (Decca 5985) 1941.
      Jimmy Wakely (Capitol 40107) 1948.
○ Elvis recorded this title at Sun Studio, Memphis on 20 December 1954 (Sun 215, 1954) [see **4.14** for details].

MYSTERY TRAIN *(Parker/Phillips)*
Elvis' recording is a combination of two Little Junior Parker tunes — the lyrics of **MYSTERY TRAIN** *and the* **LOVE MY BABY** *guitar riff — which were issued back-to-back on Sun 192. Parker's* **MYSTERY TRAIN** *itself was based on the Carter Family's* **WORRIED MAN BLUES** *(Bluebird 6020) 1930.*

✱ Original by Little Junior's Blue Flames (Sun 192) 1953.
◆ *Elvis' source:* Little Junior's Blue Flames (Sun 192) 1953.
○ Elvis recorded this title at Sun Studio, Memphis on 11 July 1955 (Sun 223, 1955) [see **4.20** for details].

ROCK THE JOINT *(Crafton/Keane/Bagby)*
R&B hit in 1949 for Jimmy Preston (Gotham 188). If any disc can lay claim to being the first rock'n'roll record, then it must surely be Preston's recording and not Jackie Brenston's **ROCKET 88** *(Chess 1458). Unutterably wild, with a great boogie-woogie piano and sax intro, honking saxes, handclaps and screams, it's infinitely more powerful than* **ROCKET 88** *— a comparatively straight R&B number — and years ahead of its time.*

✱ Original by Jimmy Preston (Gotham 188) 1949.
◆ *Elvis' sources:* Jimmy Preston (Gotham 188) 1949.
      Bill Haley (Essex 303) 1952. *[Note: Haley changed some lyrics on his version.]*

UNCLE PEN *(Monroe)*
Song written by Bill Monroe after his uncle, Pendleton Vandiver.

★ Original by Bill Monroe – Voc. Bill Monroe & Jimmy Martin (Decca 46283) 1951.
◆ *Elvis' source:* Bill Monroe – Voc. Bill Monroe & Jimmy Martin (Decca 46283) 1951.
❂ Elvis recorded this title at Sun Studio, Memphis on 8 December 1954 (unissued) [see **4.12** for details].

◆ APPENDIX A ◆

Flatbed Truck & Honky Tonk Performances 1955

Korral Club, Houston, Texas *(Audience: 25)*
Sunday, 2 January 1955 (11.30–11.45 pm)
Elvis Presley   Vocal and acoustic guitar (model unknown)
Scotty Moore   Lead guitar (Gibson ES-295)
Bill Black   Double bass

UNKNOWN TITLES

Flatbed truck, Marianna, Arkansas
Friday, 14 January 1955 (4.30–5.00 pm)
Elvis Presley   Vocal and acoustic guitar (model unknown)
Scotty Moore   Lead guitar (Gibson ES-295)
Bill Black   Double bass

UNKNOWN TITLES

Flatbed truck, Alpine, Texas
Thursday, 10 February 1955 (6.00–6.20 pm)
Elvis Presley   Vocal and acoustic guitar (model unknown)
Scotty Moore   Lead guitar (Gibson ES-295)
Bill Black   Double bass

UNKNOWN TITLES

Honky tonk (name unknown), Abilene, Texas *(Audience: 40)*
Tuesday, 15 February 1955 (11.20–11.40 pm)
Elvis Presley   Vocal and acoustic guitar (model unknown)
Scotty Moore   Lead guitar (Gibson ES-295)
Bill Black   Double bass

UNKNOWN TITLES

Honky tonk (name unknown), Austin, Texas *(Audience: 20)*
Thursday,17 March 1955 (11.30–11.50 pm)
Elvis Presley   Vocal and acoustic guitar (model unknown)
Scotty Moore   Lead guitar (Gibson ES-295)
Bill Black   Double bass

UNKNOWN TITLES

Korral Club, Houston, Texas *(Audience: 25)*
Sunday, 20 March 1955 (11.35–11.55 pm)
Elvis Presley   Vocal and acoustic guitar (model unknown)
Scotty Moore   Lead guitar (Gibson ES-295)
Bill Black   Double bass
Darrell Newsome   Drums

Darrell Newsome was the drummer of rockabilly artist Sonny Fisher.

UNKNOWN TITLES

Flatbed truck, Gainesville, Texas
Thursday, 14 April 1955 (5.00–5.15 pm)
Elvis Presley   Vocal and acoustic guitar (model unknown)
Scotty Moore   Lead guitar (Gibson ES-295)
Bill Black   Double bass

UNKNOWN TITLES

Honky tonk (name unknown), Roscoe, Texas *(Audience: 30)*
Tuesday, 7 June 1955 (10.50–11.30 pm)
Elvis Presley   Vocal and acoustic guitar (model unknown)
Scotty Moore   Lead guitar (Gibson ES-295)
Bill Black   Double bass

UNKNOWN TITLES

Honky tonk (name unknown), Andrew, Texas *(Audience: 50)*
Thursday, 9 June 1955 (11.25–11.45 pm)
Elvis Presley   Vocal and acoustic guitar (model unknown)
Scotty Moore   Lead guitar (Gibson ES-295)
Bill Black   Double bass

UNKNOWN TITLES

Flatbed truck, Altus, Oklahoma
Friday, 24 June 1955 (7.00–7.25 pm)
Elvis Presley   Vocal and acoustic guitar (model unknown)
Scotty Moore   Lead guitar (Gibson ES-295)
Bill Black   Double bass

Later that evening, Elvis performed at the Altus club

UNKNOWN TITLES

◆ APPENDIX B ◆

The Sun Sessions – At A Glance

Below is a quick reference guide to all the songs that Elvis recorded at Sun in 1954-55. Rehearsals, jams, etc are not included unless they were recorded.

4.2	18 Jul 1953	My Happiness	Acetate, RCA
		That's When Your Heartaches Begin	Acetate, RCA
4.3	4 Jan 1954	I'll Never Stand In Your Way	Acetate, RCA
		It Wouldn't Be The Same Without You	Acetate, RCA
4.4	5 Jun 1954	Casual Love Affair	Acetate (lost)
		Careless Love	Acetate (lost)
4.5	26 Jun 1954	Casual Love Affair	Erased
4.6	5 Jul 1954	Harbor Lights	RCA
		I Love You Because	RCA
		That's All Right	Sun 209 (19 Jul 1954), RCA
		Tiger Man	Cancelled second single, RCA?
		Cool Disposition	Lost
		Hey Mama, Everything's All Right	Lost
		Rock Me Mamma	Lost
4.7	6 Jul 1954	Blue Moon Of Kentucky	Sun 209 (19 Jul 1954), RCA
4.8	19 Aug 1954	Blue Moon	Cancelled second single, RCA
		Tomorrow Night #1	RCA
		I'll Never Let You Go (Little Darlin') #1	RCA
4.9	10 Sep 1954	Satisfied	RCA
		I'll Never Let You Go (Little Darlin') #2	RCA
4.10	15 Sep 1954	I Don't Care If The Sun Don't Shine	Sun 210 (27 Sep 1954)
		Just Because	RCA
		Good Rockin' Tonight	Sun 210 (27 Sep 1954), RCA
4.11	15 Nov 1954	My Baby's Gone	RCA
		Night Train To Memphis	Lost
		Tennessee Saturday Night	Lost
4.12	8 Dec 1954	Uncle Pen	Lost
		Oakie Boogie	Lost
		Tomorrow Night #2	Lost
		Juanita	Lost

4.13	13 Dec 1954	Nine Pound Hammer	Lost
		Thunderbolt Boogie	Lost
4.14	20 Dec 1954	Milkcow Blues Boogie	Sun 215 (28 Dec 1954)
		You're A Heartbreaker #1	Sun 215 (28 Dec 1954)
4.15	3 Feb 1955	I Got A Woman	RCA
		Tryin' To Get To You #1	RCA
		Baby Let's Play House	Sun 217 (25 Apr 1955), RCA
4.16	6 Mar 1955	I'm Left, You"re Right, She's Gone	Sun 217 (25 Apr 1955), RCA
		You're A Heartbreaker #2	Lost
		How Do You Think I Feel	Lost
4.17	15 Mar 1955	Tennessee Partner	Lost
		Rockin' Little Sally	Lost
		Breakin' The Rules	Lost
4.18	? Mar 1955	Nightmare	Erased
		I Played The Fool	Erased
4.19	? Apr 1955	Mexican Joe	Erased
		Just In Case	Erased
4.20	11 Jul 1955	I Forgot To Remember To Forget	Sun 223 (1 Aug 1955), RCA
		Mystery Train	Sun 223 (1 Aug 1955), RCA
		Tryin' To Get To You #2	RCA
4.21	? Jul 1955	Down The Line	Erased
4.22	? Aug 1955	Maybellene	Erased
4.23	? Aug 1955	?	Erased
4.24	? Aug 1955	Cryin' Heart Blues	Erased
		I Almost Lost My Mind	Erased
		Somethin' Blues	Erased
4.25	1954 or 1955	Do You Know The Man	Acetate (lost)
		Somewhere In Glory	Acetate (lost)
4.26	3 Nov 1955	When It Rains It Really Pours	Sun 223 (cancelled), RCA
		We're Getting Closer To Being Apart	Sun 223 (cancelled)

◆ APPENDIX C ◆

The Sun Tapes

When Elvis signed with RCA-Victor on 21 November 1955, Sam Phillips handed over fifteen tapes of Sun recordings to his new owners as part of the deal. Producer Steve Sholes made a handwritten and not altogether accurate log of their jumbled contents sometime in late November or December, details of which are reproduced below. It's also worth noting that Phillips did not supply tapes of **I DON'T CARE IF THE SUN DON'T SHINE, MILKCOW BLUES BOOGIE** and **YOU'RE A HEARTBREAKER**, and RCA had to dub these off Sun 78s. It's unclear whether the **BLUE MOON OF KENTUCKY** tape contained the master take, or whether this too has to be dubbed from disc. Eight of the Sun tapes were subsequently sent to RCA's vault in Indianapolis, where — according to different sources — they were either destroyed in 1957 or lost. Other tapes have also since been lost, stolen or misplaced.

Understanding RCA master number prefixes

Unlike many record companies who simply allocated a sequential number to each song they cut, RCA used a complex coding system that required a change of number virtually every time a recording was released:

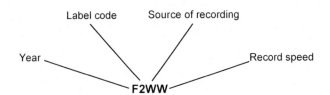

Year
The letter 'F' was used to indicate '1955'. Thus, all the Sun cuts purchased by RCA in November 1955 were allocated master numbers commencing with 'F', with the exception of **I LOVE YOU BECAUSE**, which was edited/mastered in January 1956 and allocated the number G2WB-1086. The letter 'G' was used for all of Elvis' 1956 masters including spliced takes.

Label code
The number '2' was used throughout the 1950s and up until 1962 to indicate 'RCA-Victor'. Other numbers were used for subsidiary labels.

Source of recording

The letter 'W' was used throughout the 1950s and up until 1962 to identify recordings made in RCA studios. The letter 'P' was used to identify purchased material. It is therefore something of a mystery why Steve Sholes identified the cuts that RCA acquired from Sun with a 'W' rather than a 'P' (eg F2WW instead of F2PW).

Record speed

Between 1955 and 1958, RCA used the letter 'B' to identify 78 rpm and 33⅓ rpm releases (the last RCA 78 came out in late 1958). Between 1955 and 1962, the letter 'W' was used to identify 45 rpm releases. RCA's reissues of Elvis' Sun singles appeared on both 45 and 78 rpm, which is why some sources quote F2WB- rather than F2WW- prefixes.

It's also a mystery why Steve Sholes allocated 'B' suffixes to some takes and 'W' suffixes to others. At the time he was cataloguing them, RCA had no firm plans for their their release, so how could he have known the formats?

The Sun Tapes log

		See Session
		▼

BOX 1 *Sent to Indianapolis, destroyed in 1957.*

F2WW-8000	**I FORGOT TO REMEMBER TO FORGET**	4.20
F2WW-8001	**MYSTERY TRAIN**	4.20
F2WW-8039	**TRYIN' TO GET TO YOU** *second version*	4.20

BOX 2 *Sent to Indianapolis, destroyed in 1957.*

F2WW-8040	**THAT'S ALL RIGHT**[1]	4.6
	UNKNOWN SELECTION[2]	
	UNKNOWN SELECTION[2]	

[1] *Also listed under Box 13 with the master F2WB-8040.*
[2] *Possibly not by Elvis. During the 1970s, some sources claimed that one of these selections was* **TIGER MAN**.

BOX 3 *Sent to Indianapolis, destroyed in 1957.*

F2WW-8043	**GOOD ROCKIN' TONIGHT**[1]	4.10
	JUST BECAUSE[2]	4.10

[1] *Also listed under Boxes 9 and 10 with master number F2WB-8043.*
[2] *Also listed under Boxes 9 and 10 with master number F2WB-8118.*

BOX 4 *Sent to Indianapolis, destroyed in 1957.*

F2WW-8046	**BABY LET'S PLAY HOUSE**	4.15
	I GOT A WOMAN	4.15
	TRYIN' TO GET TO YOU *first version*	4.15

BOX 5   *Lost?*

F2WW-8047   I'M LEFT, YOU'RE RIGHT, SHE'S GONE   **4.16**

BOX 6   *In RCA vaults.*

F2WW-8047   I'M LEFT, YOU'RE RIGHT, SHE'S GONE

Incorrect entry. The cut is actually **MY BABY'S GONE** *from Session* **4.11**.

BOX 7   *Lost.*

F2WB-8115   TOMORROW NIGHT *first version*   **4.8**
F2WB-8116   I'LL NEVER LET YOU GO[1] *first version*   **4.8**

[1] *This title also listed under Boxes 9 and 12.*

BOX 8   *In RCA vaults.*

F2WB-8117   BLUE MOON   **4.8**

BOX 9   *Sent to Indianapolis, destroyed in 1957.*

F2WB-8118   JUST BECAUSE[1]   **4.10**
F2WB-8116   I'LL NEVER LET YOU GO[2] *second version*   **4.9**
F2WB-[3]

[1] *Also listed under Box 3 without a master number, and under Box 10 with master number F2WB-8118.*
[2] *Master number F2WB-8116, already assigned to the first version (see Boxes 7 and 12) was also incorrectly assigned to this, the second version. This version was later given the master number OPA1-4197.*
[3] *Incomplete entry. The third song is probably* **GOOD ROCKIN' TONIGHT** — *see next box.*

BOX 10   *Lost.*

F2WB-8118   JUST BECAUSE[1]   **4.10**
8043   GOOD ROCKIN' TONIGHT[2]   **4.10**

[1] *Also listed under Box 3 without a master number, and under Box 9 with master number F2WB-8118.*
[2] *Also listed under Box 3 with master number F2WW-8043, and possibly also under Box 9.*

BOX 11   *Lost.*

WHEN IT RAINS IT REALLY POURS   **4.26**

BOX 12   *Sent to Indianapolis, destroyed in 1957.*

        F2WB-8116   **I'LL NEVER LET YOU GO**[1] *first version*   **4.8**
                      SATISFIED   **4.9**

[1] *This title also listed under Boxes 7 and 9.*

BOX 13   *Lost. Copy in RCA vaults.*

        F2WB-8040   **THAT'S ALL RIGHT**[1]   **4.6**
        G2WB-   **I LOVE YOU BECAUSE**[2]   **4.6**

[1] *Also listed under Box 2 with the master F2WW-8040.*
[2] *Sholes entered a G2WB prefix in readiness for this cut's release in 1956.*

BOX 14   *Sent to Indianapolis, destroyed in 1957.*

        F2WB-8041   **BLUE MOON OF KENTUCKY**   **4.7**

BOX 15   *Lost.*

                  HARBOR LIGHTS   **4.6**

◆ APPENDIX D ◆

Complete Show Playlists

Listed below are the complete playlists for various live shows included in Section 5. The approximate performance times stated include brief introductions, etc. (NB. In the early days, Elvis didn't indulge in long dialogues with the audience).

Bon Air Club, Memphis, TN
Saturday, 17 July 1954 (time unk)
Approx. performance time: 10 mins

That's All Right
Blue Moon Of Kentucky

Bon Air Club, Memphis, TN
Saturday, 24 July 1954 (9.00 pm)
Approx. performance time: 10-15 mins

That's All Right
I Apologize
Blue Moon Of Kentucky

Bel Air Club, Memphis, TN
Saturday, 24 July 1954
First set (10.00 pm)
Approx. performance time: 10 mins

That's All Right
Blue Moon Of Kentucky

Second set (10.45 pm)
Approx. performance time: 10-15 mins

That's All Right
Blue Moon Of Kentucky
Cry Of The Wild Goose

Bon Air Club, Memphis, TN
Saturday, 31 July 1954
First set (9.00 pm)
Approx. performance time: 10-15 mins

That's All Right
Sitting On Top Of The World
Blue Moon Of Kentucky

Second set (9.45 pm)
Approx. performance time: 10 mins

That's All Right
Blue Moon Of Kentucky

Eagle's Nest Club, Memphis, TN
Saturday, 7 August 1954
First set (9.00 pm)
Approx. performance time: 10-15 mins

That's All Right
Blue Moon Of Kentucky
Blue Moon

Second set (10.00 pm)
Approx. performance time: 10-15 mins

That's All Right
Blue Moon Of Kentucky
Tiger Man (King Of The Jungle)

Eagle's Nest Club, Memphis, TN
Monday, 16 August 1954
First set (8.45 pm)
Approx. performance time: 10-15 mins

That's All Right
Ice Cold Love
Blue Moon Of Kentucky

Second set (9.30 pm)
Approx. performance time: 10-15 mins

That's All Right
Blue Moon
Blue Moon Of Kentucky

Bel Air Club, Memphis, TN
Monday, 16 August 1954 (10.30 pm)
Approx. performance time: 15 mins

That's All Right
Blue Moon Of Kentucky
Rag Mop
That's All Right

Bel Air Club, Memphis, TN
Saturday, 21 August 1954
First set (9.00 pm)
Approx. performance time: 10-15 mins

That's All Right
John Henry
Blue Moon Of Kentucky

Second set (9.45 pm)
Approx. performance time: 10-15 mins

That's All Right
Blue Moon Of Kentucky
If I Didn't Care

Eagle's Nest Club, Memphis, TN
Friday, 27 August 1954
First set (8.45 pm)
Approx. performance time: 10-15 mins

That's All Right
Blue Moon Of Kentucky
Too Late To Worry, Too Blue To Cry

Second set (9.40 pm)
Approx. performance time: 10-15 mins

That's All Right
Blue Moon Of Kentucky
Tiger Man (King Of The Jungle)

Third set (10.15 pm)
Approx. performance time: 15 mins

That's All Right
Blue Moon
Uncle Josh
Blue Moon Of Kentucky

Eagle's Nest Club, Memphis, TN
Friday, 10 September 1954
First set (9.00 pm)
Approx. performance time: 15 mins

That's All Right
Blue Moon Of Kentucky
Good Rockin' Tonight
I Apologize
That's All Right

Second set (9.50 pm)
Approx. performance time: 15 mins

That's All Right
Good Rockin' Tonight
Blue Moon Of Kentucky
Tiger Man (King Of The Jungle)

Eagle's Nest Club, Memphis, TN
Friday, 24 September 1954
First set (9.00 pm)
Approx. performance time: 10 mins

That's All Right
Blue Moon Of Kentucky
Good Rockin' Tonight

Second set (9.40 pm)
Approx. performance time: 15 mins

That's All Right
Milkcow Blues Boogie
Good Rockin' Tonight
Blue Moon Of Kentucky

Bel Air Club, Memphis, TN
Friday, 24 September 1954 (10.45)
Approx. performance time: 15 mins

That's All Right
Good Rockin' Tonight
Blue Guitar
Blue Moon Of Kentucky
Tiger Man (King Of The Jungle)

Eagle's Nest Club, Memphis, TN
Saturday, 25 September 1954
First set (9.00 pm)
Approx. performance time: 10-15 mins

That's All Right
Good Rockin' Tonight
Blue Moon Of Kentucky

Second set (9.45 pm)
Approx. performance time: 15 mins

That's All Right
Blue Moon Of Kentucky
Milkcow Blues Boogie
Good Rockin' Tonight

Third set (10.30 pm)
Approx. performance time: 15 mins

That's All Right
Blue Guitar
Good Rockin Tonight
Blue Moon Of Kentucky
Blues Stay Away From Me

Eagle's Nest Club, Memphis, TN
Wednesday, 6 October 1954
First set (9.15 pm)
Approx. performance time: 15 mins

That's All Right
Blue Moon Of Kentucky
That's Amore
Good Rockin' Tonight

Second set (10.00 pm)
Approx. performance time: 15 mins

That's All Right
Last Train To Memphis
I Don't Care If The Sun Don't Shine
Tiger Man (King Of The Jungle)
Good Rockin' Tonight

Silver Slipper Club, Atlanta, GA
Friday, 8 October 1954
First set (8.30 pm)
Approx. performance time: 15 mins

That's All Right
Blue Moon Of Kentucky
Give Me More, More, More Of Your Kisses
I Don't Care If The Sun Don't Shine
Good Rockin' Tonight

Second set (10.30 pm)
Approx. performance time: 15 mins

That's All Right
Blue Moon
I Don't Care If The Sun Don't Shine
Blue Moon Of Kentucky
Good Rockin' Tonight

Eagle's Nest Club, Memphis, TN
Wednesday, 13 October 1954
First set (9.00 pm)
Approx. performance time: 15 mins

That's All Right
Milkcow Blues Boogie
I Don't Care If The Sun Don't Shine
Good Rockin' Tonight

Second set (9.35 pm)
Approx. performance time: 15 mins

That's All Right
Blue Moon Of Kentucky
Dark As A Dungeon
Good Rockin' Tonight

Third set (10.20 pm)
Approx. performance time: 15 mins

That's All Right
Tiger Man (King Of The Jungle)
I Don't Care If The Sun Don't Shine
Blue Moon Of Kentucky
Good Rockin' Tonight

Eagle's Nest Club, Memphis, TN
Friday, 29 October 1954
First set (9.00 pm)
Approx. performance time: 15 mins

That's All Right
Blue Moon Of Kentucky
Born To Lose
Good Rockin' Tonight

Second set (9.50 pm)
Approx. performance time: 15 mins

That's All Right
Just Because
Blue Moon Of Kentucky
I Don't Care If The Sun Don't Shine
Good Rockin' Tonight

Bel Air Club, Memphis, TN
Monday, 15 November 1954 (9.00 pm)
Approx. performance time: 15 mins

That's All Right
Blue Moon Of Kentucky
Tomorrow Night
I Don't Care If The Sun Don't Shine
Good Rockin' Tonight

Magnolia Gardens, Houston, TX
Sunday, 21 November 1954 (time unk)
Approx. performance time: 15 mins

That's All Right
I Don't Care If The Sun Don't Shine
Blue Moon Of Kentucky
My Happiness
Good Rockin' Tonight

Cook's Hoedown Club, Houston, TX
Sunday, 21 November 1954 (time unk)
Approx. performance time: 15 mins

That's All Right
Blue Moon Of Kentucky
Oakie Boogie
Milkcow Blues Boogie
Fool, Fool, Fool
Good Rockin' Tonight

Catholic Club, Helena, AR
Thursday, 2 December 1954 (time unk)
Approx. performance time: 15 mins

That's All Right
Tennessee Saturday Night
Blue Moon Of Kentucky
I'm Gonna Sit Right Down And Cry (Over You)
Good Rockin' Tonight

Municipal Auditorium, Texarkana, AR
Friday, 3 December 1954 (time unk)
Approx. performance time: 15 mins

That's All Right
Tomorrow Night
I Don't Care If The Sun Don't Shine
Blue Moon Of Kentucky
Good Rockin' Tonight
Shake, Rattle And Roll

Eagle's Nest Club, Memphis, TN
Friday, 10 December 1954
First set (9.00 pm)
Approx. performance time: 15 mins

That's All Right
Blue Moon Of Kentucky
Shake, Rattle And Roll
I Don't Care If The Sun Don't Shine
Good Rockin' Tonight

Second set (9.45 pm)
Approx. performance time: 15 mins

That's All Right
Blue Moon Of Kentucky
Money Honey
Good Rockin' Tonight

Third set (10.30 pm)
Approx. performance time: 15 mins

That's All Right
Milkcow Blues Boogie
Hearts Of Stone
Blue Moon Of Kentucky
I Don't Care If The Sun Don't Shine
Good Rockin' Tonight

Cook's Hoedown Club, Houston, TX
Tuesday, 28 December 1954 (time unk)
Approx. performance time: 15 mins

That's All Right
Blue Moon Of Kentucky
Harbor Lights
Good Rockin' Tonight
Milkcow Blues Boogie

Eagle's Hall, Houston, TX
Friday, 31 December 1954 (time unk)
Approx. performance time: 20 mins

That's All Right
Good Rockin' Tonight
Little Mama *[Clovers]*
Blue Moon Of Kentucky
The Texas Special
Hearts Of Stone
Milkcow Blues Boogie

City Auditorium, Clarksdale, MS
Wednesday, 12 January 1955 (8.00 pm)
Approx. performance time: 15 mins

That's All Right
I Don't Care If The Sun Don't Shine
Hearts Of Stone
Blue Moon Of Kentucky
Good Rockin' Tonight
Milkcow Blues Boogie

Junior College, Booneville, MS
Monday, 17 January 1955 (8.00 pm)
Approx. performance time: 15 mins

That's All Right
Blue Moon Of Kentucky
Tweedle Dee
Good Rockin' Tonight
Money Honey
Milkcow Blues Boogie

Community Center, Sheffield, AL
Wednesday, 19 January 1955 (8.00 pm)
Approx. performance time: 15 mins

That's All Right
Good Rockin' Tonight
Money Honey
I Don't Care If The Sun Don't Shine
I Got A Woman
Milkcow Blues Boogie

National Guard Armory, Sikeston, MO
Friday, 21 January 1955 (8.00 pm)
Approx. performance time: 15 mins

Blue Moon Of Kentucky
Good Rockin' Tonight
You're A Heartbreaker
I Got A Woman
Tweedle Dee
That's All Right

Humble Oil Camp, Hawkins, TX
Monday, 24 January 1955 (8.00 pm)
Approx. performance time: 20 mins

That's All Right
Money Honey
Good Rockin' Tonight
I Got A Woman
Nine Pound Hammer
You're A Heartbreaker
Blue Moon Of Kentucky

Rural Electric, Gilmer, TX
Wednesday, 26 January 1955 (7.30 pm)
Approx. performance time: 15 mins

That's All Right
I Got A Woman
Blue Moon Of Kentucky
Satisfied
Good Rockin' Tonight
Milkcow Blues Boogie

High School Auditorium, Gaston, TX
Friday, 28 January 1955 (8.00 pm)
Approx. performance time: 15 mins

That's All Right
Good Rockin' Tonight
Fireball Mail
I Don't Care If The Sun Don't Shine
Little Mama *[Clovers]*
Blue Moon Of Kentucky

High School Auditorium, Randolph, MS
Tuesday, 1 February 1955 (time unk)
Approx. performance time: 20 mins

Blue Moon Of Kentucky
Fool, Fool, Fool
Money Honey
That's All Right
You're A Heartbreaker
Milkcow Blues Boogie
Oakie Boogie

Ripley High School, Ripley, MS
Monday, 7 February 1955 (8.00 pm)
Approx. performance time: 15 mins

That's All Right
Blue Moon Of Kentucky
I Got A Woman
Mexican Joe
I Got A Woman
Milkcow Blues Boogie

Sport Arena, Carlsbad, NM
Friday, 11 February 1955 (4.00 pm)
Approx. performance time: 15 mins

Good Rockin' Tonight
That's All Right
I Got A Woman
Baby Let's Play House
Shake, Rattle And Roll
Blue Moon Of Kentucky

North Junior High, Roswell, NM
Monday, 14 February 1955 (9.30 pm)
Approx. performance time: 15 mins

That's All Right
I Don't Care If The Sun Don't Shine
I Got A Woman
Uncle Pen
Good Rockin' Tonight
Baby Let's Play House

West Monroe High School, Monroe, LA
Friday 18 February 1955 (7.30 pm)
Approx. performance time: 15-20 mins

Milkcow Blues Boogie
Good Rockin' Tonight
You're A Heartbreaker
Baby Let's Play House
That's All Right
Breakin' The Rules
Blue Moon Of Kentucky

City Auditorium, Camden, AR
Monday, 21 February 1955 (8.00 pm)
Approx. performance time: 15 mins

That's All Right
I Got A Woman
Juanita
Money Honey
Good Rockin' Tonight
Baby Let's Play House

South Side Elementary School, Bastrop, LA
Thursday, 24 Feb 1955 (7.30 pm)
Approx. performance time: 15 mins

Good Rockin' Tonight
Blue Moon Of Kentucky
You're A Heartbreaker
Milkcow Blues Boogie
Gonna Paint The Town Red
That's All Right

Porky's Rooftop Club, Newport, AR
Wednesday, 2 March 1955
First set (10.00 pm)
Approx. performance time: 15 mins

That's All Right
Money Honey
Good Rockin' Tonight
Blue Moon Of Kentucky
Baby Let's Play House
Wabash Cannonball

Second set (10.45)
Approx. performance time: 15 mins

Milkcow Blues Boogie
Blue Moon Of Kentucky
I Got A Woman
Tweedle Dee
Baby Let's Play House
That's All Right

Armory, Poplar Bluff, AR
Wednesday, 9 March 1955 (8.00)
Approx. performance time: 15 mins

Good Rockin' Tonight
Always Late (With Your Kisses)
I Got A Woman
Baby Let's Play House
Blue Moon Of Kentucky
That's All Right

Magnolia Gardens, Houston, TX
Sunday, 20 March 1955 (time unk)
Approx. performance time: 15 mins

That's All Right
Baby Let's Play House
My Baby's Gone
I Got A Woman
Blue Moon Of Kentucky
Good Rockin' Tonight

High School Gymnasium, Big Creek, MS
Monday, 28 March 1955 (time unk)
Approx. performance time: 15 mins

Milkcow Blues Boogie
Money Honey
Baby Let's Play House
Good Rockin' Tonight
Tennessee Partner
That's All Right

High School Auditorium, El Dorado, AR
Wednesday, 30 March 1955 (8.00 pm)
Approx. performance time: 15 mins

That's All Right
Blue Moon Of Kentucky
Good Rockin' Tonight
The Lovebug Itch
I Got A Woman
Baby Let's Play House

Reo Palm Isle, Longview, TX
Thursday, 31 March 1955 (9.00 pm)
Approx. performance time: 15-20 mins

That's All Right
Good Rockin' Tonight
I Don't Care
Blue Moon Of Kentucky
How Do You Think I Feel
Milkcow Blues Boogie
Baby Let's Play House

Court House, Corinth, MS
Thursday, 7 April 1955 (8.00 pm)
Approx. performance time: 15 mins

That's All Right
I Got A Woman
Blue Moon Of Kentucky
Good Rockin' Tonight
Rockin' Little Sally
Baby Let's Play House

B&B Club, Gobler, MO
Friday, 8 April 1955
First set (8.00 pm)
Approx. performance time: 15-20 mins

Good Rockin' Tonight
Baby Let's Play House
Milkcow Blues Boogie
You're A Heartbreaker
Blue Moon Of Kentucky
That's All Right

Second set (10.00 pm)
Approx. performance time: 15-20 mins

That's All Right
I Got A Woman
Good Rockin' Tonight
Rock The Joint
Money Honey
Baby Let's Play House

228

American Legion Hut, Grenada, MS
Wednesday, 20 April 1955 (8.00 pm)
Approx. performance time: 20 mins

That's All Right
Good Rockin' Tonight
I Got A Woman
I'm Left, You're Right, She's Gone
Blue Moon Of Kentucky
Milkcow Blues Boogie
Baby Let's Play House

Magnolia Garden, Houston, TX
Sunday, 24 April 1955 (3.00 pm)
Approx. performance time: 20 mins

Blue Moon Of Kentucky
Shake, Rattle And Roll
Good Rockin' Tonight
I Got A Woman
Nightmare
Baby Let's Play House
That's All Right

M-B Corral, Wichita Falls, TX
Monday, 25 April 1955 (11.00 pm)
Approx. performance time: 20 mins

Good Rockin' Tonight
I'm Left, You're Right, She's Gone
Blue Moon Of Kentucky
Thunderbolt Boogie
Money Honey
Baby Let's Play House
That's All Right

City Auditorium, Big Spring, TX
Tuesday, 26 April 1955 (8.00 pm)
Approx. performance time: 15 mins

That's All Right
Milkcow Blues Boogie
I Got A Woman
I Played The Fool
Good Rockin' Tonight
Baby Let's Play House

High School Auditorium, Baton Rouge, LA
Monday, 2 May 1955 (7.00 pm)
Approx. performance time: 15 mins

That's All Right
Blue Moon Of Kentucky
I Got A Woman
Night Train To Memphis
Good Rockin' Tonight
Baby Let's Play House

Fort Homer Hesterly Armory, Tampa, FL
Sunday, 8 May 1955
First set (2.30 pm)

No details

Second set (8.15)
Approx. performance time: 15-20 mins

Good Rockin' Tonight
Cool Disposition
Milkcow Blues Boogie
I Got A Woman
I'm Left, You're Right, She's Gone
Baby Let's Play House
That's All Right

Mosque Theater, Richmond, VA
Monday, 16 May 1955 (8.00)
Approx. performance time: 20 mins

That's All Right
I Got A Woman
I'm Left, You're Right, She's Gone
Good Rockin' Tonight
Blue Moon Of Kentucky
Baby Let's Play House
I'm Movin' On

Memorial Auditorium, Raleigh, NC
Thursday, 19 May 1955 (8.00 pm)
Approx. performance time: 15 mins

That's All Right
Money Honey
Good Rockin' Tonight
I Don't Hurt Anymore
I'm Left, You're Right, She's Gone
Baby Let's Play House

American Legion Hall, Meridian, MS
Wednesday, 25 May 1955 (9.00 pm)
Approx. performance time: 35 mins

That's All Right
Good Rockin' Tonight
Mean Mama Blues
Cold, Cold Heart
Blue Moon Of Kentucky
That's The Stuff You Gotta Watch
Baby Let's Play House
I'm Left, You're Right, She's Gone
You're A Heartbreaker
Milkcow Blues Boogie

Fair Park Auditorium, Abilene, TX
Monday, 30 May 1955 (time unk)
Approx. performance time: 15 mins

Baby Let's Play
Good Rockin' Tonight
I Got A Woman
I'm Left, You're Right, She's Gone
Gone
That's All Right

High School Auditorium, Guymon, OK
Wednesday, 1 June 1955 (8.00 pm)
Approx. performance time: 15-20 mins

That's All Right
Blue Moon Of Kentucky
Milkcow Blues Boogie
Cottonfields
I'm Left, You're Right, She's Gone
Baby Let's Play House
Good Rockin' Tonight

Texas Auditorium, Sweetwater, TX
Wednesday, 8 June 1955 (8.00 pm)
Approx. performance time: 15 mins

Baby Let's Play House
I Got A Woman
Good Rockin' Tonight
Corrine Corrina
Blue Moon Of Kentucky
That's All Right

High School Gymnasium, Belden, MS
Wednesday, 15 June 1955 (8.00 pm)
Approx. performance time: 15 mins

That's All Right
Good Rockin' Tonight
I'm Left, You're Right, She's Gone
Milkcow Blues Boogie
Down The Line
Baby Let's Play House

City Auditorium, Beaumont, TX
Tuesday, 21 June 1955 (7.00 pm)
Approx. performance time: 20 mins

I Got A Woman
Baby Let's Play House
Blue Moon Of Kentucky
Music Makin' Mama From Memphis
Good Rockin' Tonight
Money Honey
That's All Right

Southern Club, Lawton, OK
Friday, 24 June 1955 (2.00 pm)
Approx. performance time: 15 mins

That's All Right
Mean Heart Blues
I'm Left, You're Right, She's Gone
Good Rockin' Tonight
Blue Moon Of Kentucky
Baby Let's Play House

Slavonian Lodge, Biloxi, MS
Sunday, 26 June 1955 (8.00 pm)
Approx. performance time: 15-20 mins

Good Rockin' Tonight
Baby Let's Play House
Tweedle Dee
I Got A Woman
Shout Sister Shout
Blue Moon Of Kentucky
That's All Right

Radio Ranch Club, Mobile, AL
Thursday, 30 June 1955 (8.30)
Approx. performance time: 30 mins

Blue Moon Of Kentucky
I'm Left, You're Right, She's Gone
Good Rockin' Tonight
Milkcow Blues Boogie
Baby Let's Play House
Sitting On Top On The World
That's All Right
Mean Mama Boogie

Cape Arena, Cape Girardeau, MO
Wednesday, 20 July 1955 (8.30 pm)
Approx. performance time: 15 mins

That's All Right
Good Rockin' Tonight
I'm Left, You're Right, She's Gone
Baby Let's Play House
Mystery Train

Municipal Auditorium, Orlando, FL
Tuesday, 26 July 1955 (8.15 pm)
Approx. performance time: 15 mins

Mystery Train
Good Rockin' Tonight
Blue Moon Of Kentucky
Rags to Riches
Baby Let's Play House
That's All Right

New Baseball Stadium, Jacksonville, FL
Friday, 29 July 1955 (8.15 pm)
Approx. performance time: 15 mins

That's All Right
Good Rockin' Tonight
Baby Let's Play House
I Got A Woman
Rock Around The Clock
Mystery Train

Municipal Auditorium, Camden, AR
Thursday, 4 August 1955 (9.30 pm)
Approx. performance time: 20 mins

That's All Right
Baby Let's Play House
I Forgot To Remember To Forget
Blue Moon Of Kentucky
I'm Left, You're Right, She's Gone
Mystery Train
Good Rockin' Tonight

Large Auditorium, Tyler, TX
Monday, 8 August 1955 (8.00 pm)
Approx. performance time: 15 mins

Mystery Train
Baby Let's Play House
Good Rockin' Tonight
I Forgot To Remember To Forget
I'm Left, You're Right, She's Gone
That's All Right

Driller Park, Kilgore, TX
Friday, 12 August 1955 (time unk)
Approx. performance time: 15 mins

That's All Right
Baby Let's Play House
I Forgot To Remember To Forget
Maybellene
Good Rockin' Tonight
Mystery Train

Saddle Club, Bryan, TX
Tuesday, 23 August 1955 (time unk)
Approx. performance time: 15 mins

Baby Let's Play House
Blue Moon Of Kentucky
Tryin' To Get To You
I Forgot To Remember To Forget
Mystery Train
That's All Right

Baseball Park, Gonzales, TX
Friday, 26 August 1955 (8.00 pm)
Approx. performance time: 15-20 mins

That's All Right
Blue Moon Of Kentucky
Good Rockin' Tonight
I Forgot To Remember To Forget
Cryin' Heart Blues
Baby Let's Play House
Mystery Train

Arkansas Municipal Auditorium,
Texarkana, AR
Friday, 2 September 1955 (7.00 pm)
Approx. performance time: 15-20 mins

Mystery Train
Good Rockin' Tonight
Baby Let's Play House
I Forgot To Remember To Forget
Texarkana Baby
I'm Left, You're Right, She's Gone
That's All Right

Smith Stadium, Forrest City, AR
Monday, 5 September 1955 (8.00 pm)
Approx. performance time: 15 mins

That's All Right
Blue Moon Of Kentucky
Too Late To Cry
Baby Let's Play House
Good Rockin' Tonight
Mystery Train

National Guard Armory, Sikeston, MO
Wednesday, 7 September 1955 (8.00 pm)
Approx. performance time: 15-20 mins

That's All Right
Baby Let's Play House
I Forgot To Remember To Forget
Blue Moon Of Kentucky
Good Rockin' Tonight
The Covered Wagon Rolled Right Along
Mystery Train

High School Auditorium, McComb, MS
Friday, 9 September 1955 (8.00 pm)
Approx. performance time: 15-20 mins

Mystery Train
Good Rockin' Tonight
I Forgot To Remember To Forget
Baby Let's Play House
Long Tall Mama
I'm Left, You're Right, She's Gone
That's All Right

Memorial Auditorium, Raleigh, NC
Wednesday, 21 September 1955 (8.00 pm)
Approx. performance time: 15-20 mins

That's All Right
Blue Moon Of Kentucky
Baby Let's Play House
Good Rockin' Tonight
Only You
I Forgot To Remember To Forget
Mystery Train

B&B Club, Gobler, MO
Wednesday, 28 September 1955 (time unk)
Approx. performance time: 15-20 mins

Mystery Train
That's All Right
Baby Let's Play House
Blue Moon Of Kentucky
I Forgot To Remember To Forget
I'm Left, You're Right, She's Gone
My Babe

Southwest Texas State U, San Marcos, TX
Thursday, 6 October 1955 (3.00 pm)
Approx. performance time: 15 mins

Mystery Train
Baby Let's Play House
Good Rockin' Tonight
When It Rains It Really Pours
I Forgot To Remember To Forget
That's All Right

Memorial Hall, Brownwood, TX
Monday, 10 October 1955 (8.00 pm)
Approx. performance time: 15 mins

That's All Right
I Forgot To Remember To Forget
Good Rockin' Tonight
Baby Let's Play House
Mystery Train
Move It On Over / Rock Around The Clock

Missouri Theater, St. Louis, MO
Saturday, 22 October 1955 (9.30 pm)
Approx. performance time: 15-20 mins

That's All Right
Blue Moon Of Kentucky
Good Rockin' Tonight
I Forgot To Remember To Forget
Only You
Baby Let's Play House
Mystery Train

Community House, Biloxi, MS
Sunday, 6 November 1955 (8.00 pm)
Approx. performance time: 25 mins

Mystery Train
I Forgot To Remember To Forget
Good Rockin' Tonight
Blue Moon Of Kentucky
I'm Left, You're Right, She's Gone
Baby Let's Play House
That's All Right
My Baby Left Me

Sports Arena, Atlanta, GA
Friday, 2 December 1955 (time unk)
Approx. performance time: 25 mins

Mystery Train
Baby Let's Play House
Sixteen Tons
Blue Moon Of Kentucky
Heartbreak Hotel
I Forgot To Remember To Forget
Good Rockin' Tonight
That's All Right

State Coliseum, Montgomery, AL
Saturday, 3 December 1955 (time unk)
Approx. performance time: 25 mins

Mystery Train
I Forgot To Remember To Forget
Good Rockin' Tonight
Flip, Flop And Fly
Baby Let's Play House
Blue Moon Of Kentucky
That's All Right
Heartbreak Hotel

Lyric Theater, Indianapolis, IN
Monday, 5 December 1955 (time unk)
Approx. performance time: 25 mins

That's All Right
Good Rockin' Tonight
Tutti Frutti
Baby Let's Play House
I Forgot To Remember To Forget
Mystery Train
Heartbreak Hotel

Lyric Theater, Indianapolis, IN
Wednesday, 7 December 1955 (time unk)
Approx. performance time: 25 mins

Heartbreak Hotel
That's All Right
Sixteen Tons
Tutti Frutti
Rock Around The Clock
I Forgot To Remember To Forget
Good Rockin' Tonight
Mystery Train

Rialto Theater, Louisville, KY
Thursday, 8 December 1955 (time unk)
Approx. performance time: 35 mins

Mystery Train
I Forgot To Remember To Forget
Blue Moon Of Kentucky
Baby Let's Play House
Lawdy Miss Clawdy
Tutti Frutti
Good Rockin' Tonight
Heartbreak Hotel
That's All Right

B&I Club, Swifton, AR
Friday, 9 December 1955 (time unk)
Approx. performance time: 30 mins

Mystery Train
Good Rockin' Tonight
Baby Let's Play House
I Forgot To Remember To Forget
Heartbreak Hotel
Blue Moon Of Kentucky
Tutti Frutti
That's All Right

◆ APPENDIX E ◆

Amateur Films & Recordings

In the course of his investigations in 1968-70, Graham Metson established the existence of a number of amateur films of Elvis on stage, the majority of them made in Texas. These were all 8 mm films, some in black and white, some in colour.

Wednesday, 5 January 1955	City Auditorium, San Angelo, Texas.
Saturday, 26 February 1955	Circle Theater, Cleveland, Ohio (*Hillbilly Jamboree*, WERE).
Wednesday, 18 May 1955	American Legion Auditorium, Roanoke, Virginia.
Saturday, 18 June 1955	Sportatorium, Dallas, Texas (*Big D Jamboree*, KRLD) 10 mins.
Tuesday, 21 June 1955	City Auditorium, Beaumont, Texas.
Thursday, 25 August 1955	Sportcenter, Austin, Texas.
Sunday, 23 October 1955	Missouri Theater, St. Louis, Missouri.
Saturday, 19 November 1955	High School, Gladewater, Texas (*Louisiana Hayride*, KWKH).

Graham also learned that two of Elvis' shows at the Eagle's Nest in Memphis — one in October 1954 and the other in November 1954 — were recorded on tape (both lost).

The famous colour footage of Elvis, Carl Perkins, Johnny Cash and Buddy Holly shot by Lubbock, Texas radio personality/bandleader Ben Hall, which has previously been thought to be the earliest film of Elvis on stage, actually dates from 10 April 1956. The following explanation appears in *Elvis & Buddy – Linked Lives* (Music Mentor Books, 2002) by Buddy Holly expert, Alan Mann:

Hall claims to have shot the film at a concert in Lubbock in 1955, but there was never a single occasion — either in 1955 or since — when all the personalities featured appeared on the same bill. Moreover, Presley's attire is more redolent of his 1956 stage garb than the styles he wore in 1955, and Perkins' quite obvious references to his 'blue suede shoes' likewise firmly place the event post-1955.

The most likely explanation is that the Elvis footage dates from his 10 April 1956 appearance in Lubbock, and that Hall finished off his film at another Fair Park show on 26 April 1956 which included Perkins, Johnny Cash, Sonny James, Justin Tubb and the Belew Twins.

We know that Buddy and his group were present on the first of these occasions and may also have been around on the second, either as spectators or playing backup for Sonny James. However, the latter is uncertain as no record exists of them being on the bill on that date. Then again, backing bands and minor support acts were often not advertised.

Also seen bobbing about in the background during the Elvis segment of the film is a dark-haired lass in a red cowgirl outfit, who looks very much like 'Big D Jamboree' regular Helen Hall (no relation to Ben). As with Buddy, there is no evidence of her being on the bill that night.

◆ APPENDIX F ◆

Elvis' Record Collection

The following is a list of pre-1956 releases which Elvis had in his collection at the time of his death. It was compiled from various sources by English researcher Steve Cairns, and gives us another insight into the music that inspired the young Elvis. This list is by no means exhaustive, however the preponderance of vocal group records is noteworthy.

Singles

Johnny Ace - **MY SONG / FOLLOW THE RULE** (Duke 102) 1952
Johnny Ace - **PLEDGING MY LOVE / NO MONEY** (Duke 136) 1955.
Faye Adams - **SHAKE A HAND / I'VE GOTTA LEAVE YOU** (Herald 416) 1953.
Blackwood Brothers Quartet - **HIS HAND IN MINE / I'M FEELING FINE** (RCA-Victor 5709) 1954.
Blackwood Brothers Quartet - **LED BY THE MASTER'S HAND / LIVE RIGHT, DIE RIGHT**
(RCA-Victor 6048) 1955.
Buddy Blake - **ROSIE / YOU'LL CRY FOR ME** (River 499) 1955.
Charles Brown - **MERRY CHRISTMAS BABY /**
Lloyd Glenn - **SLEIGH RIDE** (Hollywood 1021) 1954.
Roy Brown - **HURRY HURRY BABY / TRAVELIN' MAN** (King 4602) 1953.
Ruth Brown - **OH WHAT A DREAM / PLEASE DON'T FREEZE** (Atlantic 1036) 1954.
Ruth Brown - **AS LONG AS I'M MOVING / I CAN SEE EVERYBODY'S BABY**
(Atlantic 1059) 1955.
Ray Charles - **I GOT A WOMAN / COME BACK BABY** (Atlantic 1050) 1955.
Clovers - **BLUE VELVET / IF YOU LOVE ME** (Atlantic 1052) 1955.
Crickets - **YOU'RE MINE / MILK AND GIN** (MGM 11428) 1953.
Crickets - **CHANGING PARTNERS / YOUR LOVE** (Jay-Dee 785) 1954.
Bing Crosby & The Andrews Sisters -
JINGLE BELLS / SANTA CLAUS IS COMIN' TO TOWN (Decca 23281) 1943.
Bing Crosby - **SILENT NIGHT / ADESTE FIDELES (O COME ALL YE FAITHFUL)**
(Decca 23777) 1946.
Bing Crosby - **WHITE CHRISTMAS / GO REST YE MERRY GENTLEMEN** (Decca 23778) 1946.
Bing Crosby - **I'LL BE HOME FOR CHRISTMAS /**
FAITH OF OUR FATHERS (Decca 23779) 1946.
Bing Crosby - **RUDOLPH THE RED NOSED REINDEER / THE TEDDY BEARS' PICNIC**
(Decca 27159) 1950.
Sammy Davis Jnr - **BECAUSE OF YOU (PARTS 1 & 2)** (Decca 29200) 1954.
Diamonds - **A BEGGAR FOR YOUR KISSES / CALL BABY CALL** (Atlantic 981) 1952.
Fats Domino - **AIN'T IT A SHAME / LA LA** (Imperial 5348) 1955.
Dominoes - **THAT'S WHAT YOU'RE DOING TO ME /**
WHEN THE SWALLOWS COME BACK TO CAPISTRANO (Federal 12059) 1952.
Drifters - **WHITE CHRISTMAS / THE BELLS OF ST. MARY'S** (Atlantic 1048) 1954.
Eagles - **TRYIN' TO GET TO YOU / PLEASE PLEASE** (Mercury 70391) 1954.
Tommy Edwards - **THE MORNING SIDE OF THE MOUNTAIN / F'R INSTANCE**
(MGM 10989) 1951.
Tommy Edwards - **IT'S ALL IN THE GAME / ALL OVER AGAIN** (MGM 11035) 1951.
Sonny Fisher - **ROCKIN' DADDY / HOLD ME BABY** (Starday 179) 1955.

Red Foley - **OUR CHRISTMAS WALTZ / HERE COMES SANTA CLAUS** (Decca 46185) 1950.
Red Foley - **RUDOLPH THE RED NOSED REINDEER / FROSTY THE SNOWMAN**
(Decca 46267) 1950.
Red Foley - **I BELIEVE / MANSION OVER THE HILLTOP** (Decca 28694) 1953.
Four Aces - **LOVE IS A MANY SPLENDORED THING / SHINE ON HARVEST MOON**
(Decca 29625) 1955.
Four Lads - **MOMENTS TO REMEMBER / DREAM ON, MY LOVE, DREAM ON**
(Columbia 40539) 1955.
Lowell Fulson - **RECONSIDER BABY / I BELIEVE I'LL GIVE UP** (Checker 804) 1954.
Arthur Gunter - **BABY LET'S PLAY HOUSE / BLUES AFTER HOURS** (Excello 2047) 1954.
Roy Hamilton - **I'M GONNA SIT RIGHT DOWN AND CRY / YOU'LL NEVER WALK ALONE**
(Epic 9015) 1954.
Roy Hamilton - **HURT / STAR OF LOVE** (Epic 9086) 1954.
Roy Hamilton - **UNCHAINED MELODY / FROM HERE TO ETERNITY** (Epic 9102) 1955.
Hilltoppers - **TO BE ALONE / LOVE WALKED IN** (Dot 15105) 1953.
Lightnin' Hopkins - **MERRY CHRISTMAS / HAPPY NEW YEAR** (Decca 48306) 1953.
Ivory Joe Hunter - **IT'S A SIN / DON'T YOU BELIEVE HER** (MGM 10818) 1950.
Jacks - **WHY DON'T YOU WRITE ME / SMACK DAB IN THE MIDDLE** (RPM 428) 1955.
Jo Stafford - **TENNESSEE WALTZ / IF YOU'VE GOT THE HONEY** (Columbia 39065) 1950.
Little Walter - **MY BABE / THUNDER BIRD** (Checker 811) 1955.
Nellie Lutcher - **I'LL NEVER GET TIRED / THAT'S A PLENTY** (Capitol 878) 1950.
Marigolds - **ROLLIN' STONE / WHY DON'T YOU** (Excello 2057) 1955.
Brownie McGhee - **I'M 10,000 YEARS OLD / CHERRY RED** (Jax 312) 1953.
McGuire Sisters - **SINCERELY / NO MORE** (Coral 61323) 1954.
Vaughn Monroe - **MISTER SANDMAN / THEY WERE DOIN' THE MAMBO**
(RCA-Victor 5767) 1954.
Orioles - **CRYING IN THE CHAPEL / DON'T YOU THINK I OUGHT TO KNOW**
(Jubilee 5122) 1953.
Patti Page - **I WENT TO YOUR WEDDING / YOU BELONG TO ME** (Mercury 5899) 1952.
Platters - **ONLY YOU / BARK, BATTLE AND BALL** (Mercury 70633) 1955.
Lloyd Price - **LAWDY MISS CLAWDY / MAILMAN BLUES** (Specialty 428) 1952.
Lloyd Price - **OOOH, OOOH, OOOH / RESTLESS HEART** (Specialty 440) 1952.
Lloyd Price - **SO LONG / WHAT'S THE MATTER NOW** (Specialty 457) 1953.
Prisonaires - **JUST WALKIN' IN THE RAIN / BABY PLEASE** (Sun 186) 1953.
Hank Snow - **I'M GONNA BID MY BLUES GOODBYE /**
JUST A FADED PETAL FROM BEAUTIFUL BOUQUET
(RCA-Victor 3126) 1948.
Spiders - **WITCHCRAFT / IS IT TRUE** (Imperial 5366) 1955.
Kay Starr - **KAY'S LAMENT / FOOL, FOOL, FOOL** (Capitol 2151) 1952.
Statesmen Quartet - **IN THE SWEET FOREVER / AN OLD LOG CABIN FOR SALE**
(Statesmen 1013/1014) 1952.
Statesmen Quartet - **GET AWAY JORDAN / I BOWED ON MY KNEES AND CRIED HOLY**
(Statesmen 1027/1028) 1952.
Statesmen Quartet - **I HAVE A DESIRE / THE OLD LANDMARK** (Statesmen 1039/1040) 1953.
Billy Tate - **SINGLE LIFE / YOU TOLD ME** (Imperial 5337) 1955.
T. Texas Tyler - **MUCH MORE THAN THE REST / FRANKIE AND JOHNNY** (4 Star 1150) 1947.
Willie Mae 'Big Mama' Thornton - **HOUND DOG / NIGHT MARE** (Peacock 1612) 1953.
Ernest Tubb - **WHITE CHRISTMAS / BLUE CHRISTMAS** (Decca 46186) 1949.
Joe Turner - **FLIP, FLOP AND FLY / TI-RI-LEE** (Atlantic 1053) 1955.
Billy Vaughn & His Orchestra - **THE SHIFTING WHISPERING SANDS (PARTS 1 & 2)**
(Dot 15409) 1955.
Billy Ward & His Dominoes - **THE BELLS / PEDAL PUSHIN' PAPA** (Federal 12114) 1952.
Billy Ward & His Dominoes - **RAGS TO RICHES / DON'T THANK ME** (King 1280) 1953.
Hank Williams - **I SAW THE LIGHT / 6 MORE MILES** (MGM 10271) 1948.
Hank Williams - **LOVESICK BLUES / NEVER AGAIN** (MGM 10352) 1949.

Albums

CBS Trumpeteers - *Milky White Way* (Grand LP-7701) 1955.
Hilltoppers - *Present Tops In Pops* (Dot DLP-3003) 1955.

SOURCES

Note: Samuel Barnes numbered his archive files, Graham Metson only noted the year.

1.1   Samuel Barnes' files (Tupelo investigations No. 284, May 1971; No. 827, October 1974; No. 980, November 1975).

1.2   Samuel Barnes' files (Tupelo investigations No. 3, April 1968 (interview with Pastor Heywood C. Brown).

1.3   Samuel Barnes' files (Tupelo investigations No. 3, April 1968, interview with Mrs. Oleta Grimes).

1.4   Samuel Barnes' files (Tupelo investigations No. 284, May 1971).

1.5   Samuel Barnes' files (Tupelo investigations No. 284, May 1971).

1.6   Samuel Barnes' files (Tupelo investigations No. 3, April 1968).

2.1   Samuel Barnes' files (Tupelo investigations No. 3, April 1968; No. 284, May 1971; No. 827, October 1974; No. 980, November 1975); Peter Guralnick, *Last Train To Memphis.*

2.2   Samuel Barnes' files (Tupelo investigations No. 3, April 1968; No. 284, May 1971; No. 827, October 1974; No. 980, November 1975).

2.3   Ibid.

2.4   Ibid.

2.5   Peter Guralnick, *Last Train To Memphis.*

2.6   Samuel Barnes' files (Tupelo investigations No. 3, April 1968; No. 284, May 1971; No. 827, October 1974; No. 980, November 1975).

2.7   Ibid.

2.8   Ibid.

2.9   Ibid.

2.10   Ibid.

2.11   Ibid.

2.12   Ibid.

2.13   Ibid.

2.14   Ibid.

2.15   Ibid.

3.1   Samuel Barnes' files (Memphis investigations No. 239, June 1970).

3.2   Samuel Barnes' files (Memphis investigations No. 241, August 1970, interview with Rev. W. Herbert Brewster).

3.3   Samuel Barnes' files (Memphis investigations No. 241, August 1970); Peter Guralnick, *Last Train To Memphis.*

3.4   Peter Guralnick, *Last Train To Memphis.*

3.5   Samuel Barnes' files (Memphis investigations No. 239, June 1970, interview with Marcus Van Story).

3.6   Samuel Barnes' files (Memphis investigations No. 240, June 1970, interview with James R. Tipler); Peter Guralnick & Ernst Jorgensen, *Elvis Day By Day.*

4.1   Colin Escott with Martin Hawkins, *Good Rockin' Tonight* (St. Martin's Press, New York, 1991); Colin Escott (Bear Family CD *The Prisonaires*, BCD-15523, 1990); Jay Warner, *Just Walkin' In The Rain* (Renaissance Books, New York) 2001; Martin Hawkins, 2004.

4.2   Marion Keisker's archives and interview by Samuel Barnes (Memphis, September 1970); Samuel Barnes file reference: Elvis' Sun Sessions No. 242, September 1970.

4.3   Ibid.

4.4	Ibid.
4.5	Ibid.
4.6	Ibid.
4.7	Ibid.
4.8	Ibid.
4.9	Ibid.
4.10	Ibid.
4.11	Marion Keisker's archives and interview by Samuel Barnes (Memphis, September 1970); Samuel Barnes file reference: Elvis' Sun Sessions No. 242, September 1970; Colin Escott (Bear Family CD *The Prisonaires*, BCD-15523, 1990).
4.12	Marion Keisker's archives and interview by Samuel Barnes (Memphis, September 1970); Samuel Barnes file reference: Elvis' Sun Sessions No. 242, September 1970.
4.13	Ibid.
4.14	Ibid.
4.15	Ibid.
4.16	Marion Keisker's archives and interview by Samuel Barnes (Memphis, September 1970); Samuel Barnes file reference: Elvis' Sun Sessions No. 242, September 1970; Colin Escott & Martin Hawkins, *Good Rockin' Tonight*.
4.17	Marion Keisker's archives and interview by Samuel Barnes (Memphis, September 1970); Samuel Barnes file reference: Elvis' Sun Sessions No. 242, September 1970.
4.18	Ibid.
4.19	Ibid.
4.20	Marion Keisker's archives and interview by Samuel Barnes (Memphis, September 1970); Samuel Barnes file reference: Elvis' Sun Sessions No. 242, September 1970; Adam Komorowski, 1996.
4.21	Marion Keisker's archives and interview by Samuel Barnes (Memphis, September 1970); Samuel Barnes file reference: Elvis' Sun Sessions No. 242, September 1970.
4.22	Ibid.
4.23	Ibid.
4.24	Ibid.
4.25	Marion Keisker's archives and interview by Samuel Barnes (Memphis, September 1970); Samuel Barnes file reference: Elvis' Sun Sessions No. 242, September 1970; Cedric J. Hayes & Robert Laughton, *Gospel Records 1943-69*.
4.26	Marion Keisker's archives and interview by Samuel Barnes (Memphis, September 1970); Samuel Barnes file reference: Elvis' Sun Sessions No. 242, September 1970.
5.1	Graham Metson's copyright research, 1969.
5.2	Ibid.
5.3	Ibid.
5.4	Ibid.
5.5	Ibid.
5.6	Graham Metson's interview with Roy Brown, Los Angeles, 1968.
5.7	Graham Metson's copyright research, 1969.
5.8	Ibid.
5.9	Ibid.
5.10	Ibid.
5.11	Ibid.

5.12   Ibid.
5.13   Ibid.
5.14   Ibid.
5.15   Ibid.
5.16   Graham Metson's copyright research, 1969; Samuel Barnes' files (Nashville investigations: May 1978, interview with Felton Jarvis).
5.17   Graham Metson's copyright research, 1969.
5.18   Ibid.
5.19   Ibid.
5.20   Ibid.
5.21   Ibid.
5.22   Graham Metson's copyright research, 1969; Billy Vera, 2003.
5.23   Graham Metson's copyright research, 1969.
5.24   Ibid.
5.25   Ibid.
5.26   Ibid.
5.27   Ibid.
5.28   Ibid.
5.29   Ibid.
5.30   Ibid.
5.31   Ibid.
5.32   Ibid.
5.33   Ibid.
5.34   Ibid.
5.35   Ibid.
5.36   Ibid.
5.37   Ibid.
5.38   Ibid.
5.39   Ibid.
5.40   Ibid.
5.41   Ibid.
5.42   Ibid.
5.43   Ibid.
5.44   Ibid.
5.45   Ibid.
5.46   Ibid.
5.47   Ibid.
5.48   Ibid.
5.49   Ibid.
5.50   Ibid.
5.51   Ibid.
5.52   Ibid.
5.53   Ibid.
5.54   Ibid.
5.55   Ibid.
5.56   Ibid.
5.57   Ibid.
5.58   Samuel Barnes, No. 262 (February 1971); data from various collectors in the 1970s.
5.59   Graham Metson's copyright research, 1969.
5.60   Ibid.
5.61   Ibid.
5.62   Ibid.

5.63	Ibid.
5.64	Ibid.
5.65	Ibid.
5.66	Ibid.
5.67	Ibid.
5.68	Ibid.
5.69	Ibid.
5.70	Ibid.
5.71	Ibid.
5.72	Ibid.
5.73	Ibid.
5.74	Ibid.
5.75	Ibid.
5.76	Ibid.
5.77	Ibid.
5.78	Ibid.
5.79	Ibid.
5.80	Ibid.
5.81	Ibid.
5.82	Ibid.
5.83	Ibid.
5.84	Ibid.
5.85	Ibid.
5.86	Ibid.
5.87	Ibid.
5.88	Ibid.
5.89	Ibid.
5.90	Ibid.
5.91	Ibid.
5.92	Ibid.

6.1 Samuel Barnes' files (Memphis investigations No. 241, August 1970); Peter Guralnick, *Last Train To Memphis*.

6.2 Samuel Barnes' files (Memphis investigations, No. 714, December 1973 [research carried out in June/July 1973]).

6.3 Graham Metson's jam research 1968-1970.

6.4 Ibid.

6.5 Ibid.

6.6 Ibid.

6.7 Ibid.

6.8 Ibid.

6.9 Ibid.

6.10 Samuel Barnes' files (Memphis investigations No. 286, June 1971 and No. 829, December 1974).

6.11 Ibid.

6.12 Ibid.

6.13 Ibid.

6.14 Samuel Barnes' files (Memphis investigations No. 1, April 1968; No. 2, April 1968; No. 239, June 1970; No. 241, August 1970; No. 242, September 1970, No. 286, June 1971; No. 714, December 1973 (research carried out in June/July 1973); No. 829, December 1974).

7.1 Graham Metson's copyright research, 1969. Wanda Feathers, 2003.

7.2 Peter Guralnick & Ernst Jorgensen, *Elvis Day By Day*.

7.3   Peter Guralnick & Ernst Jorgensen, *Elvis Day By Day*; Ernst Jorgensen, *Elvis Presley: A Life In Music*; Ernst Jorgensen archives; Dave Thompson (sleevenotes to Stardust CD *Elvis Broadcasts On Air*); Joseph Tunzi, *Elvis Sessions II*.

7.4   KWKH archives; *www.elvisrecords.com* website

7.5   Peter Guralnick & Ernst Jorgensen, *Elvis Day By Day*; Ernst Jorgensen archives; Joseph Tunzi, *Elvis Sessions II*; Billy Vera, 2003.

7.6   Peter Guralnick & Ernst Jorgensen, *Elvis Day By Day*; Ernst Jorgensen archives.

7.7   Peter Guralnick & Ernst Jorgensen, *Elvis Day By Day*; Ernst Jorgensen archives; Joseph Tunzi, *Elvis Sessions II*.

7.8   Graham Metson's copyright research, 1969.

7.9   Ibid.

7.10   Ibid.

7.11   Peter Guralnick & Ernst Jorgensen, *Elvis Day By Day*; Ernst Jorgensen archives.

7.12   Ibid.

7.13   Peter Guralnick & Ernst Jorgensen, *Elvis Day By Day*; Ernst Jorgensen archives; Joseph Tunzi, *Elvis Sessions II*.

7.14   Graham Metson's copyright research, 1969.

7.15   Ibid.

7.16   Peter Guralnick & Ernst Jorgensen, *Elvis Day By Day*; Ernst Jorgensen archives; Joseph Tunzi, *Elvis Sessions II*.

7.17   Ibid.

7.18   Graham Metson's copyright research, 1969.

7.19   Peter Guralnick & Ernst Jorgensen, *Elvis Day By Day*.

7.20   Graham Metson's copyright research, 1969.

7.21   Ernst Jorgensen archives.

7.22   Graham Metson's copyright research, 1969.

7.23   Peter Guralnick & Ernst Jorgensen, *Elvis Day By Day*; Ernst Jorgensen archives; Joseph Tunzi, *Elvis Sessions II*.

7.24   Peter Guralnick & Ernst Jorgensen, *Elvis Day By Day*.

7.25   Peter Guralnick & Ernst Jorgensen, *Elvis Day By Day*; Ernst Jorgensen archives; Joseph Tunzi, *Elvis Sessions II*; data from various collectors in the 1970s.

7.26   Peter Guralnick & Ernst Jorgensen, *Elvis Day By Day*.

7.27   Ernst Jorgensen archives.

7.28   Peter Guralnick & Ernst Jorgensen, *Elvis Day By Day*; Ernst Jorgensen, *Elvis Presley: A Life In Music*; Ernst Jorgensen archives; Joseph Tunzi, *Elvis Sessions II*.

7.29   Data from various collectors in the 1970s and 1980s.

7.30   Peter Guralnick & Ernst Jorgensen, *Elvis Day By Day*; Ernst Jorgensen archives.

7.31   Graham Metson's research in Odessa and Midland, 1968 and 1969.

7.32   Peter Guralnick & Ernst Jorgensen, *Elvis Day By Day*; Ernst Jorgensen archives; Joseph Tunzi, *Elvis Sessions II*.

7.33   Ibid.

7.34   Peter Guralnick & Ernst Jorgensen, *Elvis Day By Day*; data from various collectors in the 1970s.

7.35   Peter Guralnick & Ernst Jorgensen, *Elvis Day By Day*.

7.36   Peter Guralnick & Ernst Jorgensen, *Elvis Day By Day*; Ernst Jorgensen, *Elvis Presley: A Life In Music*.

7.37   Graham Metson's copyright research, 1969.

7.38   Ibid.
7.39   Ibid.
7.40   Peter Guralnick & Ernst Jorgensen, *Elvis Day By Day.*
7.41   Peter Guralnick & Ernst Jorgensen, *Elvis Day By Day*; data from various collectors in the 1970s.
7.42   Graham Metson's research in Odessa and Midland, 1968 and 1969.
7.43   Graham Metson's copyright research, 1969.
7.44   Ibid.
7.45   Peter Guralnick & Ernst Jorgensen, *Elvis Day By Day.*
7.46   Graham Metson's copyright research, 1969.
7.47   Peter Guralnick & Ernst Jorgensen, *Elvis Day By Day.*
7.48   Peter Guralnick & Ernst Jorgensen, *Elvis Day By Day*; data from various collectors in the 1970s.
7.49   Graham Metson's copyright research, 1969.
7.50   Peter Guralnick & Ernst Jorgensen, *Elvis Day By Day*; Ernst Jorgensen archives; Joseph Tunzi, *Elvis Sessions II.*
7.51   Graham Metson's copyright research, 1969.
7.52   Peter Guralnick & Ernst Jorgensen, *Elvis Day By Day.*
7.53   Unknown fanzine.
7.54   Peter Guralnick & Ernst Jorgensen, *Elvis Day By Day.*
7.55   Peter Guralnick & Ernst Jorgensen, *Elvis Day By Day*; Kay Wheeler, former president of Elvis' fan club in Dallas, Texas.
7.56   Graham Metson's copyright research, 1969.
7.57   Peter Guralnick & Ernst Jorgensen, *Elvis Day By Day.*
7.58   Peter Guralnick & Ernst Jorgensen, *Elvis Day By Day*; Joseph Tunzi, *Elvis Sessions II.*
7.59   Peter Guralnick & Ernst Jorgensen, *Elvis Day By Day.*
7.60   Graham Metson's copyright research, 1969.
7.61   Peter Guralnick & Ernst Jorgensen, *Elvis Day By Day*; data from various collectors in the 1970s.
7.62   Peter Guralnick & Ernst Jorgensen, *Elvis Day By Day.*
7.63   Ibid.
7.64   Graham Metson's copyright research, 1969.
7.65   Peter Guralnick & Ernst Jorgensen, *Elvis Day By Day.*
7.66   Ibid.
7.67   Graham Metson's research in Odessa and Midland, 1968 and 1969.
7.68   Ibid.
7.69   Peter Guralnick & Ernst Jorgensen, *Elvis Day By Day*; data from various collectors in the 1970s.
7.70   Peter Guralnick & Ernst Jorgensen, *Elvis Day By Day.*
7.71   Ibid.
7.72   Graham Metson's copyright research, 1969.
7.73   Peter Guralnick & Ernst Jorgensen, *Elvis Day By Day.*
7.74   Peter Guralnick & Ernst Jorgensen, *Elvis Day By Day*; Ernst Jorgensen archives; Joseph Tunzi, *Elvis Sessions II.*
7.75   Peter Guralnick & Ernst Jorgensen, *Elvis Day By Day.*
7.76   Graham Metson's copyright research, 1969.
7.77   Peter Guralnick & Ernst Jorgensen, *Elvis Day By Day.*
7.78   Graham Metson's copyright research, 1969.
7.79   Peter Guralnick & Ernst Jorgensen, *Elvis Day By Day*; Ernst Jorgensen archives; Joseph Tunzi, *Elvis Sessions II.*
7.80   Peter Guralnick & Ernst Jorgensen, *Elvis Day By Day*; Ernst Jorgensen, *Elvis Presley: A Life In Music*; data from various collectors in the 1970s.

7.81   Graham Metson's copyright research, 1969; data from various collectors in the 1970s.

App A   Graham Metson's concert research 1968-70.

App B   Extracted from *Section 4*.

App C   Ernst Jorgensen, *Elvis Presley: A Life In Music*; Joseph Tunzi, *Elvis Sessions II*.

App D   Graham Metson's concert research 1968-70.

App E   Ibid.

App F   Original research by Steve Cairns and George R. White; *Virtual Graceland* CD-ROM (1996); *Q Magazine* (2001); *The Rough Guide To Elvis* by Paul Simpson (2002); *Elvis – The Man & His Music* (September and December 2003).

PRINCIPAL WORKS CONSULTED

Burk, Bill E. - *The Tupelo Years* (Propwash, Memphis) 1994.
Burton, Jack with additions by Larry Freeman - *The Blue Book Of Broadway Musicals*
       (Century House, New York) 1969.
Clee, Ken - *The Directory of American 45 rpm Records [5 volumes]*
       (Stak-O-Wax, Philadelphia, Pennsylvania) 1976-2000.
Cohn, Lawrence - *Nothing But The Blues* (Abbeville Press, New York) 1993.
Dixon, Robert M.W., John Godrich & Howard W. Rye -
     Blues & Gospel Records 1890-1943 (Oxford University Press) 1997.
Docks, Les - *American Premium Record Guide* (Krause Publications, Iola, WI) 1997.
Escott, Colin, & Martin Hawkins - *Good Rockin' Tonight*
       (St. Martin's Press, New York) 1991.
Escott, Colin, & Martin Hawkins - *Sun Records: The Discography*
       (Bear Family, Vollersode, West Germany) 1987.
Guralnick, Peter - *Last Train To Memphis: The Rise of Elvis Presley*
       (Little, Brown & Co, London) 1994.
Guralnick, Peter, & Ernst Jørgensen - *Elvis – Day By Day* (Ballantine, New York) 1999.
Hayes, Cedric J., & Robert Laughton - *Gospel Records 1943-69 [2 volumes]*
       (Record Information Services, London) 1992.
Jorgensen, Ernst - *Elvis Presley: A Life In Music* (St. Martin's Press, New York) 1998.
Kinkle, Roger D. - *The Complete Encyclopedia of Popular Music & Jazz 1900-50*
       (Arlington House, New Rochelle, NY) 1974 *[4 volumes]*.
Leadbitter, Mike, & Neil Slaven - *Blues Records A-K (1943-70)*
       (Record Information Services, London) 1987
Leadbitter, Mike, Leslie Fancourt & Paul Pelletier - *Blues Records L-Z (1943-70)*
       (Record Information Services, London) 1994
Malone , Bill C. - *Country Music USA* (University of Texas Press) 1985.
Murrells, Joseph - *Daily Mail Book of Golden Discs* (McWhirter Twins, London) 1966.
Neely, Tim - *Country & Western Music Price Guide*
       (Krause Publications, Iola, WI) 2001.
Osborne, Jerry P., & Bruce Hamilton - *55 Years of Recorded Country & Western Music*
       (O'Sullivan, Woodside & Co, Phoenix, Arizona) 1976.
Osborne, Jerry P., & Bruce Hamilton - *Popular & Rock Price Guide For 45s*
       (O'Sullivan, Woodside & Co, Phoenix, Arizona) 1981.
Mike Paikos - *R&B Covers & Re-recordings* (self-published, Moraga, CA) 1993.
Pavlow, Big Al - *The R&B Book – A Disc-History of Rhythm & Blues*
       (Music House Publishing, Providence, RI) 1983.
Rust, Brian - *The American Dance Band Discography 1917-42*
       (Arlington House, New Rochelle, NY) 1975 *[2 volumes]*
Tunzi, Joseph A. - *Elvis Sessions II* (JAT Productions, Chicago) 1996.
Joel Whitburn - *Pop Memories 1890-1954*
       (Record Research, Menomonee Falls, WI) 1986.
Joel Whitburn - *Top Country Singles 1944-88*
       (Record Research, Menomonee Falls, WI) 1989.
Joel Whitburn - *Top Pop 1955-82*
       (Record Research, Menomonee Falls, WI) 1983.
Joel Whitburn - *Top R&B Singles 1944-88*
       (Record Research, Menomonee Falls, WI) 1988.

The following websites were also extensively consulted:

The Cyber Hymnal
http://www.cyberhymnal.org

negrospirituals.com
http://www.negrospirituals.com

The Online 78 rpm Discographical Project
http://settlet.fateback.com

INDEX OF PEOPLE'S NAMES

Excluding Elvis, who is of course omnipresent.

Evans, Sherwin 1.4
Excelsior Quartet 6.14
Fairburn, Werly 6.14
Fairfield Four 1.2, 6.2, 6.14
Faith, Percy 6.14
Famous Blue Jay Singers
    Of Birmingham, Alabama 6.2, 6.14
Famous Jubilee Singers 1.2
Faren Twins 5.67
Farley, Jesse 6.14
Fate Marable Society Syncopators 6.2
Feathers, Charlie 4.20, 4.26, 5.71, 5.72, 6.8,
    6.14, 7.61, 7.69, 7.81
Fisher, Eddie 6.14
Fisher, Sonny 7.49, A.6
Fisher Brothers 6.14
Fisk University Jubilee Quartet 1.1, 3.1, 6.7,
    6.14
Fitzgerald, Ella 3.3, 3.6, 4.2, 4.5, 5.20
Five Blind Boys Of Mississippi 1.1, 4.5, 6.12
    See also Original Five Blind Boys
Five Keys 6.4
Five Scamps 4.5
Five Soul Stirrers 5.67, 6.14
    See also Soul Stirrers
Five Trumpets 6.14
Flamingos 4.5, 6.2
Flanagan, Ralph 3.3, 4.5, 4.6, 5.8, 5.25
Flatt, Lester 7.27
Flying Clouds Of Detroit 5.67, 6.14
Foley, Red 2.1, 2.5, 3.3, 4.5, 4.11, 4.17, 5.22,
    5.44, 5.45, 5.67, 6.2, 6.12, 6.14
Fontana, D.J. 5.72-5.77, 5.84-5.92, 7.3,
    7.11-7.13, 7.16, 7.23-7.27,
    7.30, 7.32, 7.33, 7.35, 7.40,
    7.45, 7.47, 7.50, 7.52-7.54,
    7.56, 7.57, 7.59, 7.69-7.80
Fontane, Tony 5.57, 6.13
Fontane Sisters 3.3, 5.24, 5.57, 6.13, 7.13,
    7.16, 7.17
Ford, Tennessee Ernie
    4.17, 5.3, 5.44, 5.87, 7.79
Four Aces 4.5, 6.2
Four Kings Of Harmony Of Miami, Fla. 4.5
Four Knights 6.14
Four Lads 1.3, 6.13, 7.69
Four Tunes 3.3, 4.4
Fowler, Wally 5.67
Fox, Roy 4.5, 4.6, 5.25
Frizzell, Lefty 5.16, 5.42, 7.4
Fulson, Lowell 6.2, 6.13, 6.14
Fulton, Jack 1.3
Gale, Sunny 6.14
Garland, Judy 1.3
Gates, Rev. J.M. 3.1
Gaylord, Charles 1.3
Georgia Tom 5.61
    See also Dorsey, Rev. Thomas A.
Georgia Yellow Hammers 6.12

Gibbs, Georgia 4.5, 5.28, 7.17, 7.23, 7.25,
    7.36
Gilkyson, Terry 5.3
Glenn, Darrell 4.5
Glover, Rev. Charles 6.14
Gluck, Alma 6.14
Godfrey, Arthur 7.29
Golden Echoes 6.14
Golden Echo Quartet 1.3
Golden Gate (Jubilee) Quartet
    1.1-1.3, 3.1, 3.2, 4.5, 5.67, 6.7, 6.14
Golden Wing Quartet 6.14
Goodman, Benny 1.5, 4.5, 4.7, 4.8, 6.13
Gordon, Curtis 5.66
Gordon, Rosco 4.17, 4.24, 5.47, 6.2, 6.14
Gospel Harmonettes 6.2, 6.14
Graves, Blind Roosevelt 1.2
Graves, Uaroy 1.2
Gray, Barry 4.5, 4.6, 5.25
Gray, Glen 4.5, 4.7, 4.8
Greene, Gene 1.3
Greer, Big John 5.22, 7.5
Greer, Jo Ann 4.14, 4.16, 5.30, 7.32
Griffin, Ken 4.5, 4.6, 5.25
Grimes, Oleta 1.3, 1.4, 2.5
Grimes, Tiny 1.6, 6.14
Grissom, Jimmy 5.7
Gunter, Arthur 4.15, 5.36, 5.58, 7.28, 7.42,
    7.48, 7.50, 7.58, 7.74, 7.79
Guthrie, Jack 4.12, 5.21, 5.34
Haley, Bill 5.23, 5.48, 5.58, 5.70, 5.84, 5.90,
    7.13, 7.15, 7.25, 7.32, 7.69, 7.74,
    7.81
Hamblen, Stuart 5.67, 6.12
Hamill, Rev. James E. 3.1
Hamilton, Roy 5.22, 6.9, 7.5
Hammond, Rev. 6.14
Hampton, Lionel 4.5, 4.24, 5.8
Handy, W.C. 1.6, 4.4
Harmonaires 3.1, 3.2, 6.7
Harmoneers *[black group]* 1.1, 6.14
Harmoneers Quartet *[white group]* 5.67
Harmonicats 3.4, 3.6, 4.5, 4.6, 5.25
Harmonizing Four 1.1, 3.2, 5.67
Harris, Marion 1.3
Harris, Phil 4.5
Harris, (Rev.) R.A. 6.12, 6.14
Harris, Ray 4.10
Harris, R.H. 6.14
Harris, Wynonie 4.10, 5.11, 5.58, 7.28, 7.42,
    7.50, 7.69
Hastings, Thomas 6.14
Hawkins, Erskine 3.3
Hawkins, Martin 4.1
Hayes, Tamara 4.5, 6.1
Hazelwood, Eddie 5.77
Heap, Jimmy 4.14, 4.16, 5.30, 6.2, 7.32
Heavenly Gospel Singers 3.2, 5.67, 6.14
Heidt, Horace 3.3, 4.5, 4.8, 4.12, 5.19, 6.1

INDEX OF SONGS & ALBUM TITLES

◘ = EP title   ■ = LP Title   ◎ = CD title   [▣] = videotape

Bold references indicate songs listed with full detail.

257

INDEX OF FILMS & SHOWS

Bold references indicate shows examined in detail.

OTHER TITLES FROM MUSIC MENTOR BOOKS

(35 Years of) British Hit EPs
George R. White
ISBN 0-9519888-1-6 *(pbk, 256 pages)* 2001 RRP £16.99

At last, a chart book dedicated to British hit EPs! Includes a history of the format, an artist-by-artist listing of every 7-inch EP hit from 1955 to 1989 (with full track details for each record), analyses of chart performance, and — for the first time ever — the official UK EP charts reproduced in their entirety. Profusely illustrated with *over 600* sleeve shots. A collector's dream!

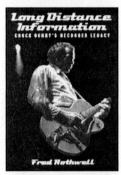

Long Distance Information: Chuck Berry's Recorded Legacy
Fred Rothwell
ISBN 0-9519888-2-4 *(pbk, 352 pages)* 2001 RRP £18.99

Detailed analysis of every recording Chuck Berry has ever made. Includes an overview of his life and career, his influences, the stories behind his most famous compositions, full session details, listings of all his key US/UK vinyl and CD releases (including track details), TV and film appearances, and much, much more. Over 100 illustrations including label shots, vintage ads and previously unpublished photos.

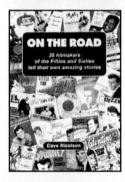

On The Road
Dave Nicolson
ISBN 0-9519888-4-0 *(pbk, 256 pages)* 2002 RRP £16.99

Gary 'US' Bonds, Pat Boone, Freddy Cannon, Crickets Jerry Allison, Sonny Curtis and Joe B. Mauldin, Bo Diddley, Dion, Fats Domino, Duane Eddy, Frankie Ford, Charlie Gracie, Brian Hyland, Marv Johnson, Ben E. King, Brenda Lee, Little Eva, Chris Montez, Johnny Moore (Drifters), Gene Pitney, Johnny Preston, Tommy Roe, Del Shannon, Edwin Starr, Johnny Tillotson and Bobby Vee tell the fascinating stories of their careers as hitmakers and beyond. Over 150 illustrations.

Elvis & Buddy — Linked Lives
Alan Mann
ISBN 0-9519888-5-9 *(pbk, 160 pages)* 2002 RRP £12.99

The achievements of Elvis Presley and Buddy Holly have been extensively documented, but until now little if anything has been known about the many ways in which their lives were interconnected. For the first time anywhere, rock & roll expert Alan Mann, author of *The A–Z Of Buddy Holly*, takes a detailed look at each artist's early years, comparing their backgrounds and influences, chronicling all their meetings and examining the many amazing parallels in their lives, careers and tragic deaths. Over 50 illustrations including many rare/previously unpublished.

American Rock'n'Roll – The UK Tours 1956-72
Ian Wallis
ISBN 0-9519888-6-7 *(pbk, 424 pages)* **2003   RRP £21.99**

The first-ever detailed overview of every visit to these shores by American (and Canadian!) rock'n'rollers. Includes full tour itineraries, supporting acts, show reports, TV appearances and other items of interest. Illustrated with vintage ads, original tour programmes and atmospheric live shots. A fascinating and nostalgic insight into a bygone era.

Let The Good Times ROCK!
Bill Millar
ISBN 0-9519888-8-3 *(pbk, 360 pages)* **2004   RRP £18.99**

A thematic compilation of articles and sleevenotes by the doyen of British rock writers, covering rock'n'roll, hillbilly, rockabilly, doo-wop, R&B, swamp pop and soul. Includes essays on the doo-wop renaissance, acappella, the swamp pop phenomenon and blue-eyed soul, and detailed profiles of some of the most fascinating and influential personalities of the era. Passionate and informative, music journalism rarely comes much better than this. Over 60 illustrations.

**Music Mentor books
are available from all good bookshops
or by mail order from:**

Music Mentor Books
69 Station Road
Upper Poppleton
YORK YO26 6PZ
England

Telephone/Fax: 01904 330308
International Telephone/Fax: +44 1904 330308
email: music.mentor@ntlworld.com
website: http://musicmentor0.tripod.com